IMAGES of America

MONTAGUE

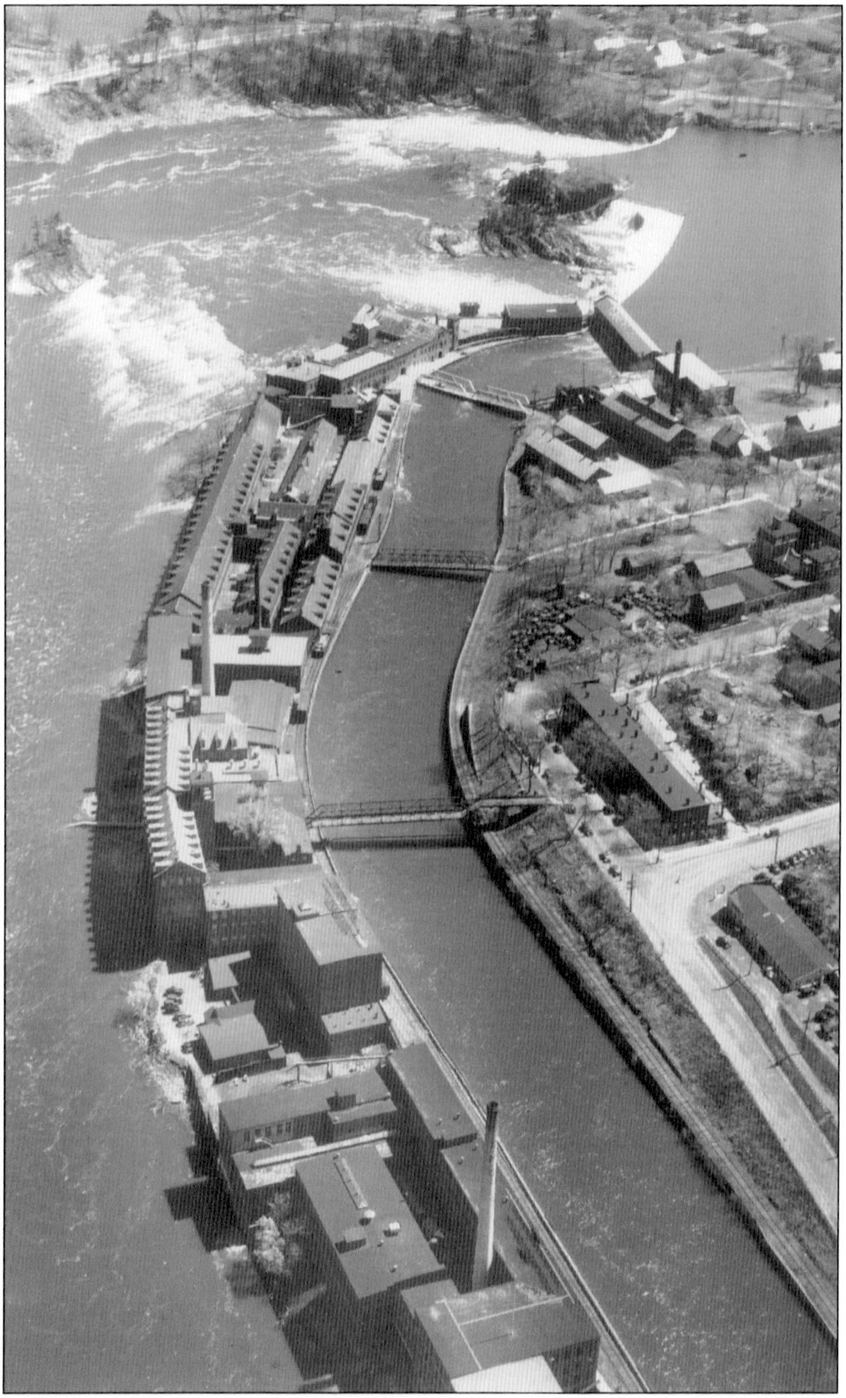

This aerial view taken on May 8, 1935, shows the mill complex from Esleeck, the Keith Paper Mill, Russell Cutlery, and the International Paper Company to the dam. The old dam and the Riverside area of Gill can be seen. Across the canal to the right is the old Turners Falls Foundry area. The Blassberg Scrap Yard is visible in the photograph on Second Street as well as the Keith Block. (Courtesy WMECO.)

IMAGES
of America

MONTAGUE

Peter S. Miller and Kyle J. Scott

ARCADIA
PUBLISHING

ISBN 978-0-7385-0443-8

Published by Arcadia Publishing
Charleston, South Carolina

Printed in the United States of America

Library of Congress Catalog Card Number: 00104084

For all general information contact Arcadia Publishing at:
Telephone 843-853-2070
Fax 843-853-0044
E-mail sales@arcadiapublishing.com
For customer service and orders:
Toll-Free 1-888-313-2665

Visit us on the Internet at www.arcadiapublishing.com

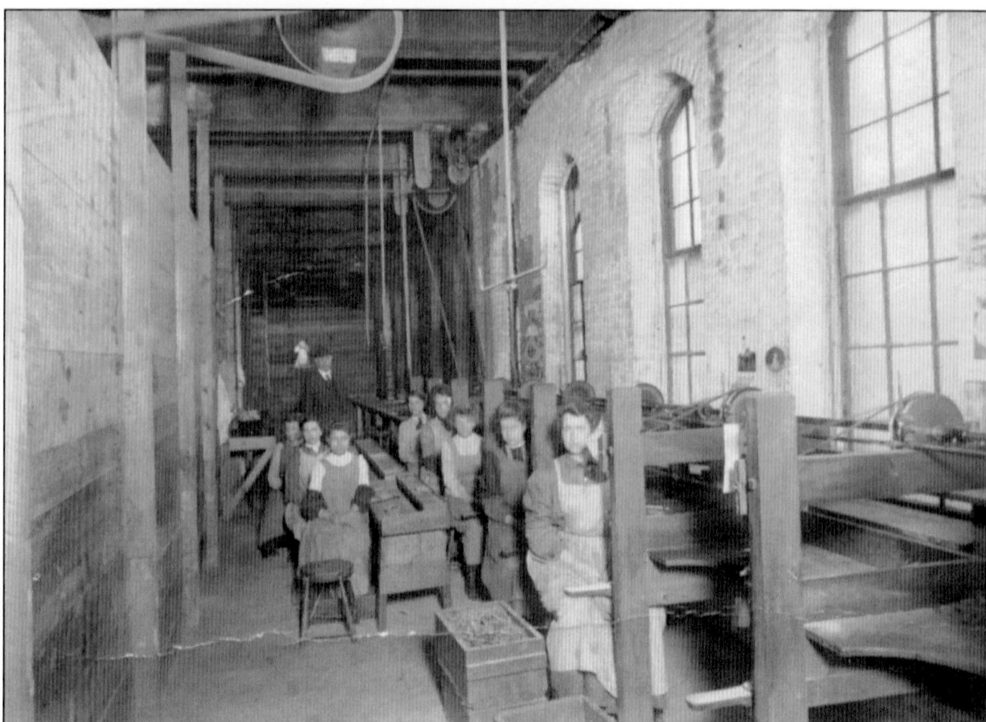

In this photograph of women working at the John Russell Cutlery Company, note the man standing in the background and the power belts. The belts were powered by a drive-shaft system that used power generated from the canals. This system also powered the equipment used by the individual workers. (Courtesy Turners Falls Library.)

Contents

ACKNOWLEDGMENTS

The authors wish to express their sincere appreciation to the Montague and Gill Historical Societies, the Western Massachusetts Electric Company (WMECO) and Northeast Utilities, the Montague Library System (Turners Falls and Millers Falls Branches), and the Town of Montague for sharing the use of their vast collections of Montague photographs. Both the authors made use of their own individual collections of Montague images. The Russell-Harrington Cutlery Company is also to be given special recognition for going the extra lengths to get the authors copies of vintage pictures of the John Russell Cutlery Company. The Montague Machine Company, the Millers Falls Paper Company, the Turners Falls Fire Department, and the Turners Falls Police Department lent the authors photographs. Mrs. Pamela Hubert, Dr. Arthur Charron, William Peloskey, John Carey, Frank Abbondanzio, John Dolan, and Rev. Charles DiMascola of Our Lady of Czestochowa let us use some of their material. We owe many thanks to Louise Shattuck of Lake Pleasant not only for the use of her vast collection of Lake Pleasant material, but also her suggestions for the captions to her material. Lillian Fiske is to be remembered for her captioning of the Montague Center material and for aiding in the search of Montague photographs. Many thanks are in order to the Historical Society of Greenfield for the use of Benton Hall. We also wish to thank Alfred Desautel, a dear friend of Kyle J.Scott, for his early encouragement of this project. Thanks go to Carl J. Schuhle of Greenfield, stepfather to Peter S. Miller, for his recollections of more than 100 years of events in his native town of Turners Falls.

This book is dedicated to all the photographers of Montague, such as Judy Radebaugh, who recorded its proud history and to the people who helped in the making of Montague what it once was and what it could be in the future.

INTRODUCTION

The picturesque town of Montague, Massachusetts, was founded in 1754 on the eastern banks of the Connecticut River. The town consists of five villages, each with its own unique characteristics—Turners Falls, Millers Falls, Lake Pleasant, Montague Center, and Montague City. Montague Center was the founding village center. The Connecticut River and, to a lesser degree, the Millers Falls River played important roles in the development of the town. In the early years, Native Americans lived, fished, traded goods, and traveled along the river. The Great Falls, at the present site of the dam, were of great importance. When the fish were running, peace was always at hand among the various tribes at this site. Later came the Europeans, who also lived, fished, traded, and traveled along the river, but had a very different concept of ownership and how things were done. In the late 18th century and early 19th century, rafts and steamboats went up and down the river. In the late 1790s, the Upper Canal Company was formed to develop a canal around the Great Falls. A dam and a barge canal, between the falls and the present sewer plant opposite the entrance to the Deerfield River, were built. To be able to pass through the rapids above the present French King Bridge, another dam and a canal were built farther up the river. During this time, the Cheapside section of Deerfield (now Greenfield) became a busy river port.

In 1846, the coming of the railroad north from Northampton in short order killed the busy river traffic. In the mid-1860s, Col. Alvah Crocker of Fitchburg, Massachusetts, had visions of developing the waterpower at Turners Falls. Thus was created a planned industrial town. He rebuilt the ruined dam at the falls, rebuilt the upper section of the canal, and sold off industrial sites. The first plant built was the John Russell Cutlery Company, which later became world famous for its products.

Eventually five other large plants were built—the Griswold Cotton Mill and the Montague, Keith, Esleeck, and Turners Falls Paper Mills. Other manufacturing plants were later built elsewhere. In the late 19th century and early 20th century, there were log drives down the river. Some of the logs went to a mill in Riverside Gill, and the rest went downriver to Easthampton. Around 1912, the dam and canal were again rebuilt and enlarged in order to develop a hydroelectric plant at the new end of the canal.

Today, only the Esleeck Paper Mill and two earlier power plants are still in operation. (The Indeck Electrical Plant, built on the site of the Russell Cutlery plant, stopped production in 1997.) The village of Millers Falls lies in the towns of Erving and Montague. The Montague side of the village was originally named Grout's Corner. To take advantage of the waterpower of the Millers Falls River, the well-known Millers Falls Tool Company relocated to the Erving side from its original Greenfield home. Having two intersecting railroads, the Montague side of town became a railroad center. The Millers Falls Paper Company came to the Erving side in 1900 and closed in August 2000.

In 1870, men from the Greenfield and Fitchburg Railroad developed the area around Lake Pleasant. This area became well known for tent camping. Shortly thereafter, cabins replaced the tents on the lake. It became a spiritualist center as well as a very popular place to summer and have a very good time. The fire of 1907 destroyed most of this village. Buildings were rebuilt, but the village never fully recovered to what it was before the fire, and a long decline occurred.

Montague City was originally built around the canal. The well-known Montague Rod and Reel Company was located here as well as several brickyards. Millions of bricks were made and shipped all over the Northeast. These bricks were used in the construction of the Hoosic Tunnel. Barnard Farren summered in Montague City. Among many other things, he was very much involved with developing Turners Falls. He also constructed and donated a hospital named for his late son.

Montague Center has remained an agricultural center. Montague has a very interesting and important past. The purpose of this book is to show this past and to stimulate people to record this past in print. We hope that you will enjoy this book.

—Kyle J. Scott and Peter S. Miller

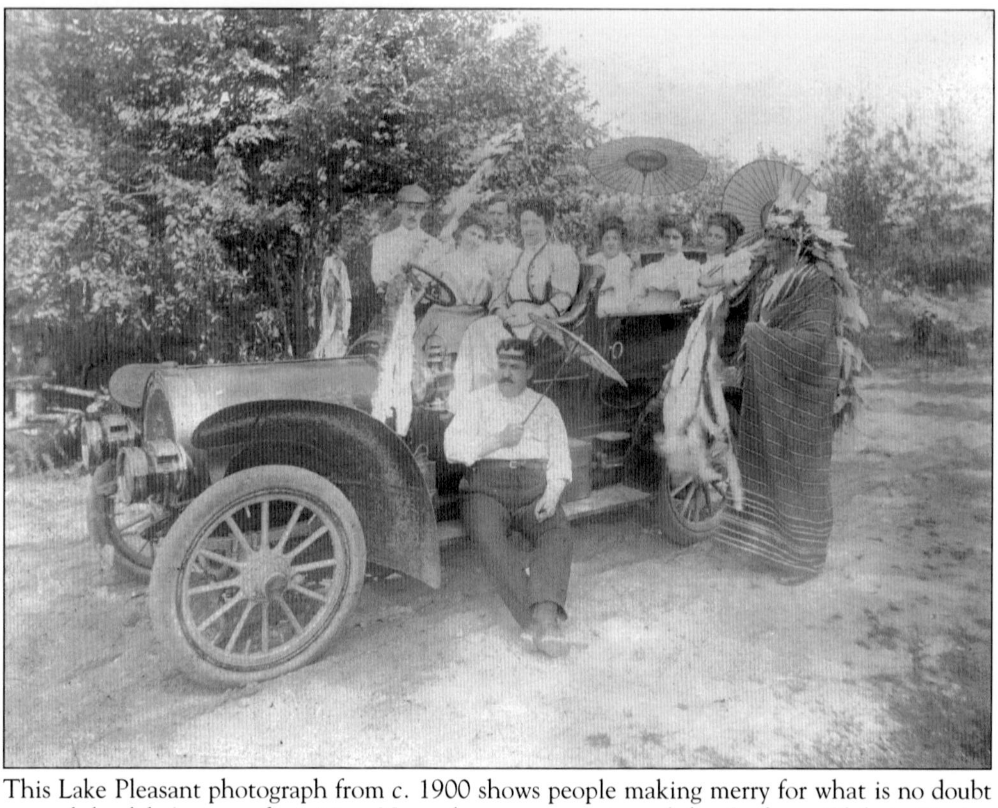

This Lake Pleasant photograph from c. 1900 shows people making merry for what is no doubt one of the lake's many festivities. Note the representative of the Scalpers Club in Native American garb. (Photograph by O.C. Leonard; courtesy Louise Shattuck.)

One

TURNERS FALLS

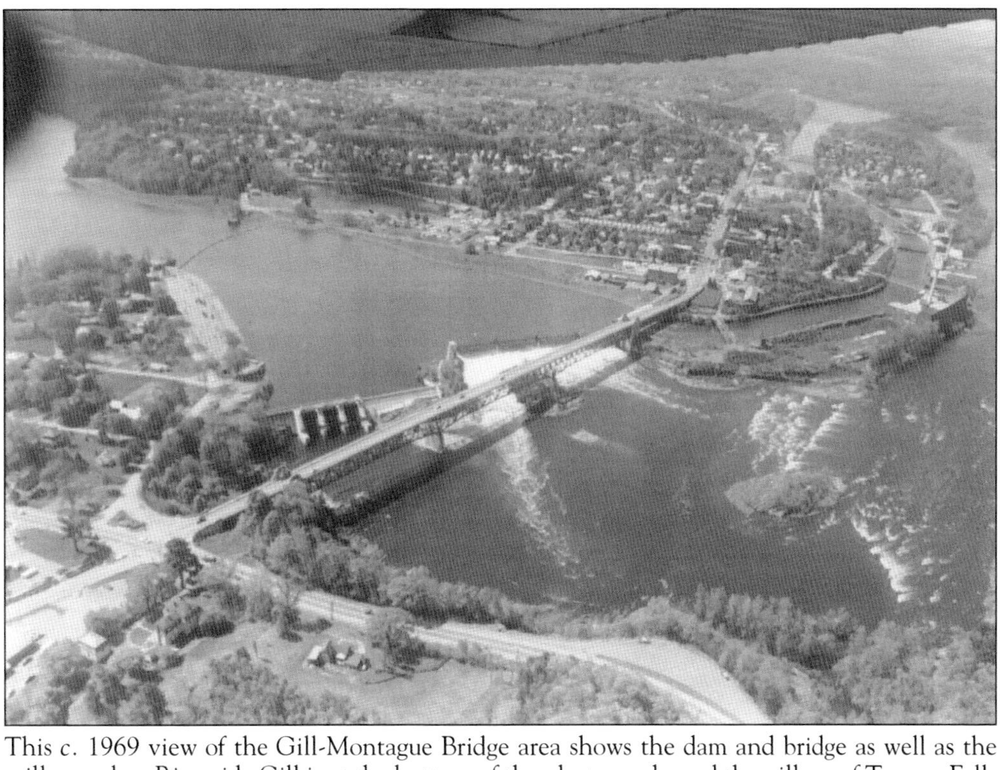

This c. 1969 view of the Gill-Montague Bridge area shows the dam and bridge as well as the mill complex. Riverside Gill is at the bottom of the photograph, and the village of Turners Falls is at the top. (Courtesy WMECO.)

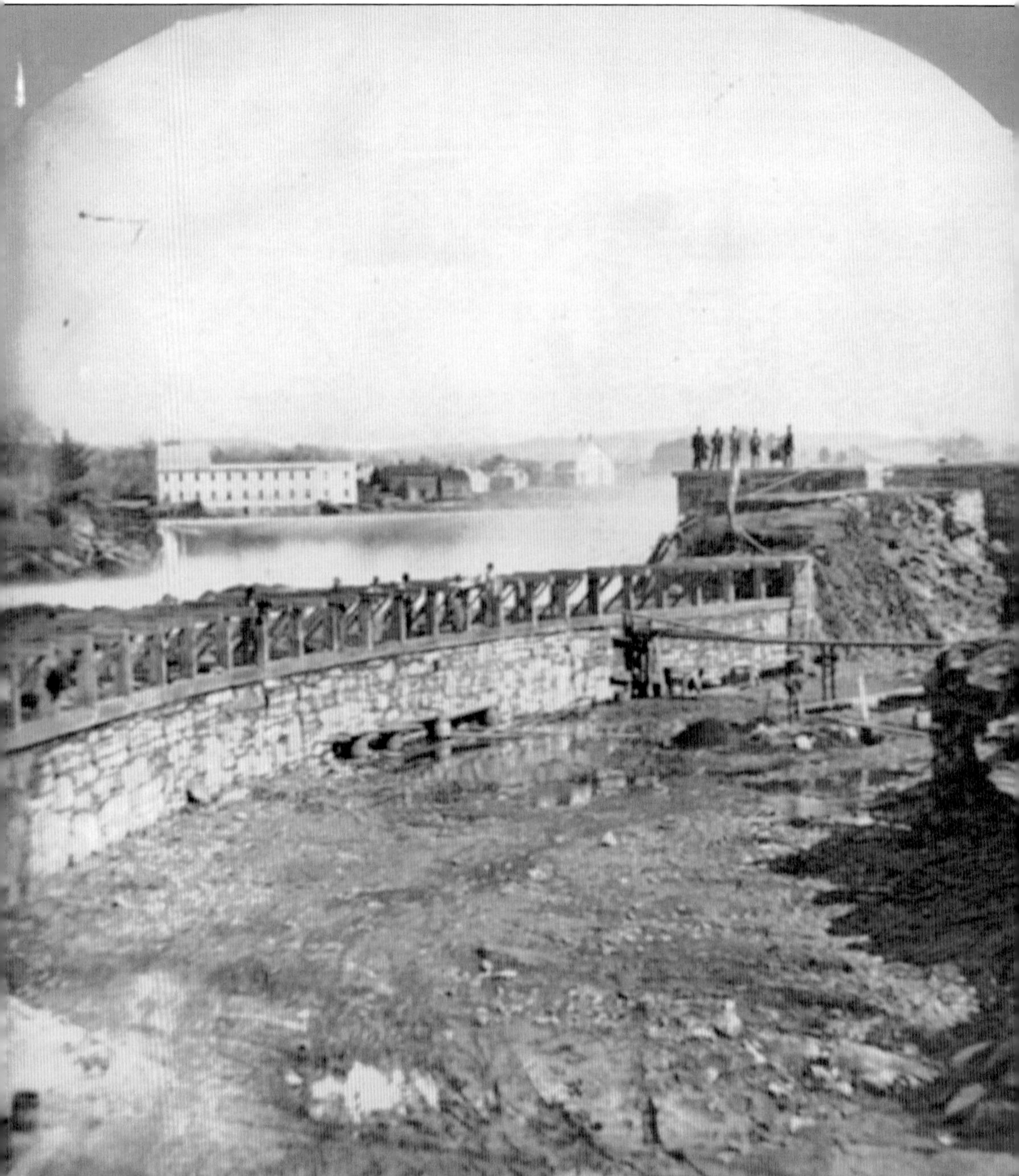

This *c.* 1869 view shows the widening of the original canal just below the gatehouse. Note the work on top of the canal wall. Riverside Gill can be seen across the river, and five people from the Turners Falls side can also be seen on the dam abutment. (Photograph by Horton and Davis; courtesy Peter S. Miller.)

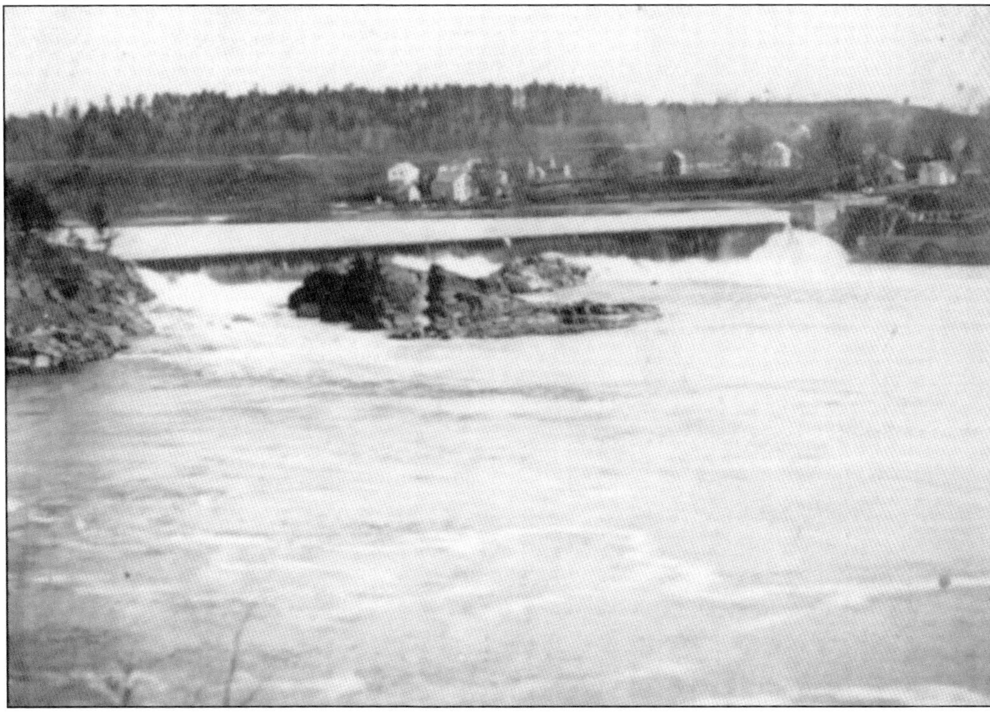

In this *c.* 1869 view of the new log dam at Turners Falls, note the small gatehouse and that no mill has yet been built here. When the photograph was taken, Turners Falls had only a few homes. (Courtesy Peter S. Miller.)

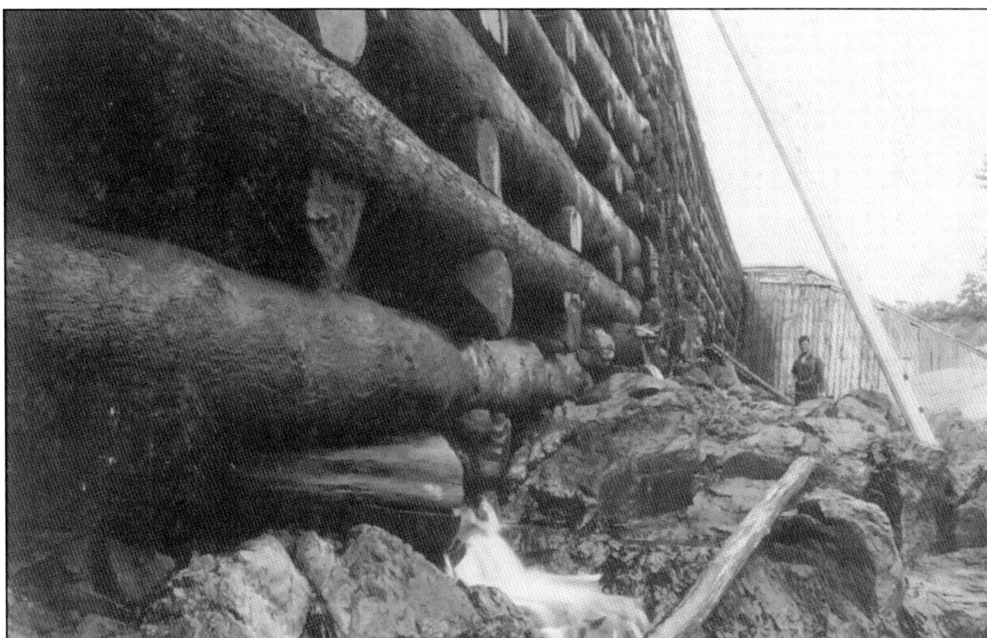

A view of the log crib dam, looking from the Gill side, shows the island in the background. A freshet took out the dam on October 31, 1866. By March 22, 1867, a new dam made of logs and stone had been built. (Courtesy WMECO.)

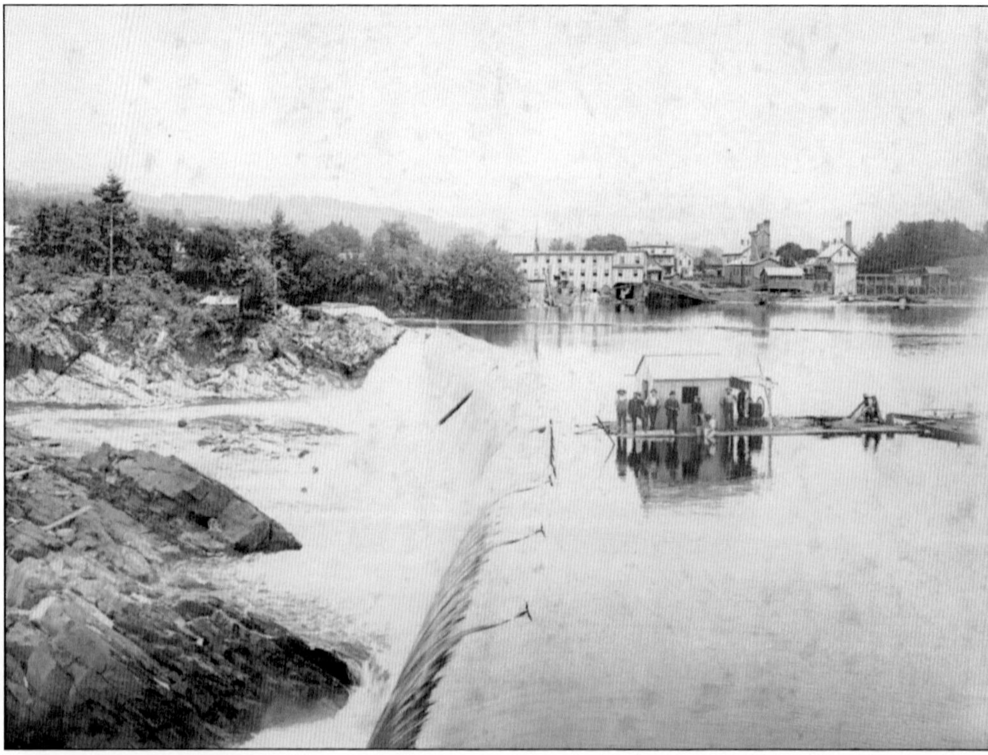

In this view, work is being performed by men on the dam. Note the diver wearing a helmet in the center of the barge building with the air pump to the right. The Turners Falls Lumber Mill is in the background. (Photograph by Temple; courtesy Gill Historical Society.)

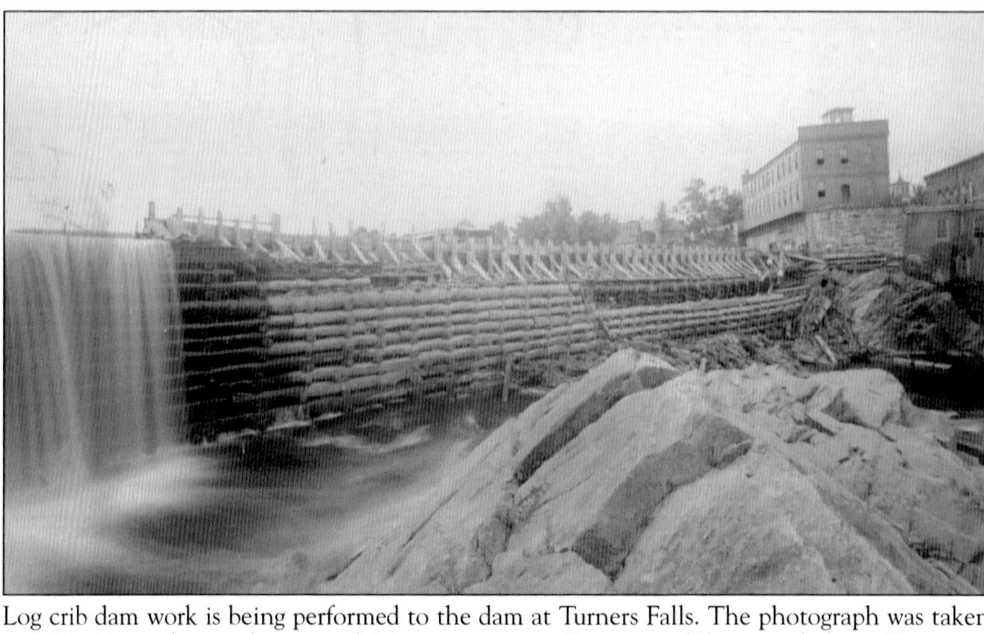

Log crib dam work is being performed to the dam at Turners Falls. The photograph was taken c. 1871. Note the gatehouse and Montague Paper Company. (Photograph by C.W. Berry; courtesy Turners Falls Library.)

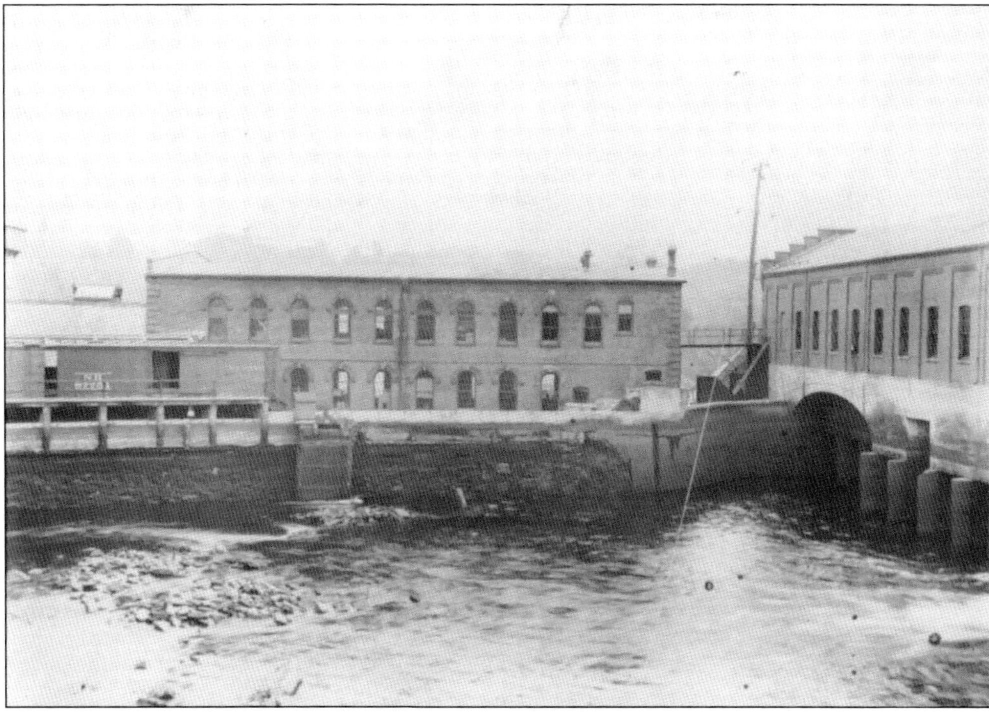

Shown is the rear of the gatehouse for the canal before the canal was rebuilt, widened, and made deeper, *c.* 1912. In the background is the International Paper Company. A portion of the current Gill Montague Bridge runs through this area. (Courtesy WMECO.)

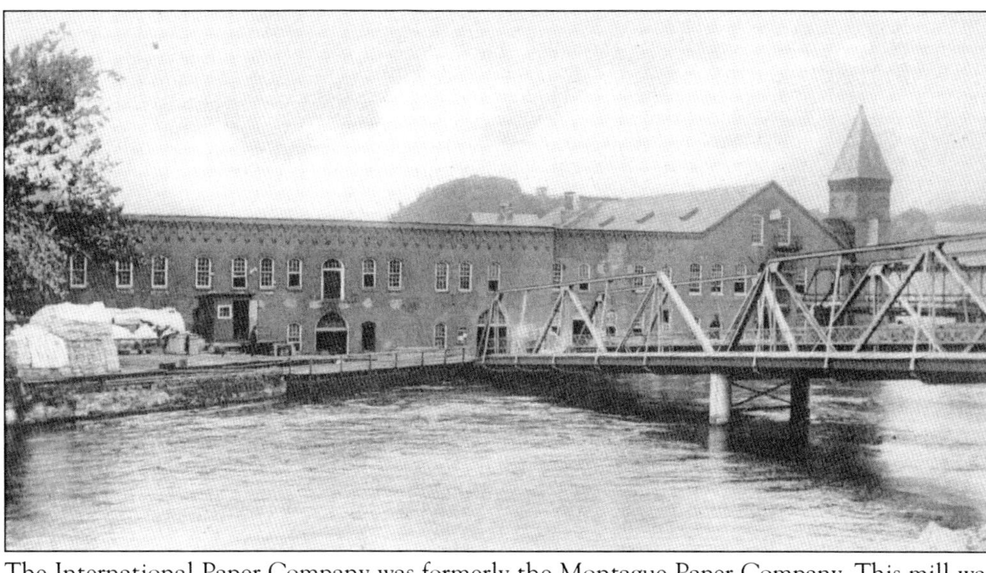

The International Paper Company was formerly the Montague Paper Company. This mill was built *c.* 1870 by Alvah Crocker and Edward Buckley to help stimulate the construction of more mills on the canal. (Courtesy Peter S. Miller.)

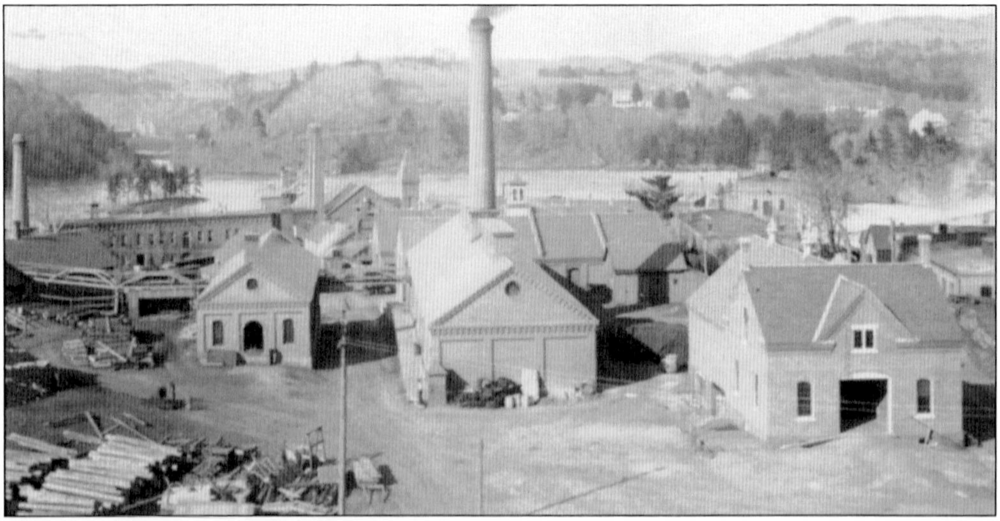

The Clark Machine Company/Turners Falls Machine Company is shown in the foreground; it changed names and ownership many times. Later this company became the Montague Machine Company and relocated to Avenue A. In the rear and on the other side is the Montague Paper Company. The small building to the left of the machine company still stands. It once housed Thomas and Thomas Rod Makers and was recently remodeled. Avenue A as it is today would run through part of the building on the far left. (Photograph taken *c.* 1890 by A.W. Howes and Company; courtesy Turners Falls Library.)

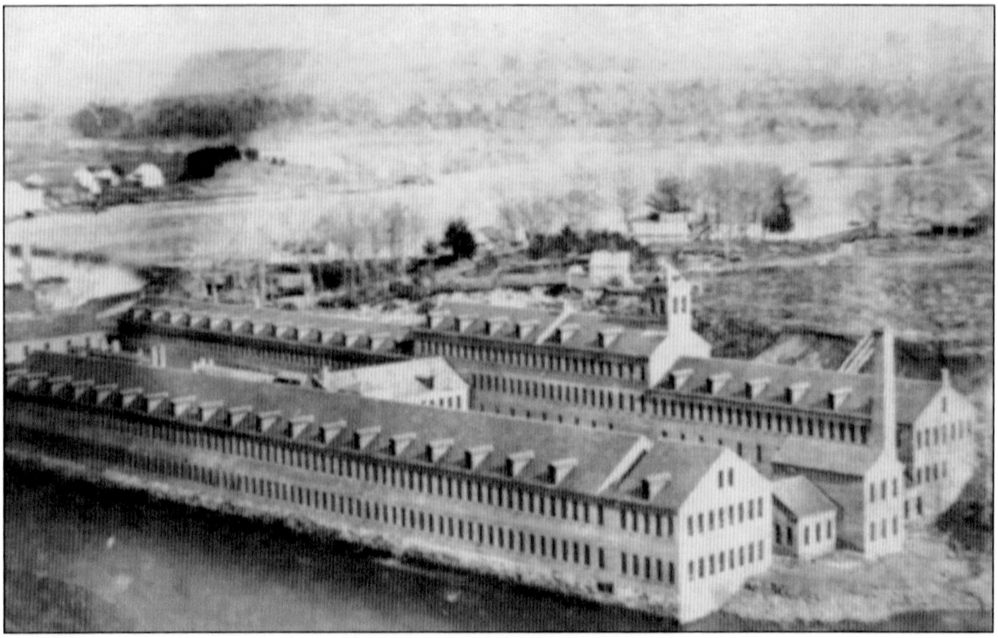

This view of the John Russell Cutlery Company was taken shortly after construction. The company had just moved from its former home on the banks of the Green River in the Deerfield section of Greenfield. The buildings were originally constructed in a parallelogram fashion with a structure across the center. The buildings' two main areas were each thought to be 600 feet long and 50 feet wide. Constructed of stone bases and brick walls, the buildings could house 1,200 employees. (Photograph by Horton and Davis; courtesy Peter S. Miller.)

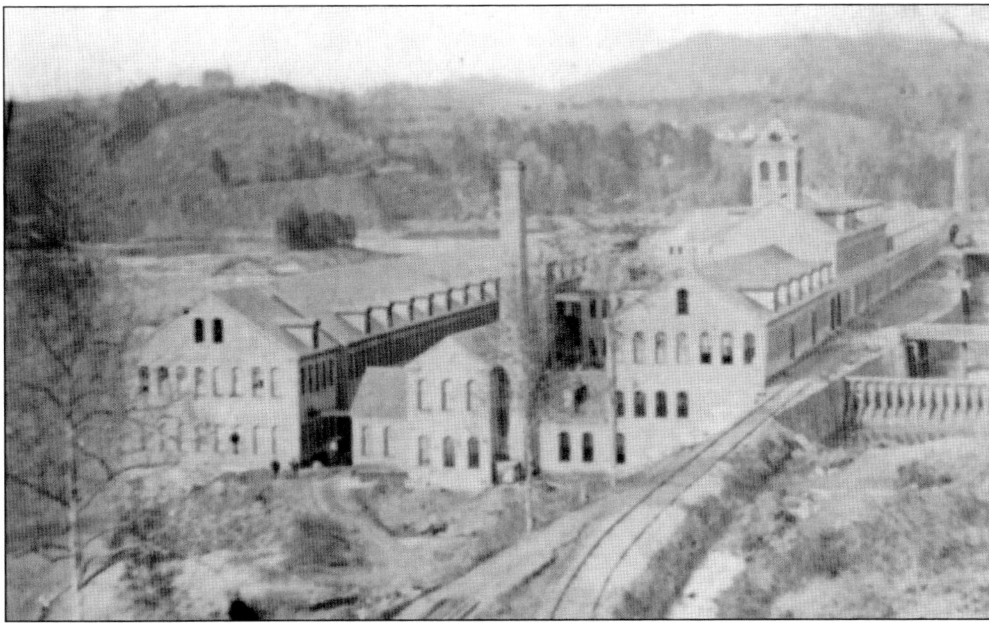

Shown is the newly constructed John Russell Cutlery Company and the canal to the cutlery. In 1873, the company was reorganized into the John Russell Cutlery Corporation. In 1933, the company merged with Harrington to form the Russell-Harrington Cutlery Company. The company moved its operation to Southbridge, Massachusetts, in 1936 because a flood that year had badly damaged the buildings. (Photograph by Horton and Davis; courtesy Peter S. Miller.)

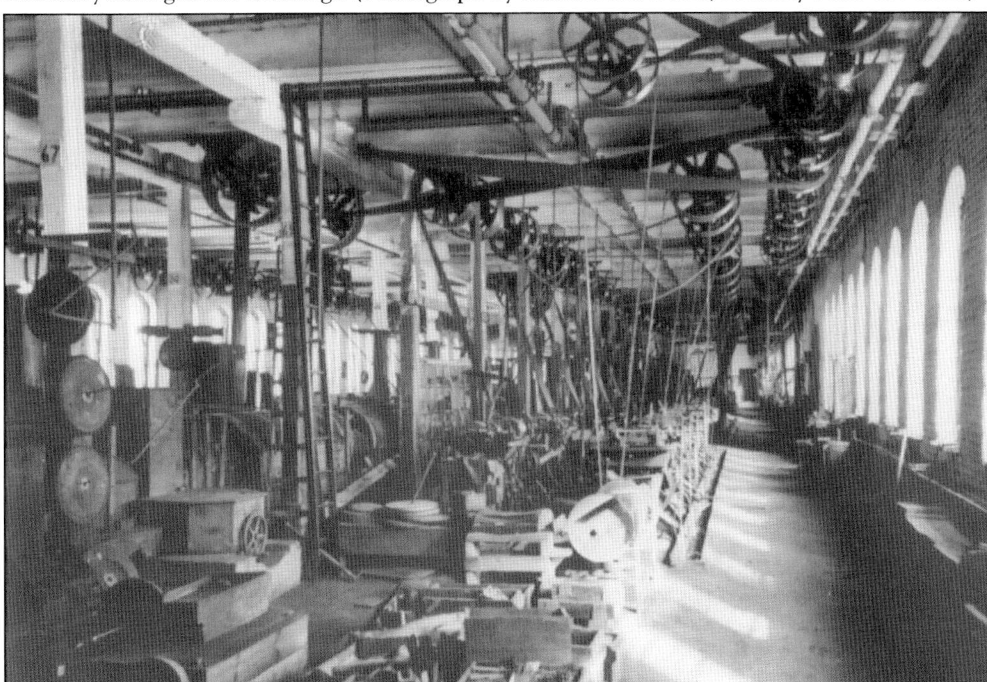

This photograph shows the polishing room of the John Russell Cutlery Company. (Courtesy Russell-Harrington Cutlery Company.)

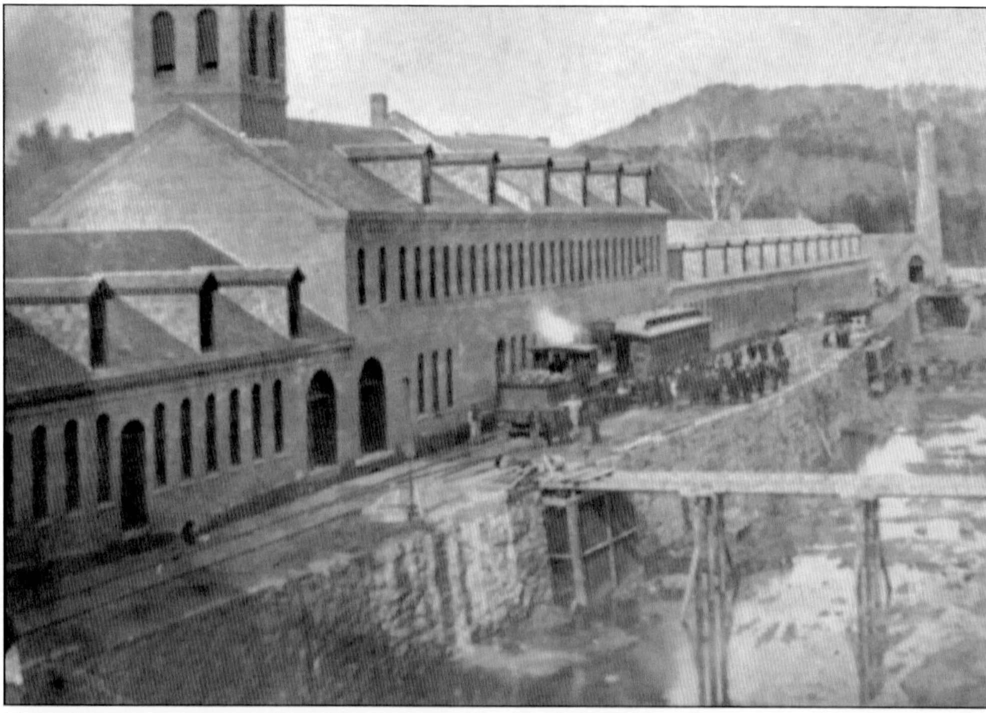

Note the steam engine pushing the passenger car to the plant in this c. 1870 photograph of the newly constructed Russell Cutlery building. Many of the workmen at the plant lived in Deerfield and Greenfield and were transported by rail to work each day. Rail passenger service to Turners Falls ended in 1936, when the cutlery moved out of town. (Photograph by Horton and Davis.)

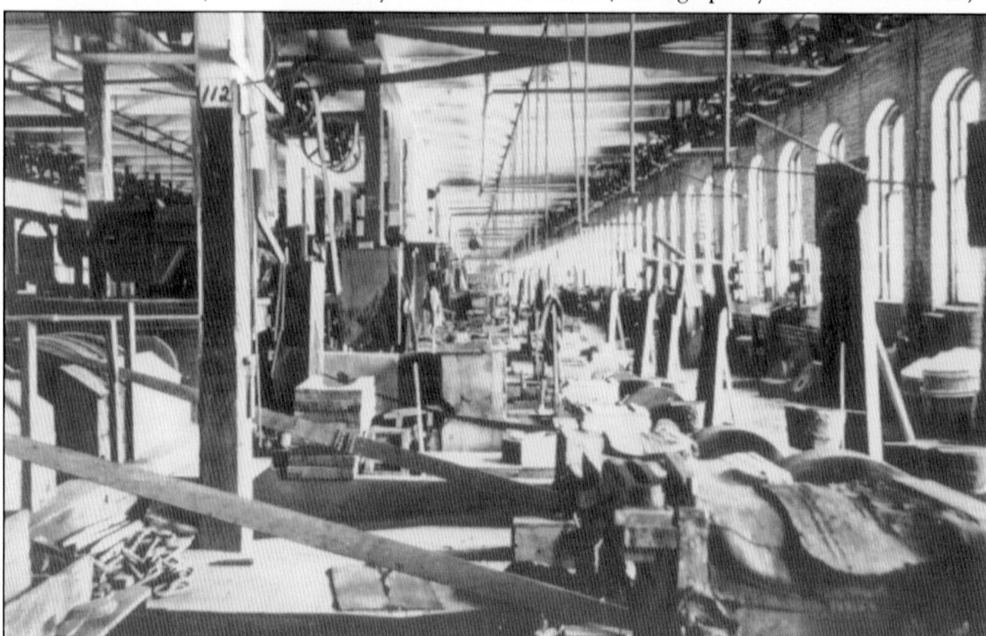

This is the machine grinding room at the John Russell Cutlery Company. In this room, blades were ground and knives were sharpened. (Courtesy Russell-Harrington Cutlery Company.)

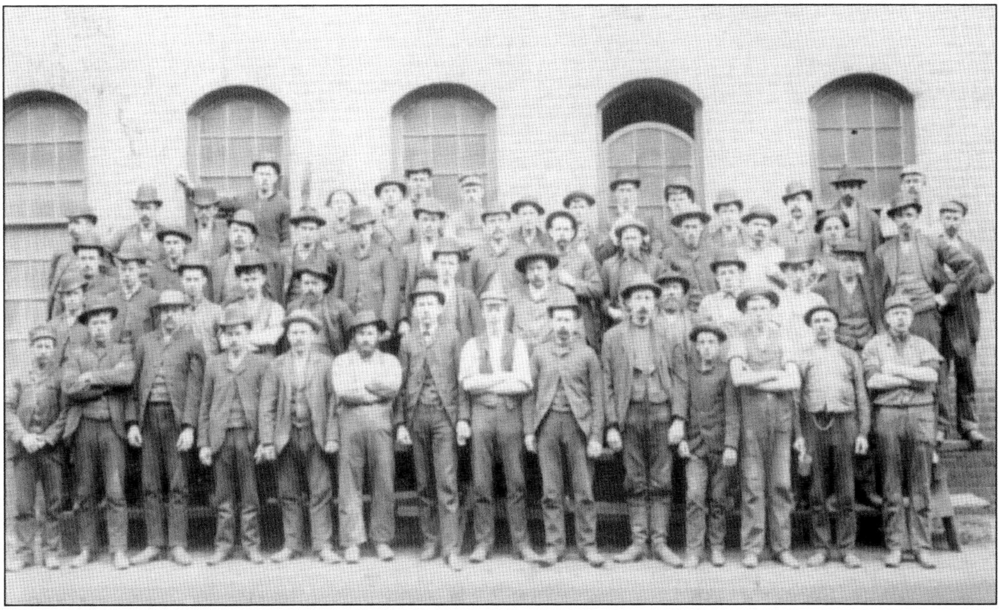

In this image of workmen at John Russell Cutlery Company, note the two boys in the front. The man with the mark above his head (third row, fourth from left) is Albert Bierkle (1864–1892). Mr. Bierkle and two others drowned while trying to shoot the rapids near the French King Rock. They were in a canoe loaded with wine grapes. (Photograph by A.W. Howes and Company; courtesy Peter S. Miller.)

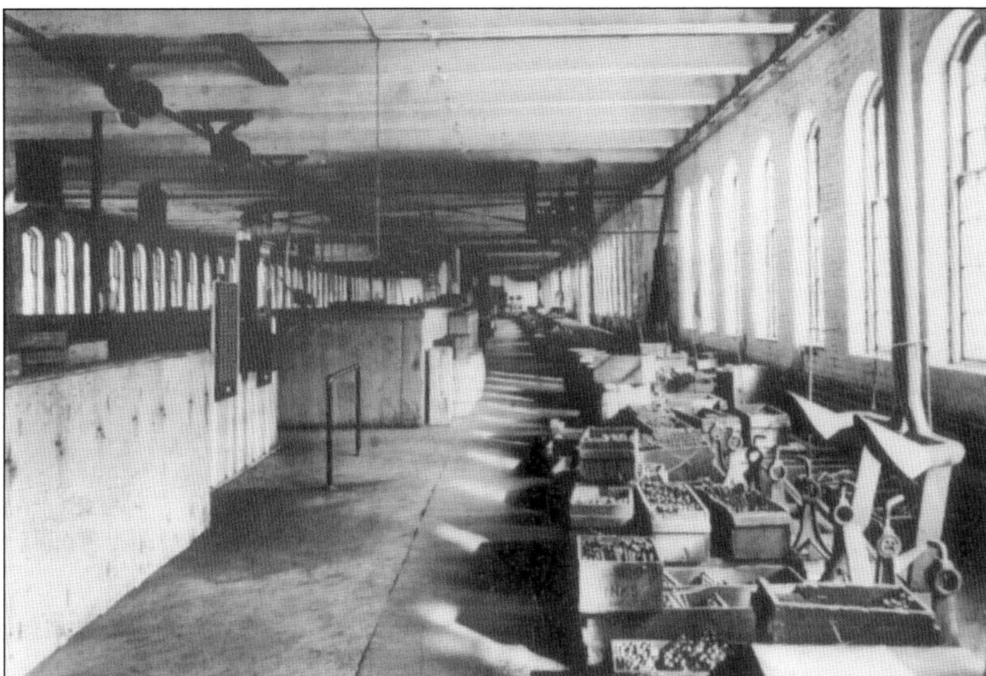

This image shows the polishing and finishing room at the John Russell Cutlery Company (Courtesy Russell-Harrington Cutlery Company.)

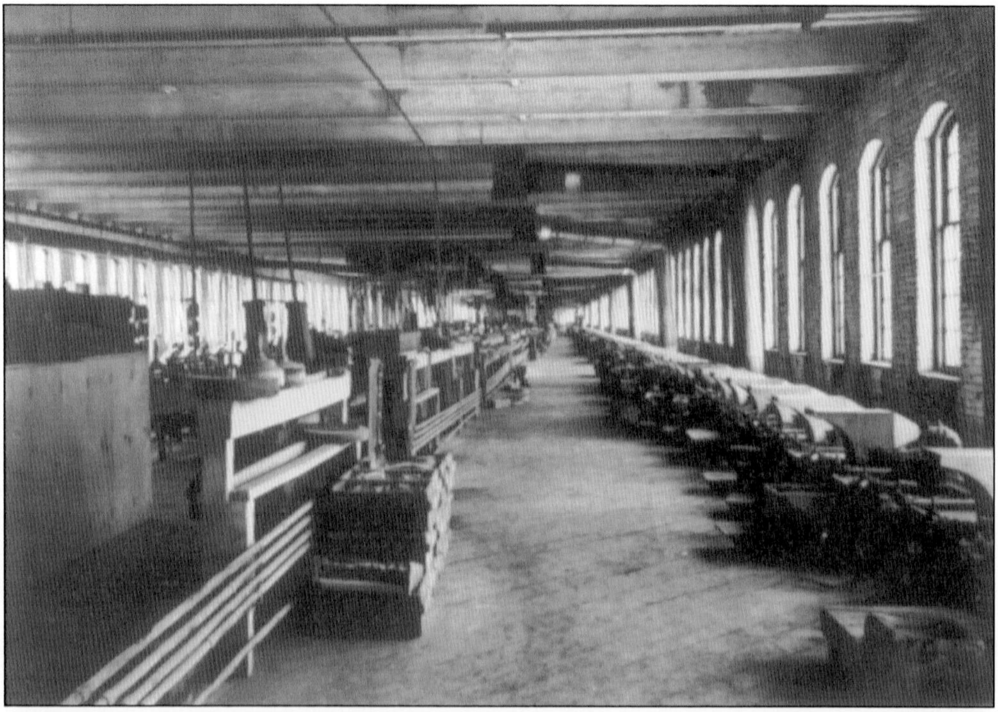
In the handle finishing room at the John Russell Cutlery Company, workers smoothed the rough edges of knife handles. (Courtesy Russell-Harrington Cutlery Company.)

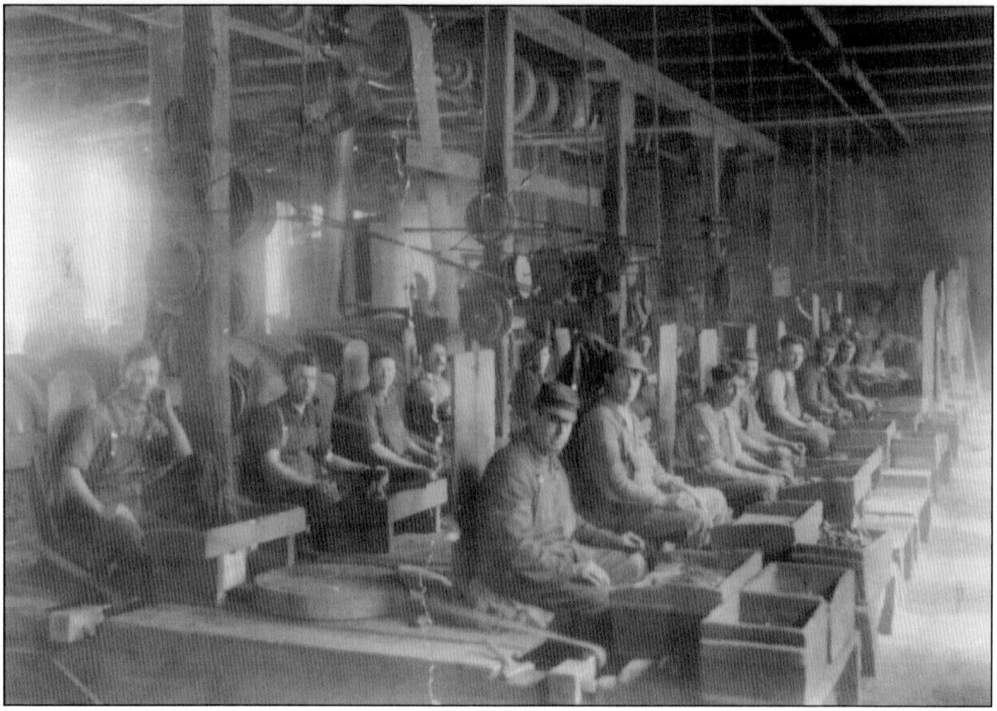
Shown is the machine grinding room at the John Russell Cutlery Company. (Courtesy Russell-Harrington Cutlery Company.)

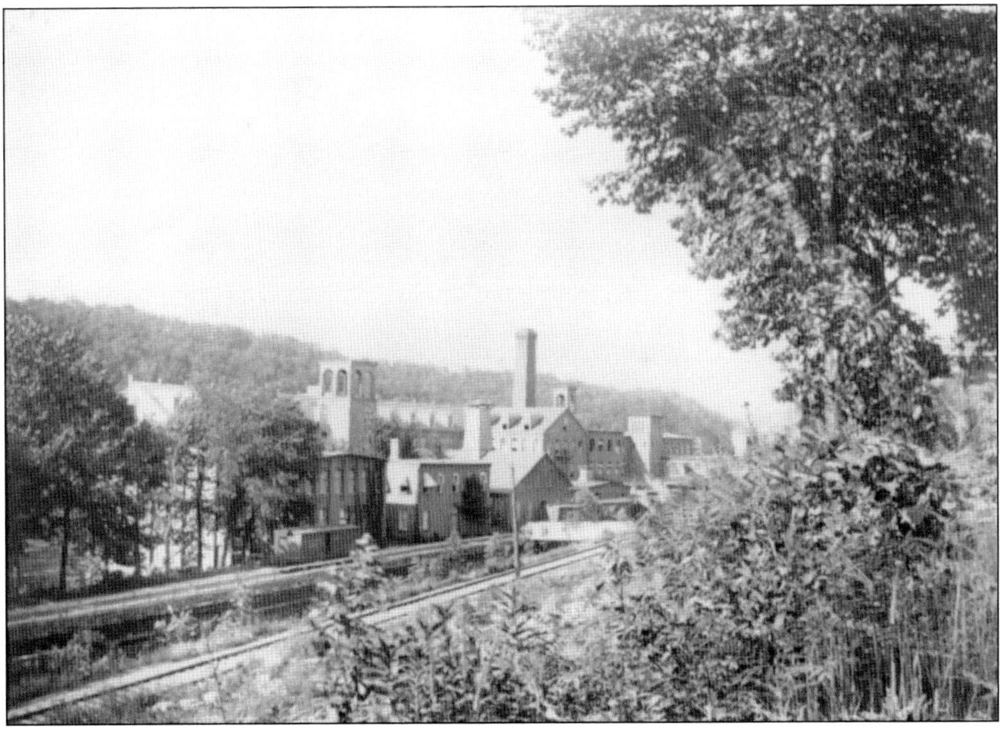

This view of the Keith Paper Mill was most likely taken in the 1890s, before the northern addition to the Esleeck Mill was added. Note the two railroads. The western side of the canal was the Fitchburg Railroad and later the Boston and Maine Railroad. The eastern side was the New York, New Haven, and Hartford Railroad. (Courtesy Turners Falls Library.)

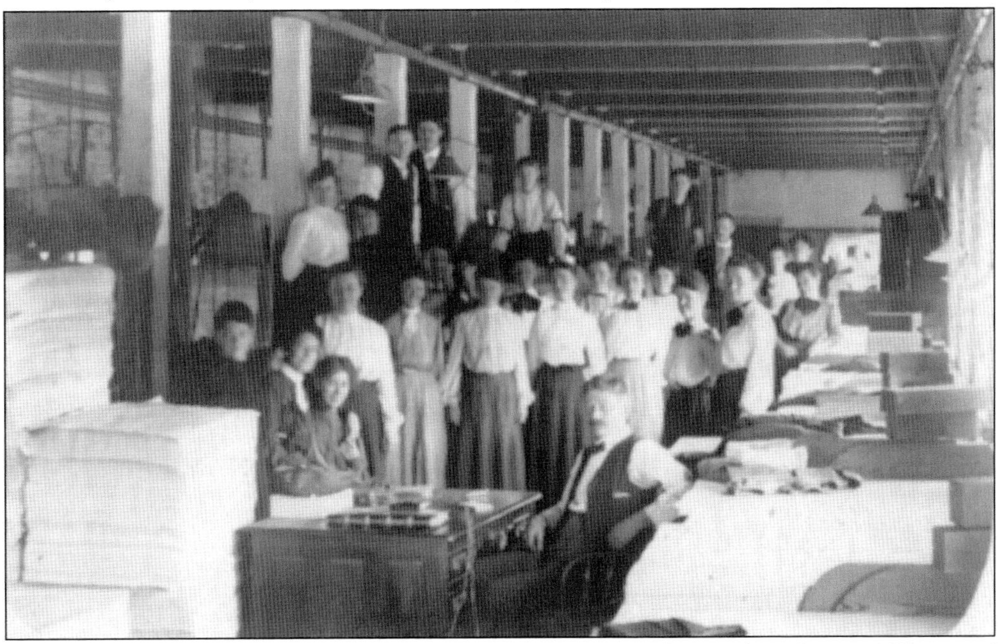

Note the large stacks of paper and how the workers are so well attired in this c. 1905 view of the interior of the Keith Paper Mill. (Courtesy Kyle J. Scott.)

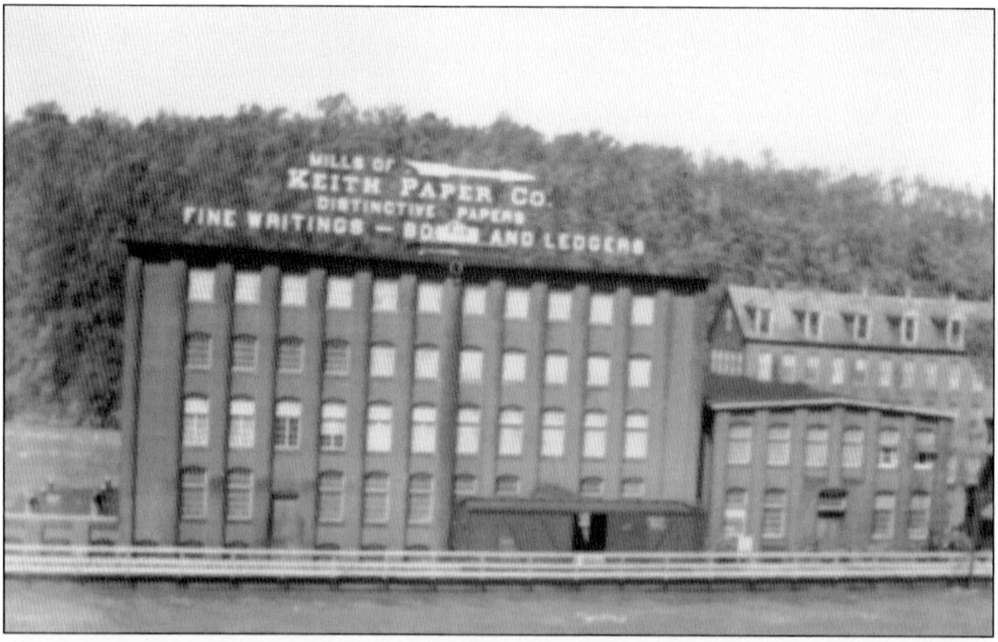

The Keith Paper Company Mill was located along the canal and Connecticut River in Turners Falls, *c.* 1930. Built in 1871–1873, the building partially burned in 1877. (Courtesy Turners Falls Library.)

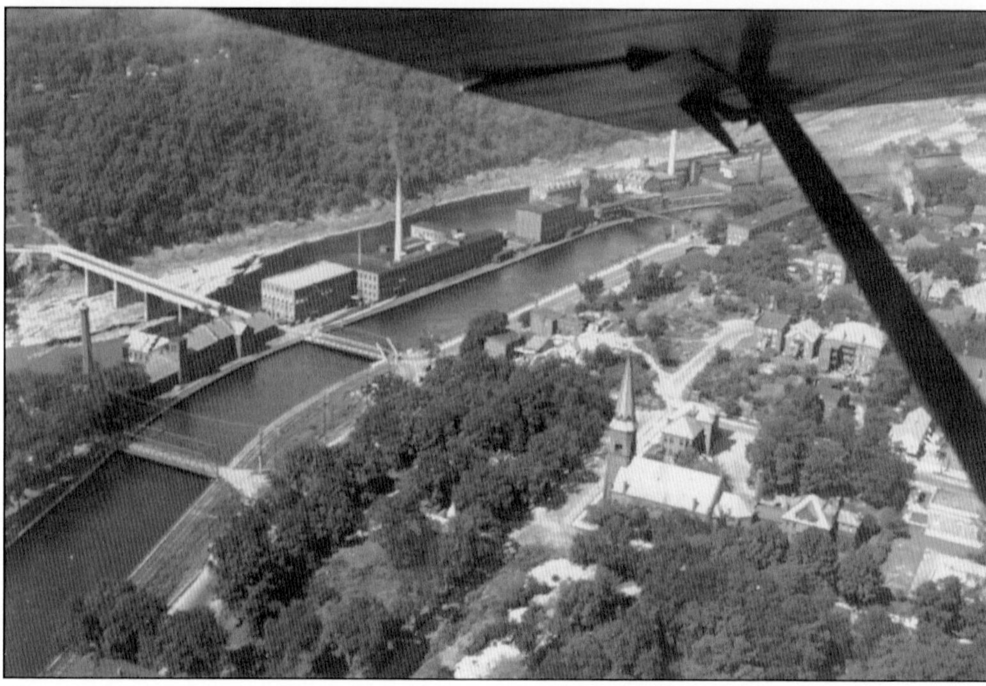
This aerial view of the mill complex of the Turner Falls Paper company was taken in 1937. To the left is the Esleeck Paper Manufacturing Company before its addition. The Keith Paper Company and the John Russell Cutlery Company can also be seen. St. Anne's Church and rectory is in the right foreground; nearby is St. Anne's School. (Courtesy WMECO.)

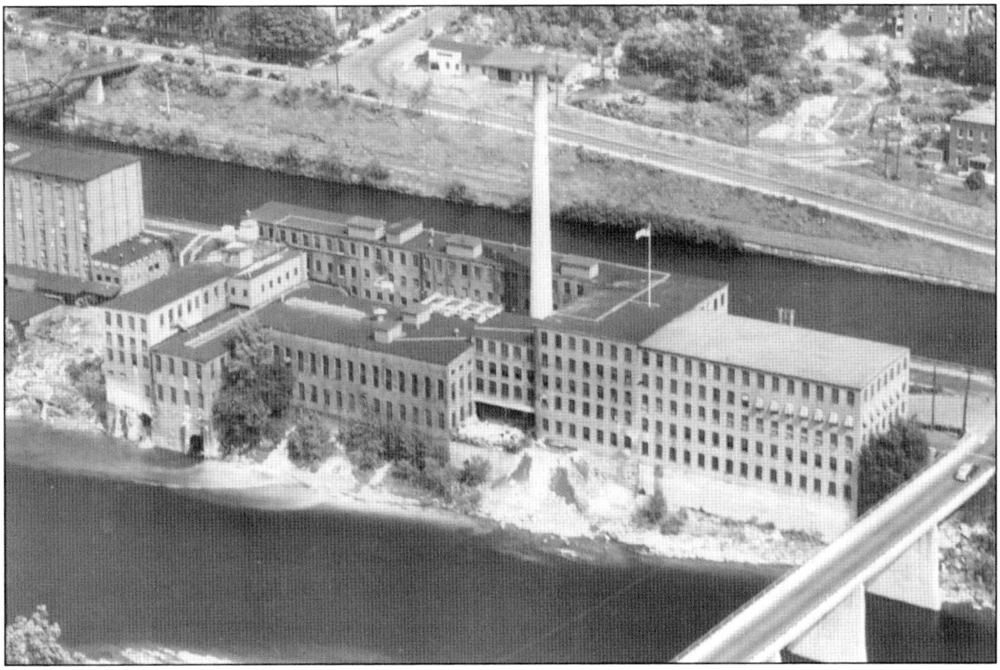

This 1947 aerial view, looking east, shows the Esleeck Paper Mill. Note the temporary bridge across the river replacing the White Suspension Bridge, which had been damaged in the flood of 1936. (Courtesy Turners Falls Library.)

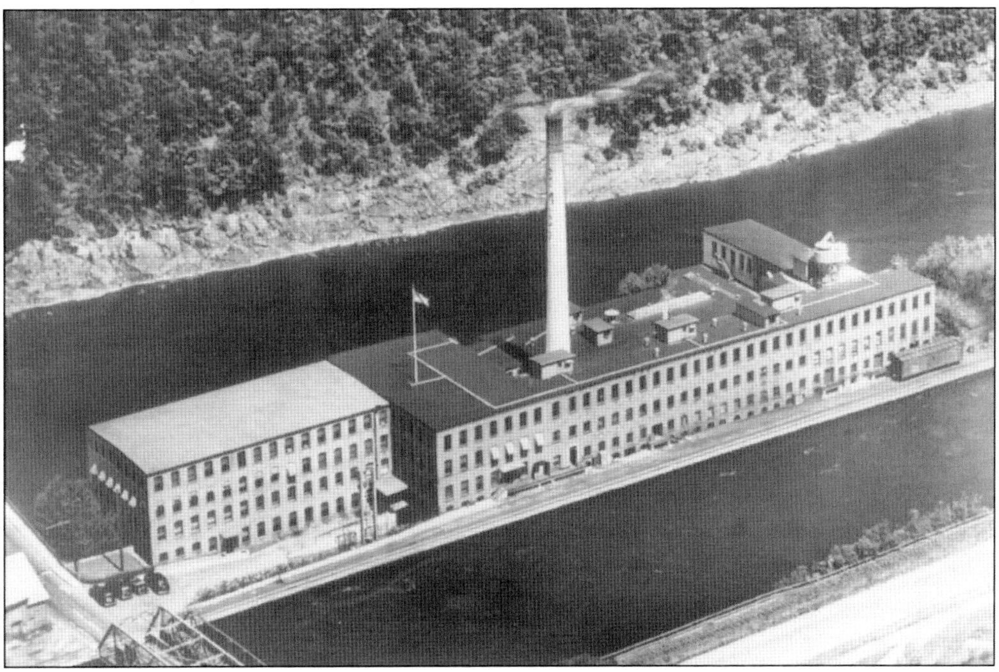

The Esleeck Paper Mill is shown in this view looking west. The Esleeck Manufacturing Company complex has had many additions; the original portion was constructed *c.* 1895 by Frank J. Marshall. In 1900, Augustine W. Esleeck took over the mill and started manufacturing fine paper at the plant. (Courtesy Turners Falls Library.)

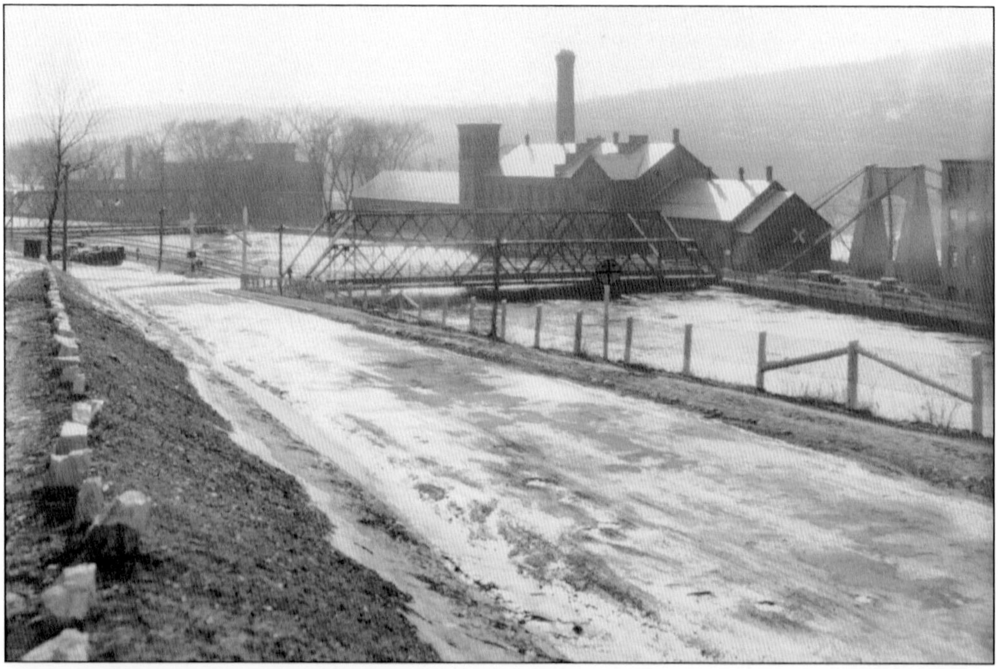

This view, showing the Griswold Cotton Mill, the Turners Falls Paper Company, and the White Suspension Bridge also shows the very edge of the Esleeck Manufacturing Company building. (Photograph by Alex M. Gamelen; courtesy Western Massachusetts Electric Company.)

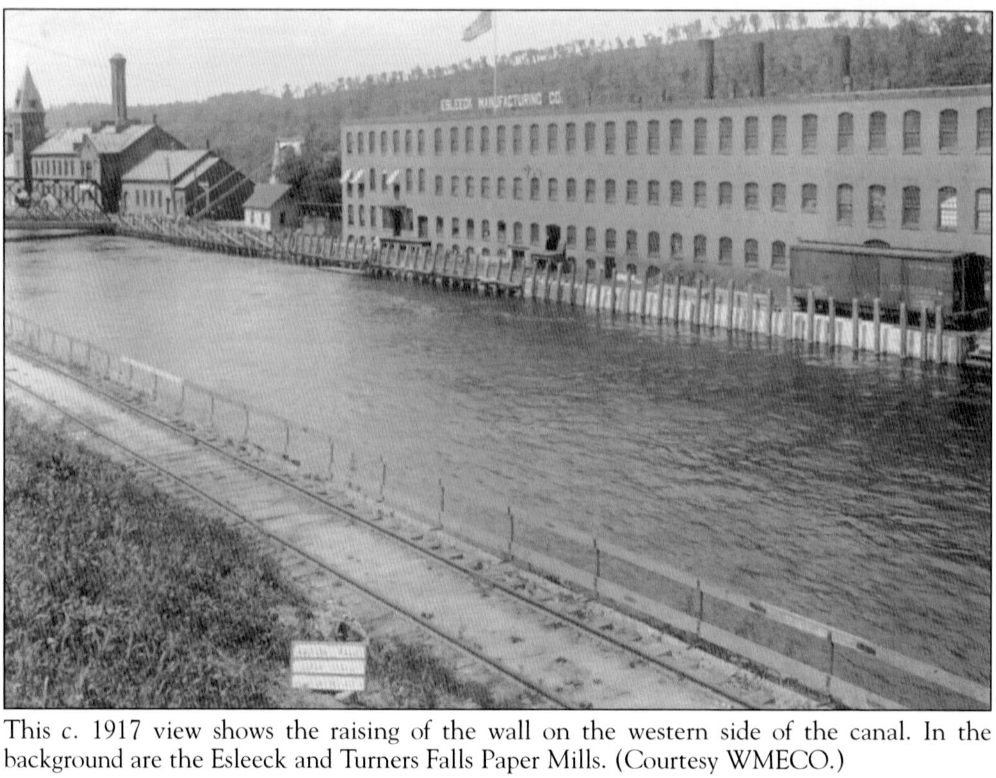

This c. 1917 view shows the raising of the wall on the western side of the canal. In the background are the Esleeck and Turners Falls Paper Mills. (Courtesy WMECO.)

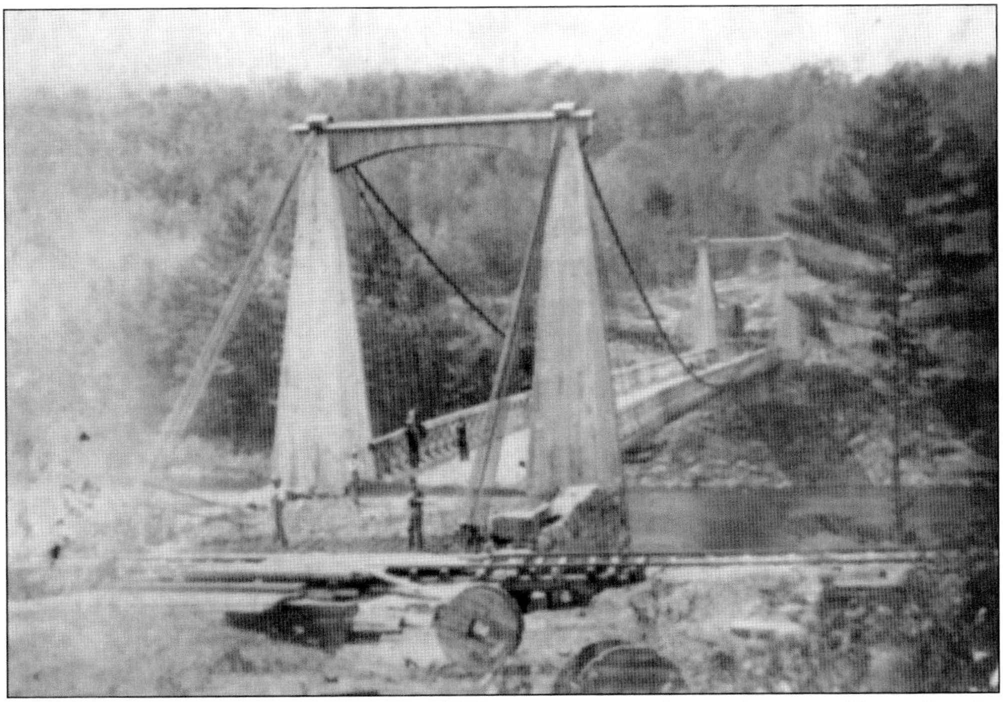

The White Suspension Bridge, shown in 1872, was constructed so workmen could travel to the developing Turners Falls from Greenfield. The bridge was started on November 16, 1871, and finished in the spring of 1872. Its cost was $36,000. The bridge spanned some 445 feet. It was damaged in the flood of 1936 and was removed. (Photograph by Horton and Davis; courtesy Peter S. Miller.)

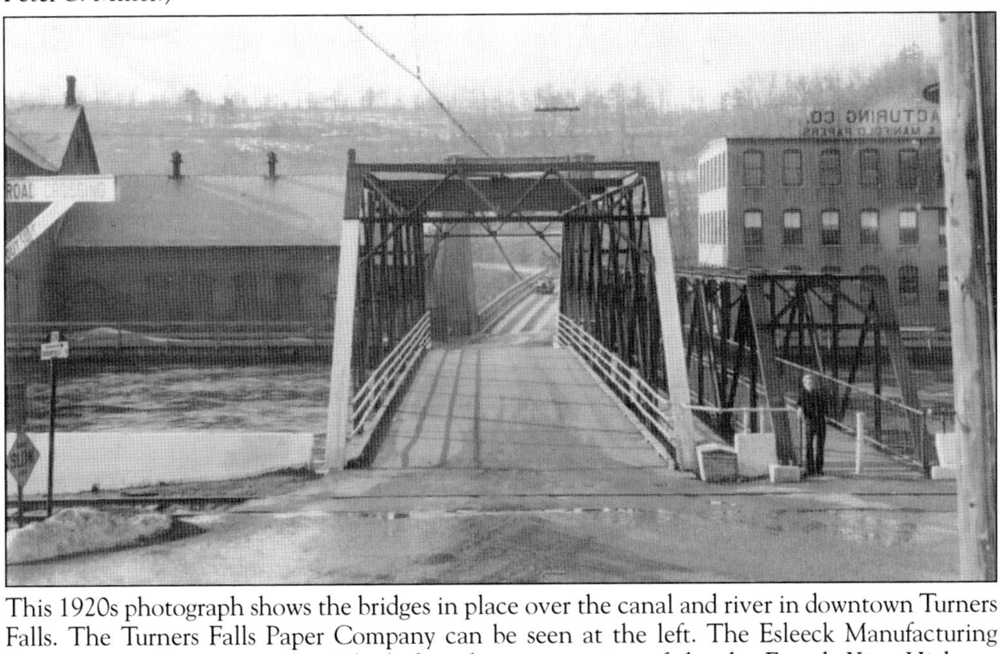

This 1920s photograph shows the bridges in place over the canal and river in downtown Turners Falls. The Turners Falls Paper Company can be seen at the left. The Esleeck Manufacturing Company can be seen at the right before the construction of the the French King Highway (Route 2) passed over these bridges. (Photograph by Alex Gamelin; courtesy WMECO.)

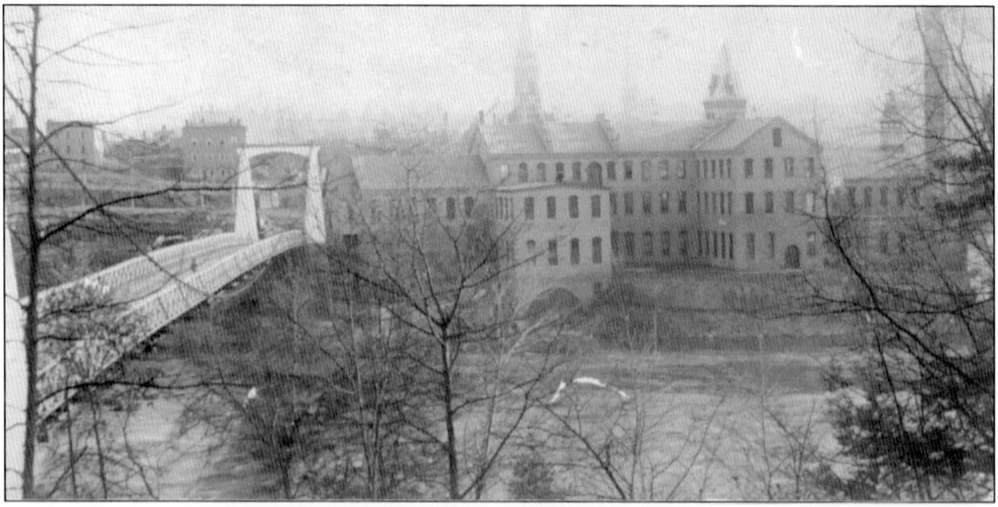

The Turners Falls Paper Company was built *c*. 1879 and was purchased by the International Paper Company in 1898. Most of this complex was taken down long ago. The very southern part of the building is now home to the Franklin County Regional Housing Authority and a warehouse for the Couture Brothers. This photograph was taken in 1890. (Courtesy Montague Library System.)

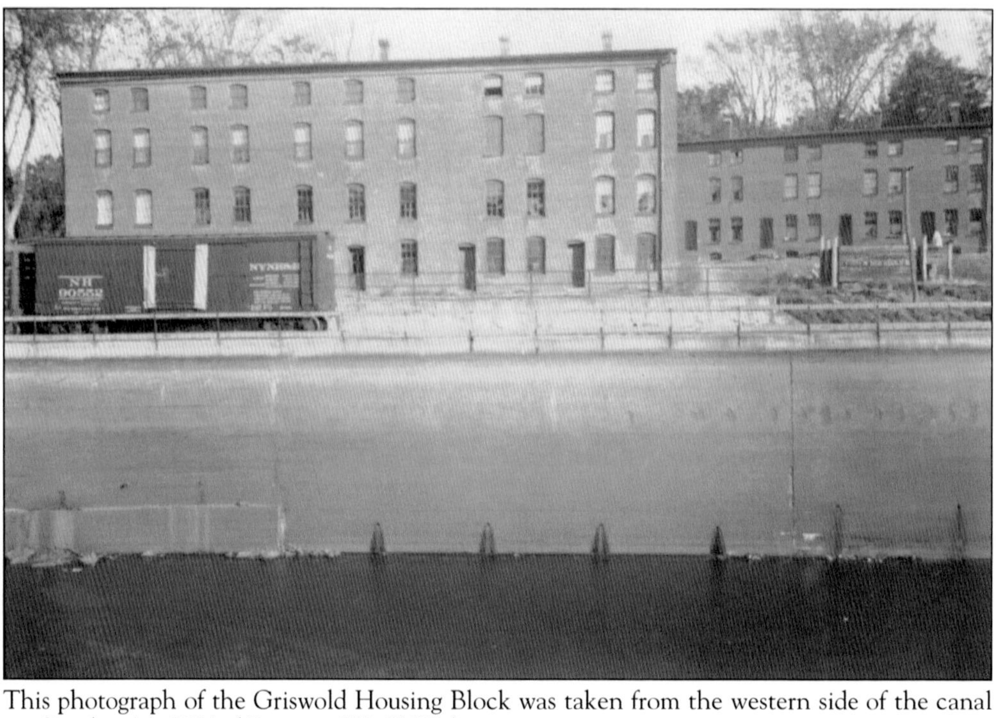

This photograph of the Griswold Housing Block was taken from the western side of the canal on October 14, 1921. (Courtesy WMECO.)

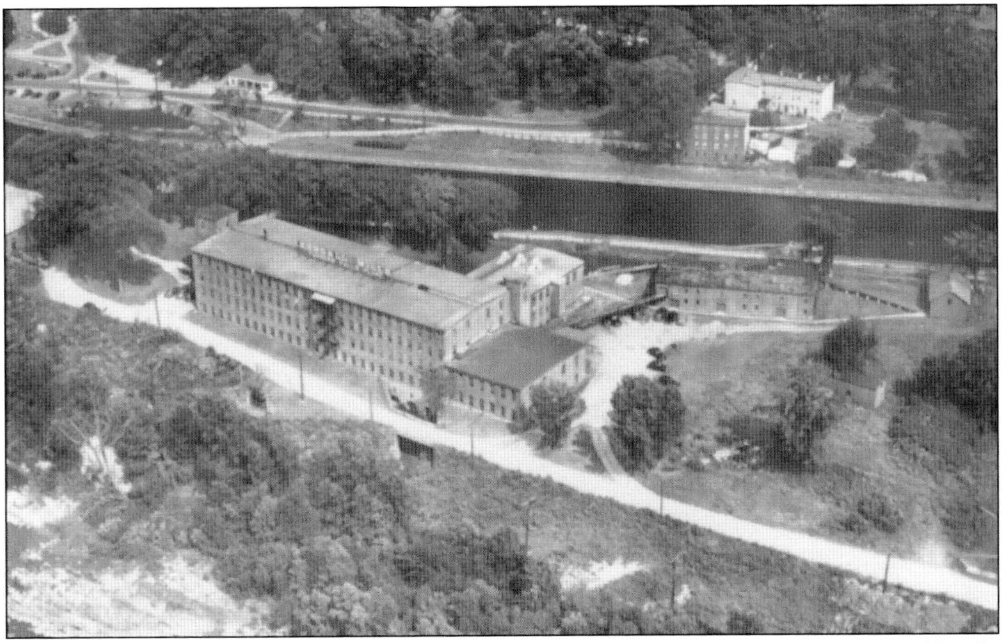

This is an aerial view of the Kendall Cotton Mill, which was built in 1873 using special bricks manufactured by the company, by Joseph Griswold of Colrain, Massachusetts. Prior to Kendell's ownership, the mill was known as the Griswold Cotton Mill. Later, the mill was used for retail stores such as Rockdale and Railroad Salvage Store. (Courtesy Peter S. Miller.)

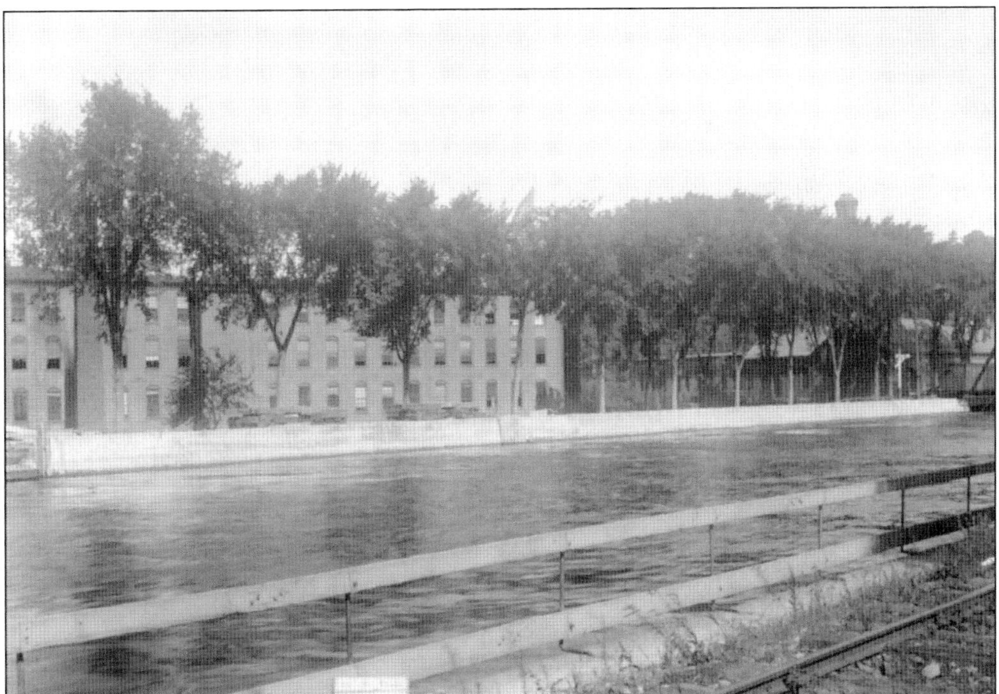

This photograph, taken on September 7, 1917, shows the northern section of the Griswold Cotton Mill along the canal. (Courtesy WMECO.)

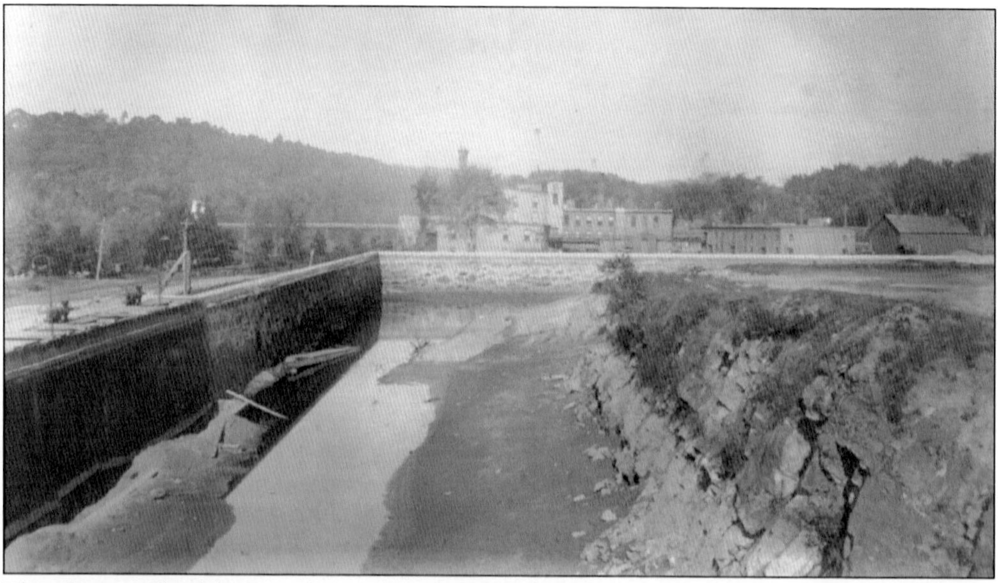

This photograph of the Branch Canal Power Station No. 1 was taken on October 16, 1920. The Kendell Mills complex is visible in the background. The White Suspension Bridge can also be seen. (Courtesy WMECO.)

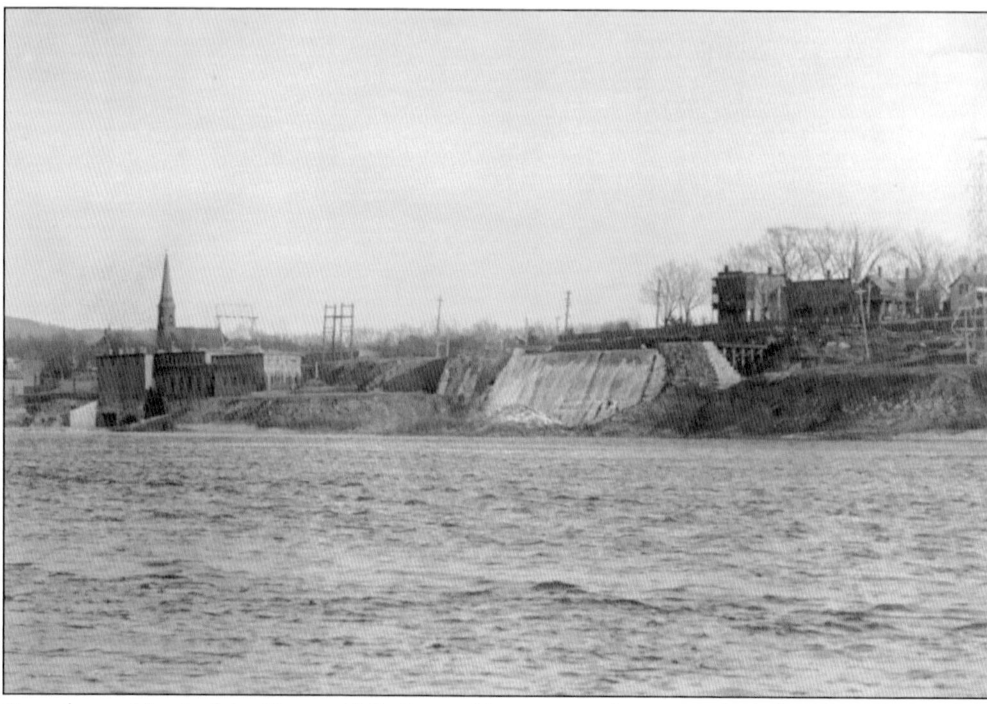

Powerhouse No. 1 of the Turners Falls Power Company is shown on the left of this photograph. The spillway over the dam is on the right. The steeple of St. Anne's can be seen in the background. (Courtesy WMECO.)

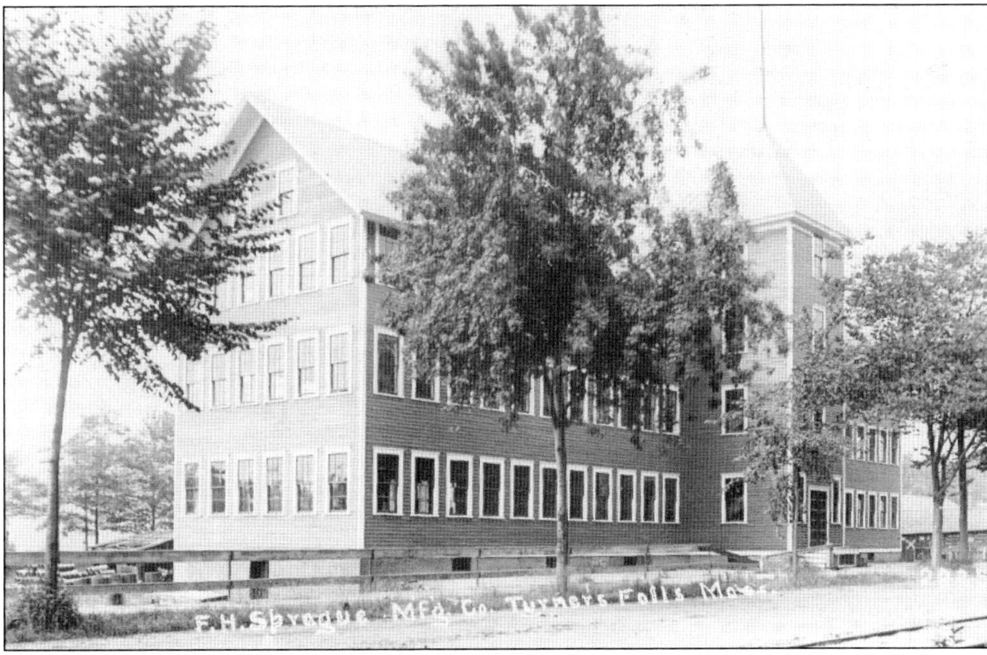

The F.H . Sprague Manufacturing Company, located on Avenue A in Turners Falls, was photographed *c.* 1909. (Courtesy Peter S. Miller.)

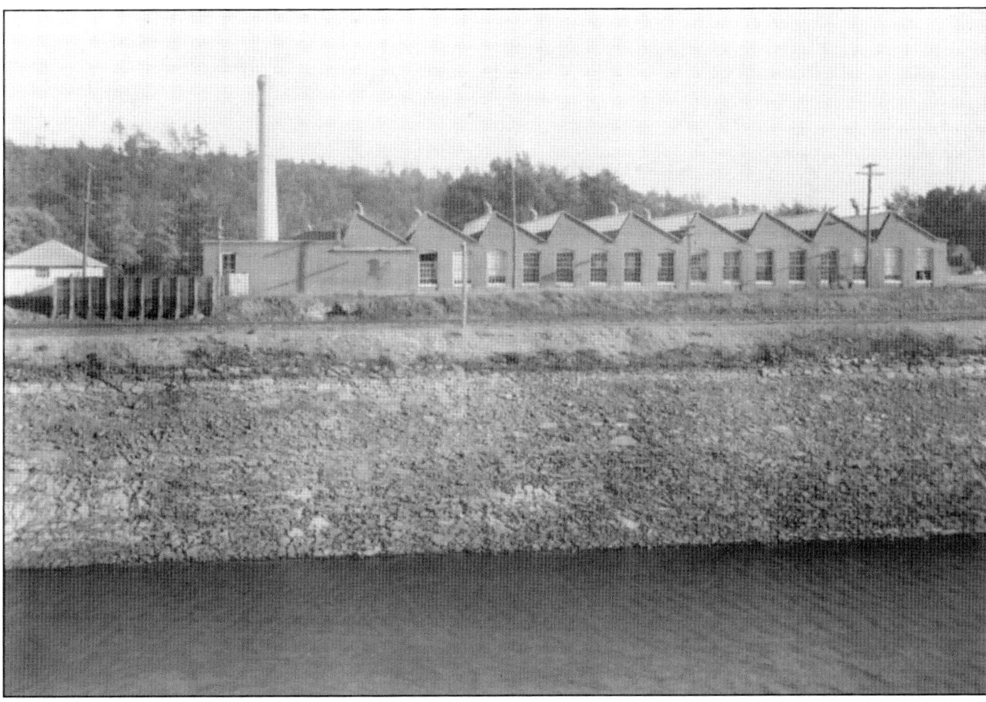

This photograph showing the McLane Silk Mill Company and the canal was taken from the south side of the canal on October 14, 1921. This mill started production in October 1914 and stopped *c.* 1928 (Courtesy WMECO.)

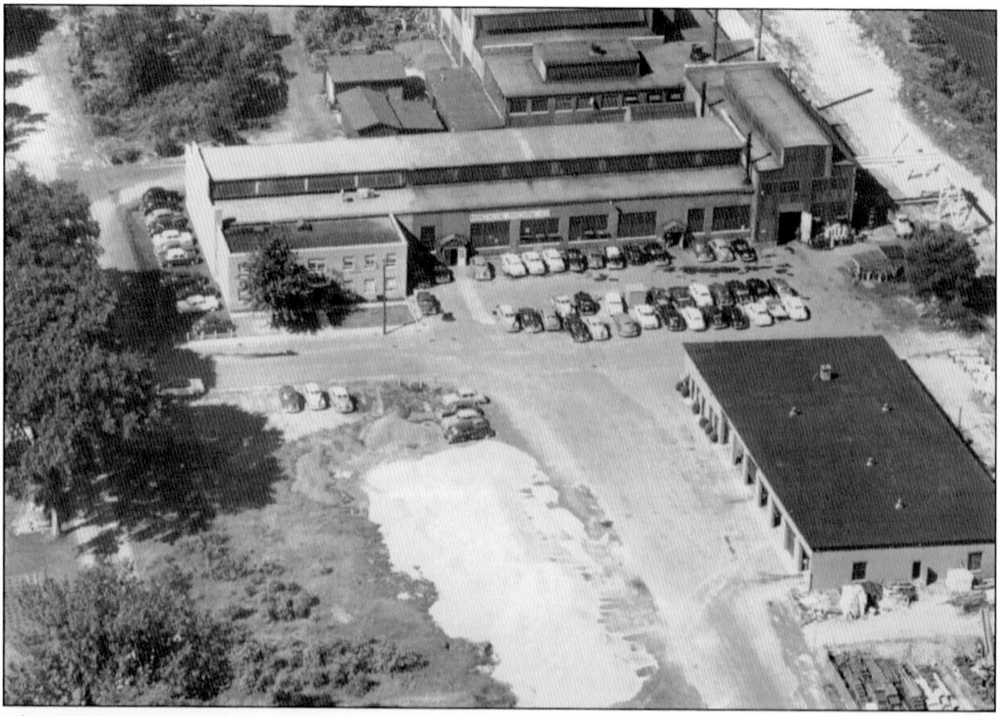

The Montague Machine Company (formerly known as Clark and Chapman and also the Turners Falls Machine Company) was previously located on the canal across from the International Paper Companies Mill. The new plant was constructed in the 1920s. This aerial view was taken *c.* 1951 (Courtesy Montague Machine Company.)

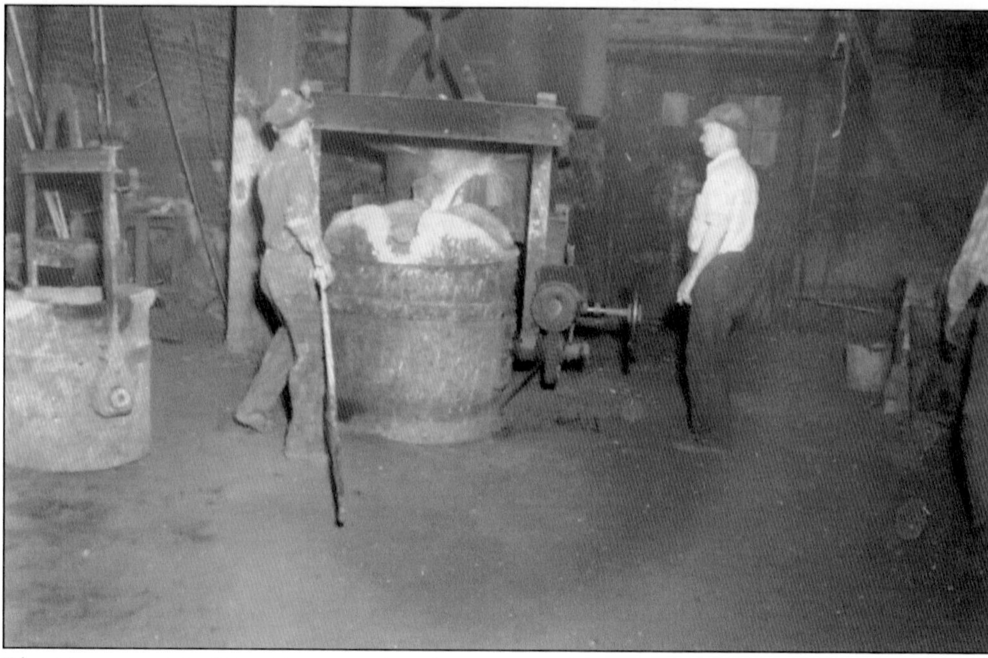

The Montague Machine Company foundry room is shown in its current Avenue A location in 1969.

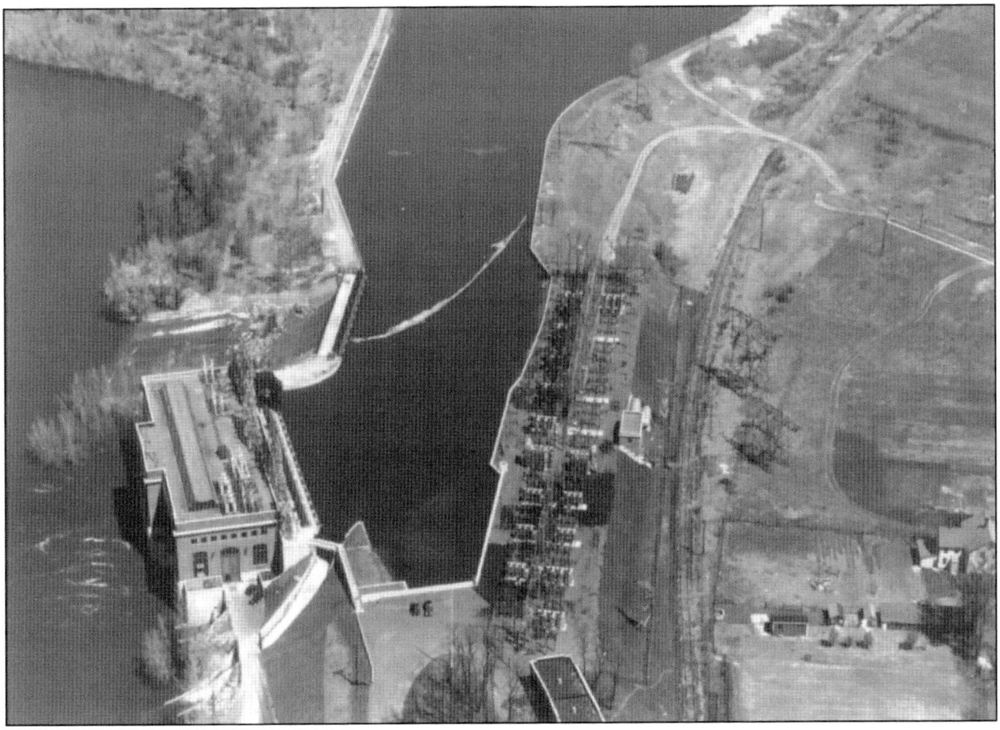

Cabot Station, located in Montague City, was built *c.* 1912. North of the station is the spillway to the canal. Nearby are tracks of the Boston and Maine Railroad. (Photograph taken May 8, 1935; courtesy WMECO.)

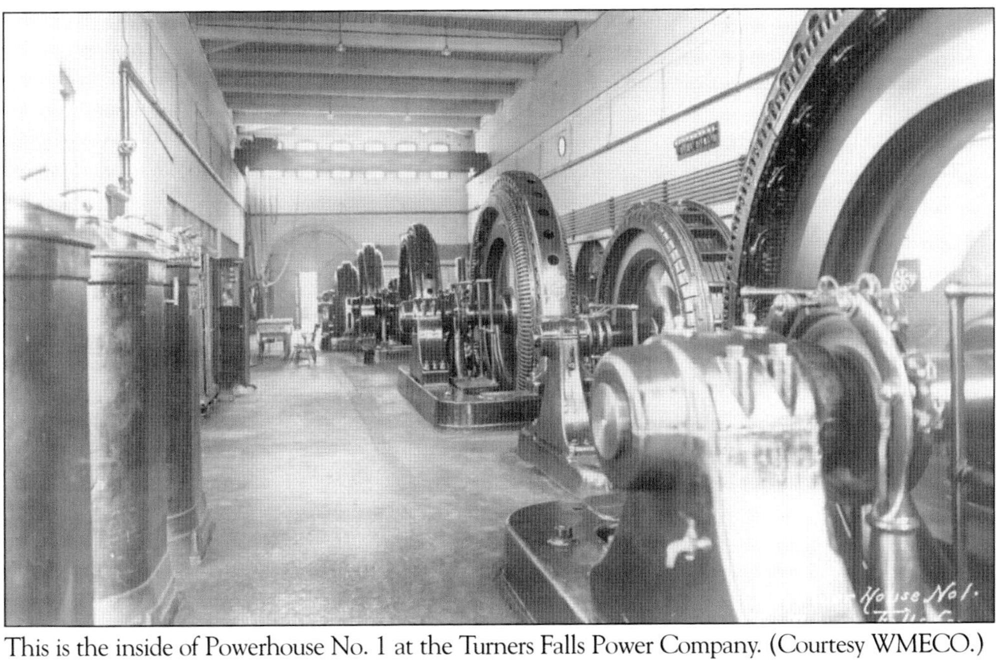

This is the inside of Powerhouse No. 1 at the Turners Falls Power Company. (Courtesy WMECO.)

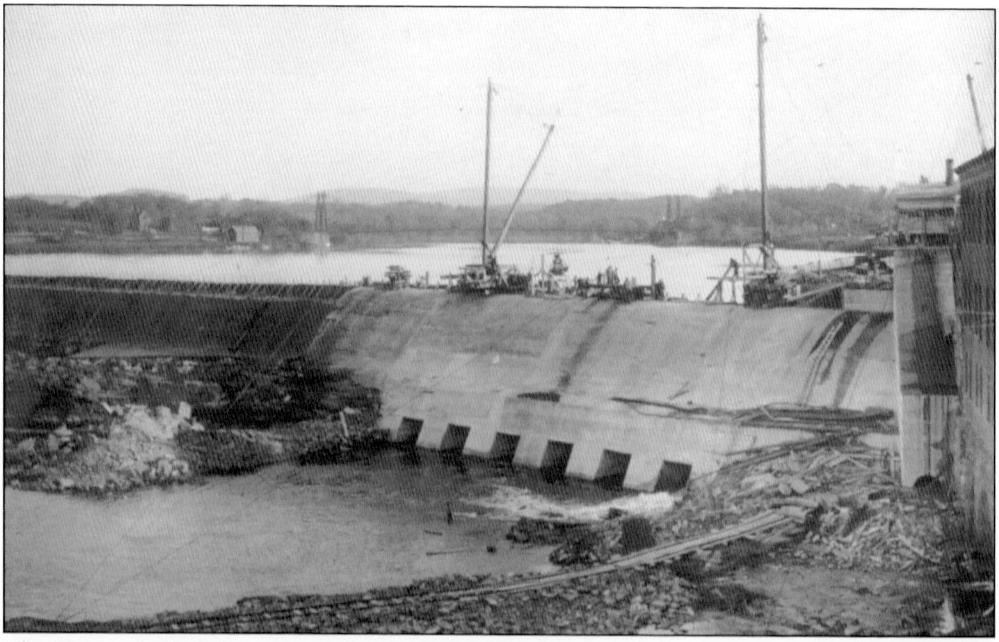

The Turners Falls Dam is shown here when its reconstruction was almost complete. The 1912 dam shows 3-foot lower abutments and downstream openings of six sluice gates. Note the extra heightening of the dam by the use of pipes that could bend and the use of flash boards. (Photograph taken 1912; courtesy WMECO.)

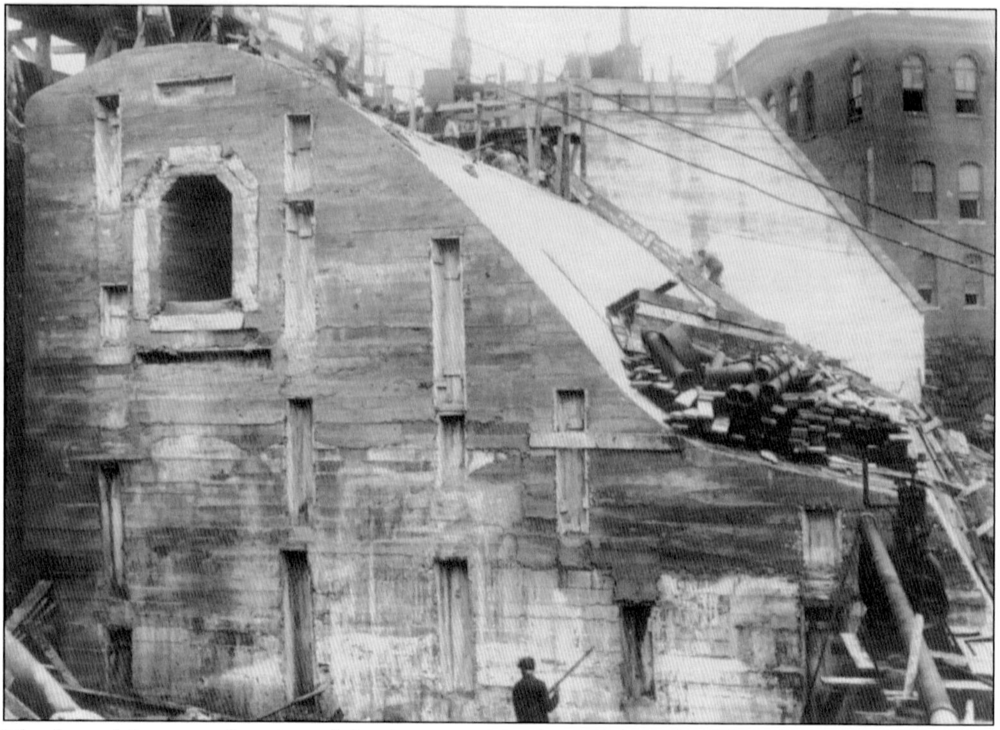

The face of the second section of the dam contains Gates 2, 3, and 4. This photograph shows the lead for the tunnel expansion joint. (Photograph taken September 5, 1913; courtesy WMECO.)

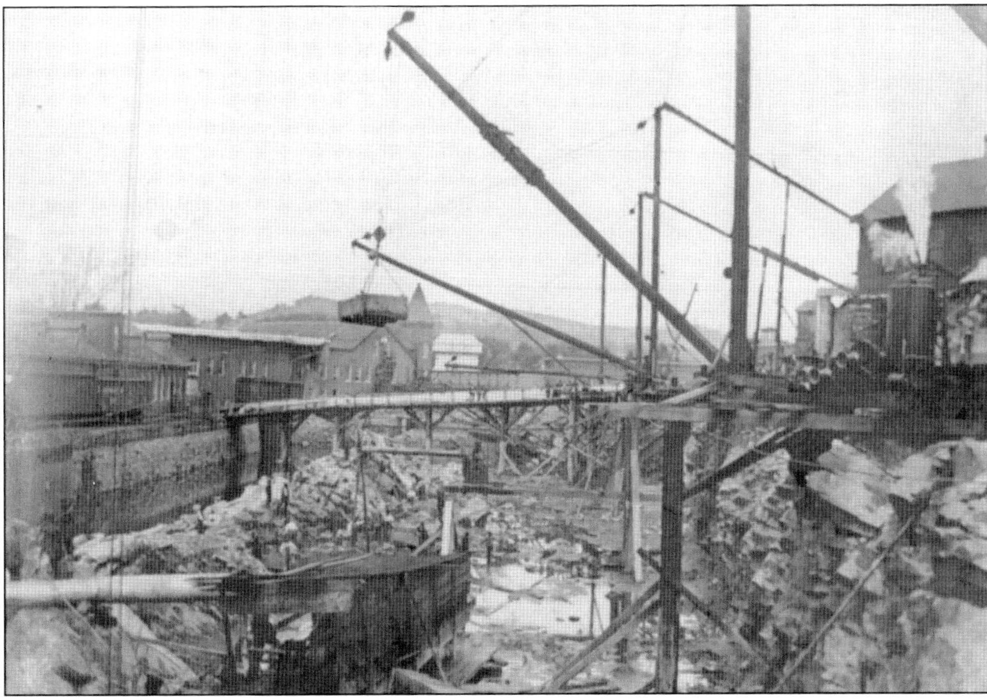

This scene shows the expansion and widening of the canal by the section of John Russell Cutlery Company. In the background is the International Paper Company. Also note the stone wall on the west side of the canal as well as the railroad spur. (Courtesy Gill Historical Society.)

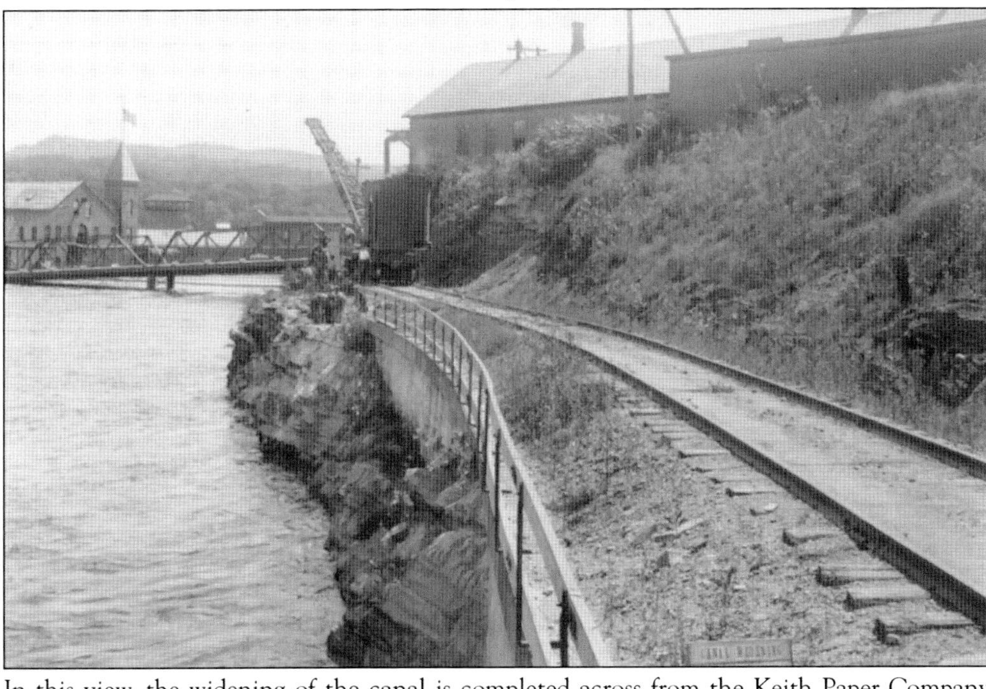

In this view, the widening of the canal is completed across from the Keith Paper Company. The Montague Paper Company (later the International Paper Company) is visible in the background of this c. 1912 photograph. (Courtesy WMECO.)

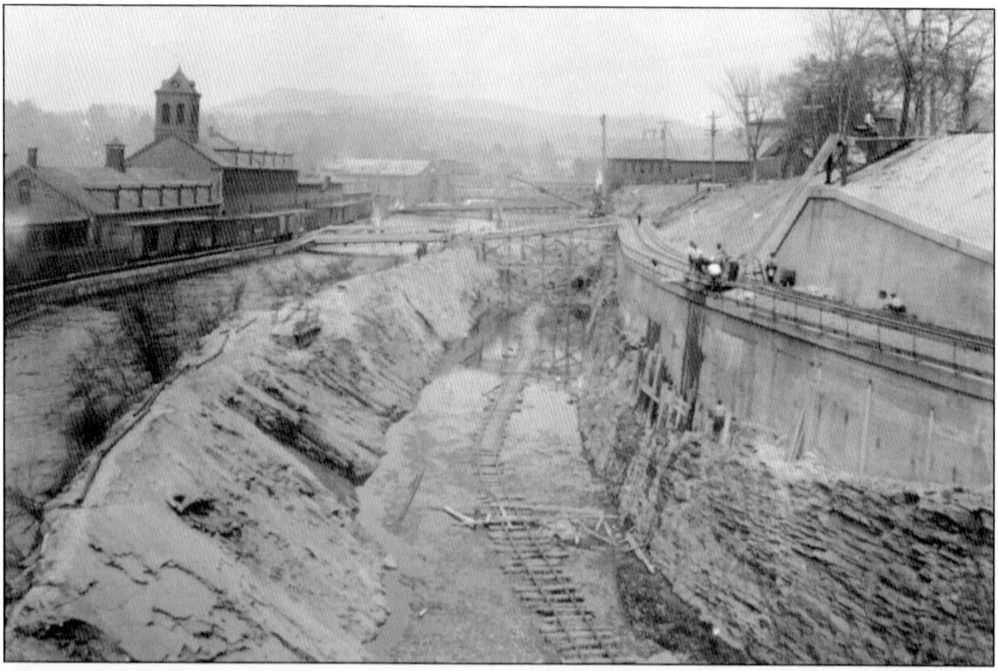

This view from the Keith Bridge at the Keith Paper Mill looks upstream. It shows the digging out of an addition to the canal while the the older portion of the canal is still being used. (Photograph taken February 26, 1913; courtesy WMECO.)

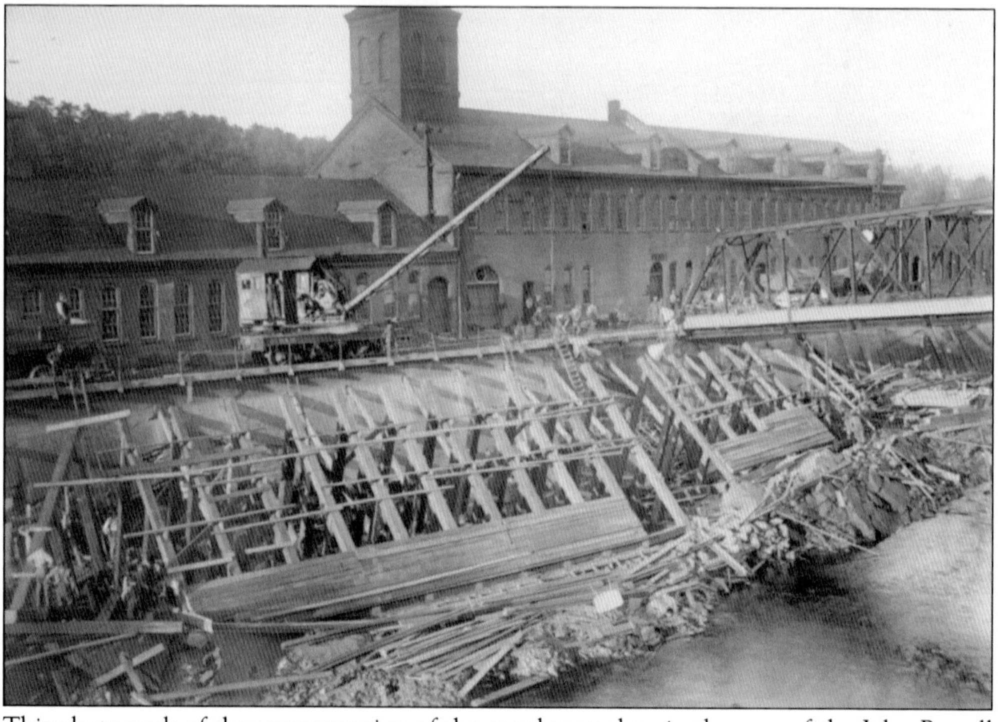

This photograph of the reconstruction of the canal was taken in the area of the John Russell Cutlery Company on October 15, 1921. (Courtesy Kyle J. Scott.)

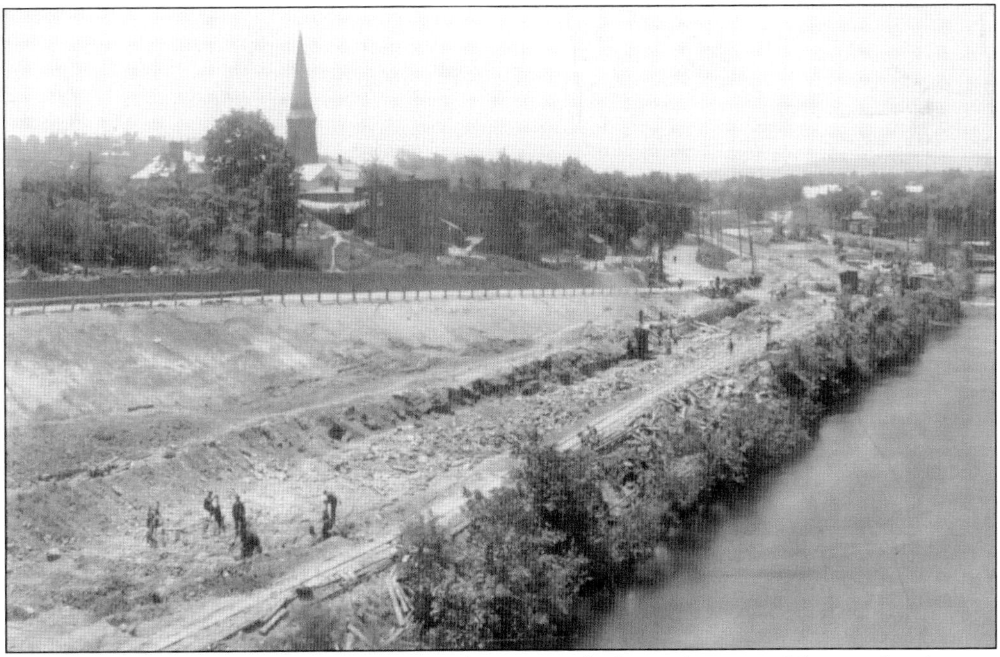

This photograph, taken across from the Keith Paper Mill, shows the start of the canal widening. St. Anne's Church can be seen in the background. (Courtesy WMECO.)

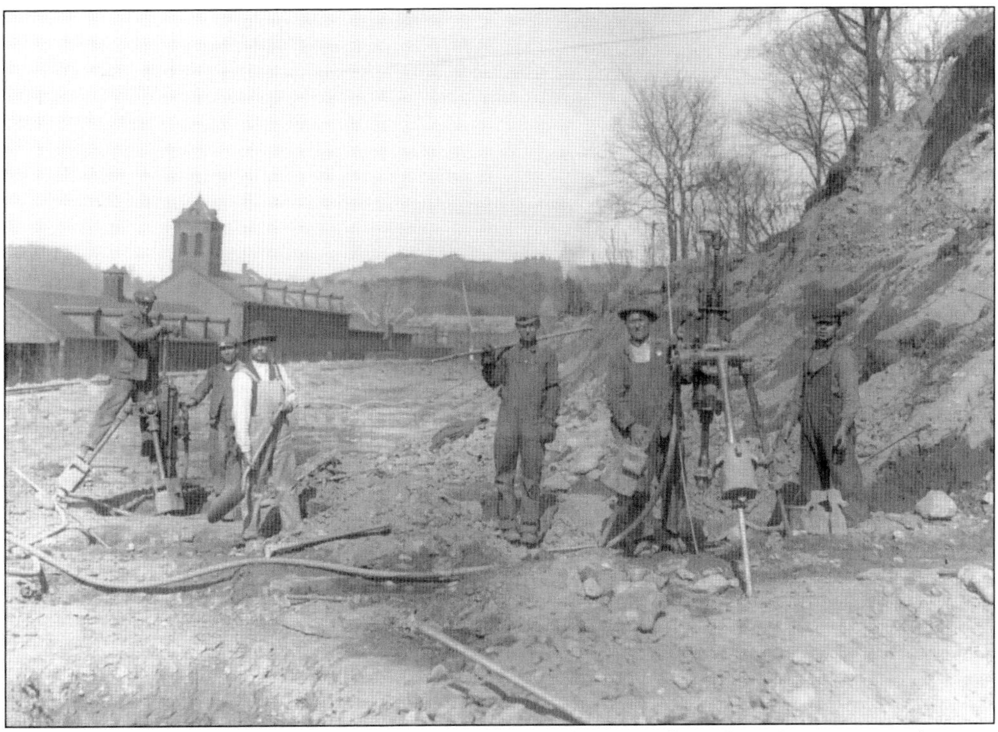

In this photograph of men at work on the canal, the John Russell Cutlery Company can be seen in the background. (Courtesy Turners Falls Library.)

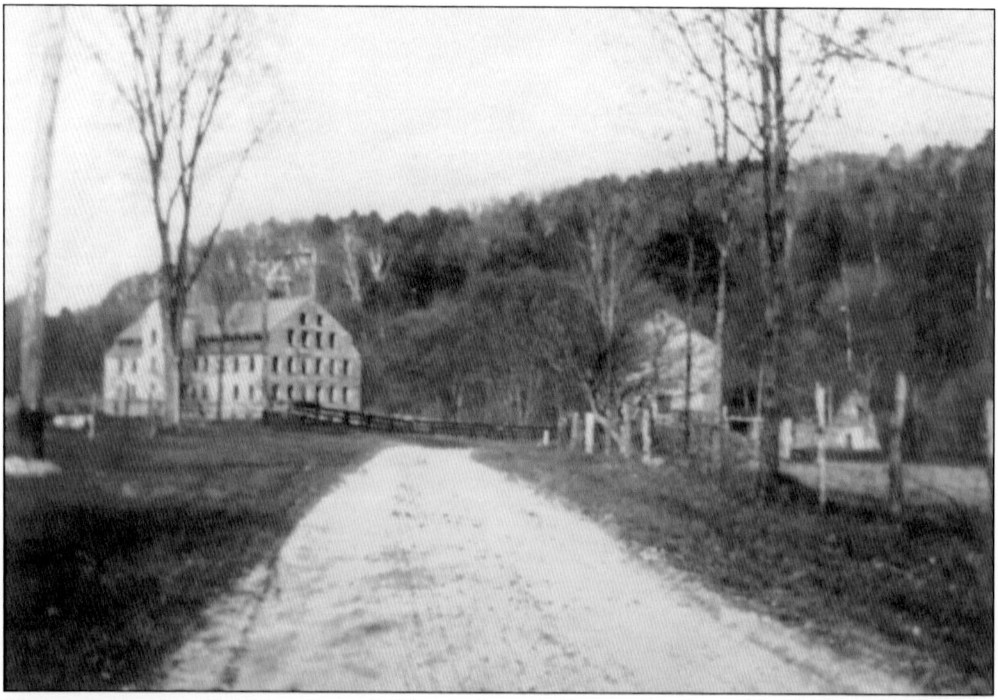

The Main Road to Gill from Greenfield goes through Factory Hollow. The old woolen mill is to the left. The mill was torched on July 4, 1933. The partially hidden building on the right was associated with the mill. The old iron bridge over the Fall River was torn down *c.* 1960, and the road became a dead end. (Courtesy Gill Historical Society.)

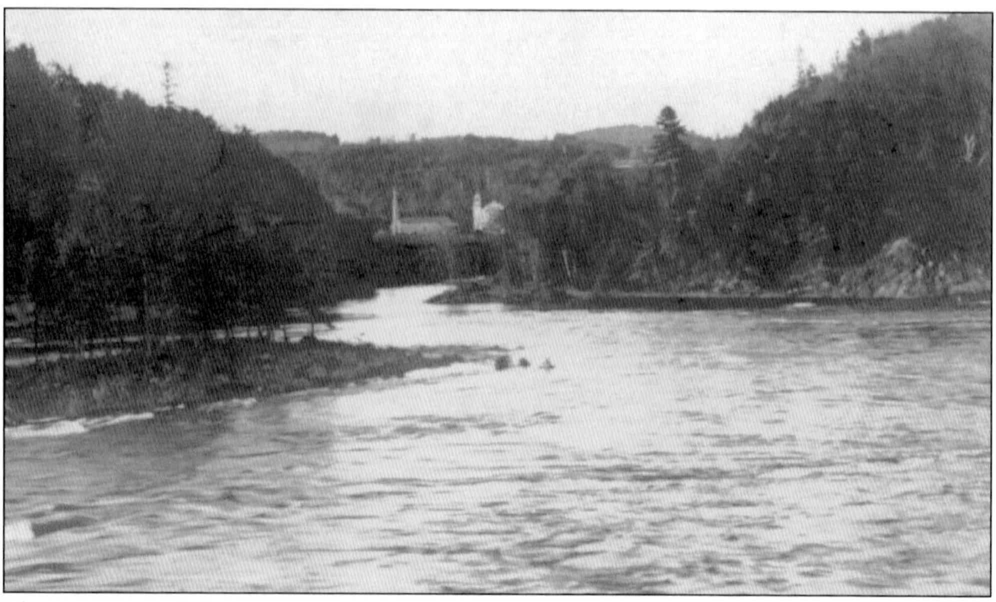

The entrance to Fall River was just below the dam on the Connecticut River. In the background are two of the buildings that were a part of the Factory Hollow Mill complex. The mill on the right was the main woolen mill. (Courtesy Montague Historical Society.)

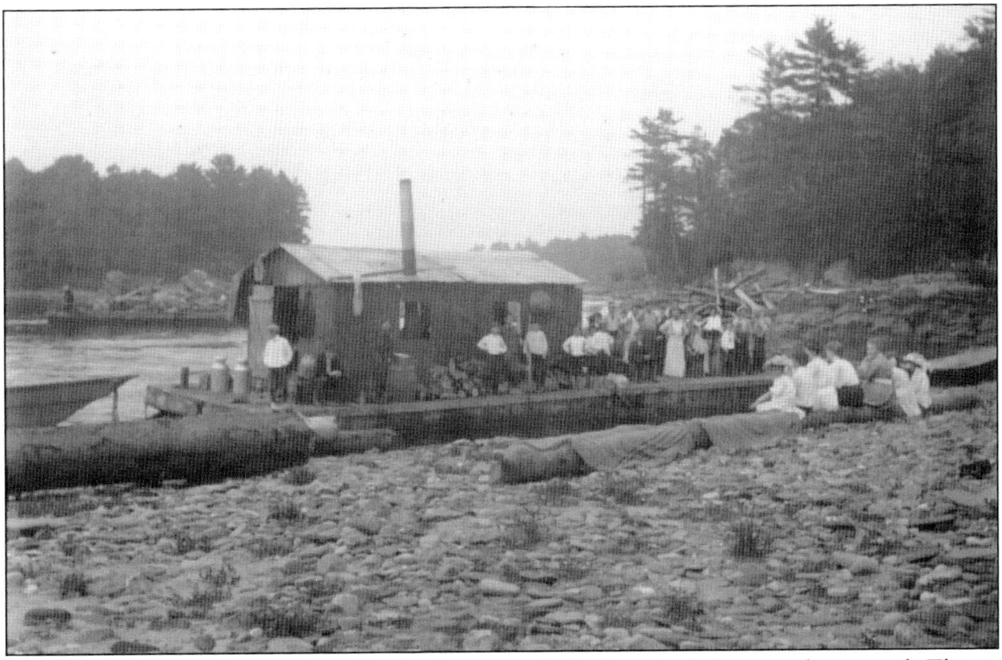

The cook shack or "wannegen" on the barge could be knocked down and removed. This is where the loggers slept and where the cooking was done. They ate at 9:30 a.m., 12:30 p.m., and had dinner after work. (Courtesy Montague Historical Society.)

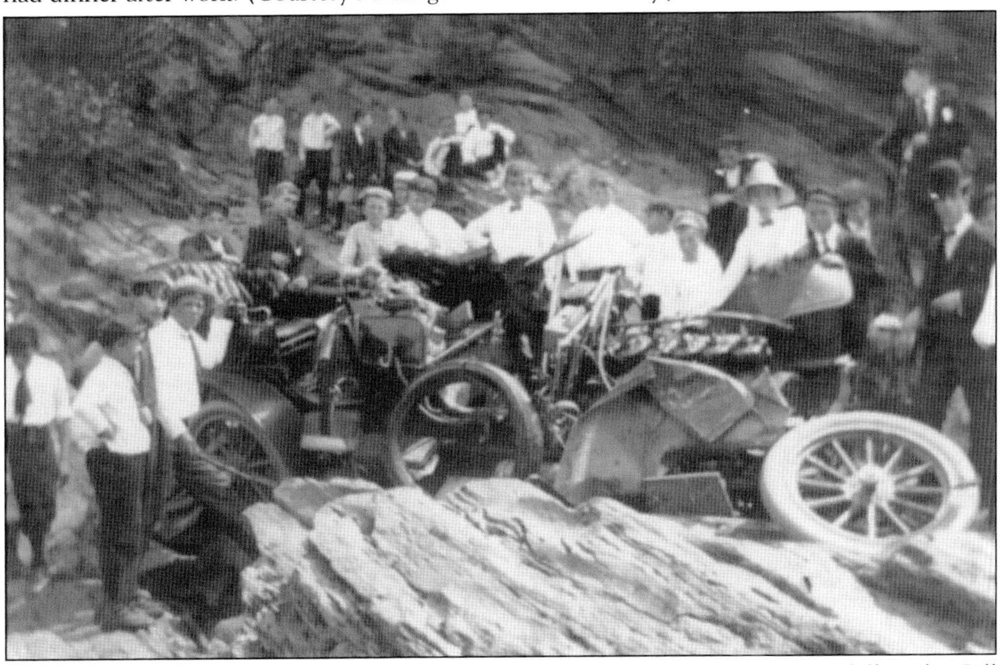

This is the wreckage of George Van Dyke's car after it went over the side of the cliff on the Gill side of the river. The accident occurred on August 8, 1909. Van Dyke was the head of a logging drive that came down the Connecticut River that year and years before. Van Dyke jumped from the car before it went over the cliff, but he was too close to the cliff edge and went over as well. His chauffeur, Shorty, also died as a result of the accident. (Courtesy Peter S. Miller.)

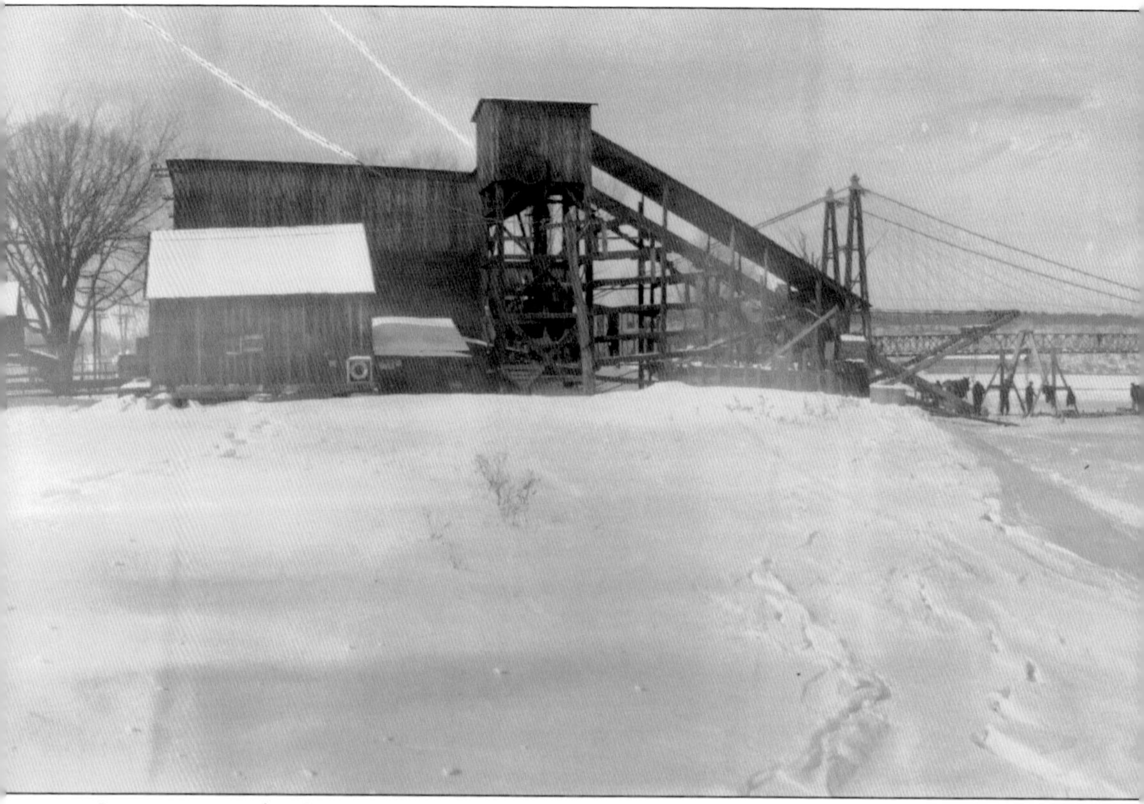

Ice cutting on the Connecticut River is shown in this view. Turners Falls is on the right and Riverside Gill on the left. The ice, which was stored to be sold at a later date, would be loaded

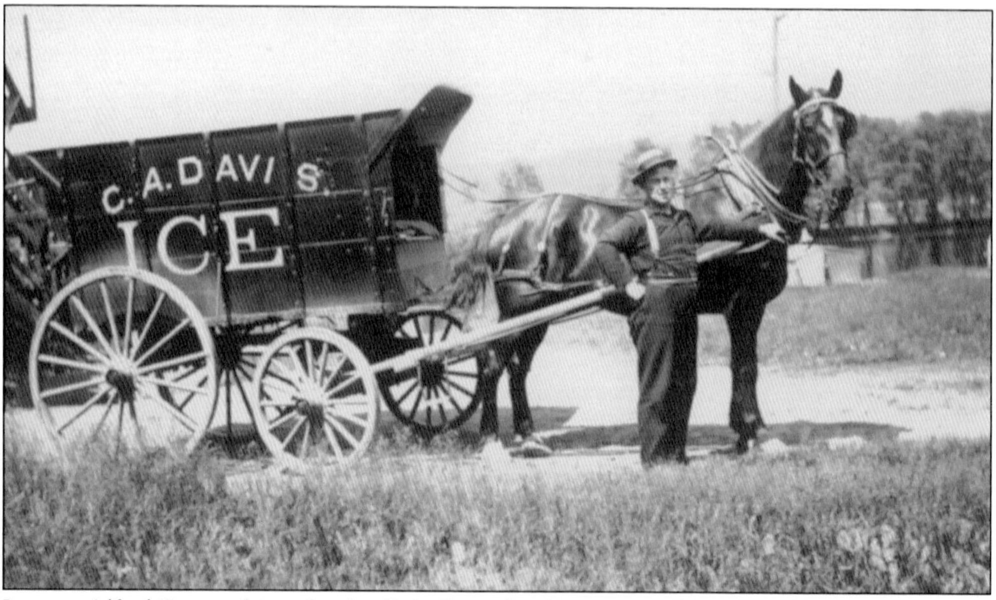

Iceman Alfred Carter, driver for the C.A. Davis Ice Company of Turners Falls, is shown in this photograph. Customers would place a card in the front window of their home showing how much ice by weight they wanted the iceman to bring. (Courtesy Gill Historical Society.)

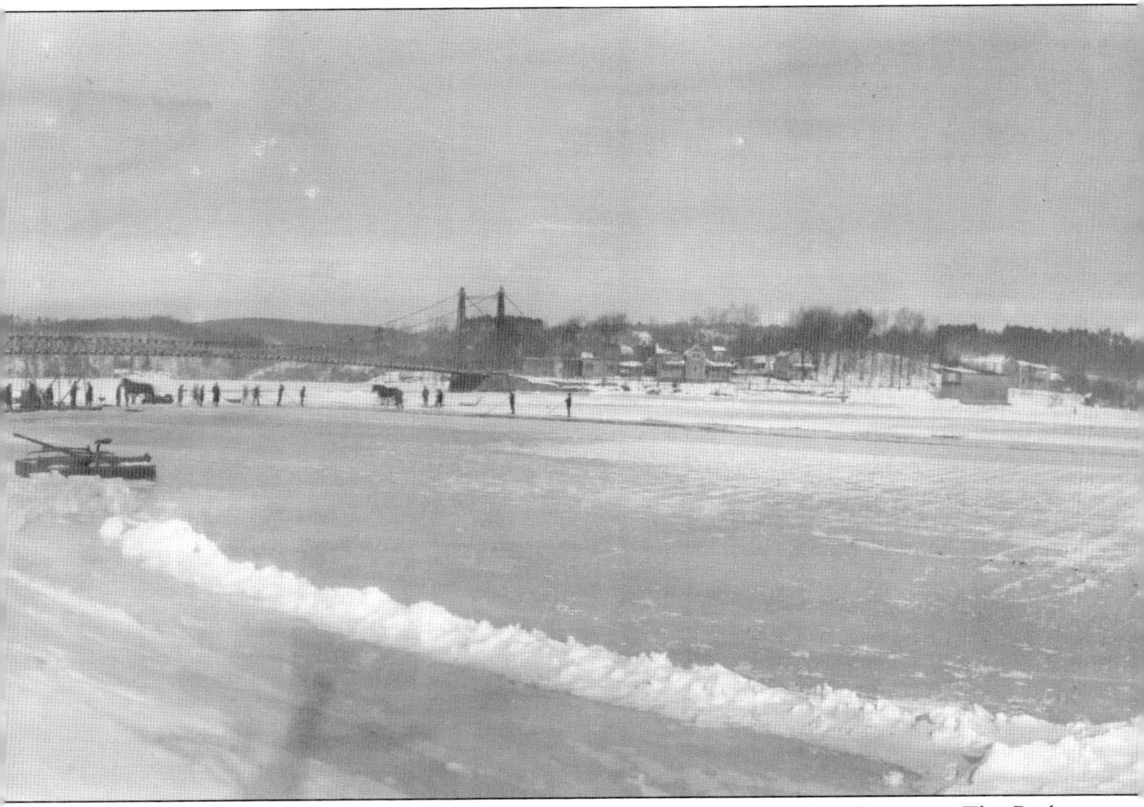

on the conveyor belt and carried into the icehouse of the C.A. Davis Ice Company. The Red Suspension Bridge is shown in the background. (Courtesy Montague Historical Society.)

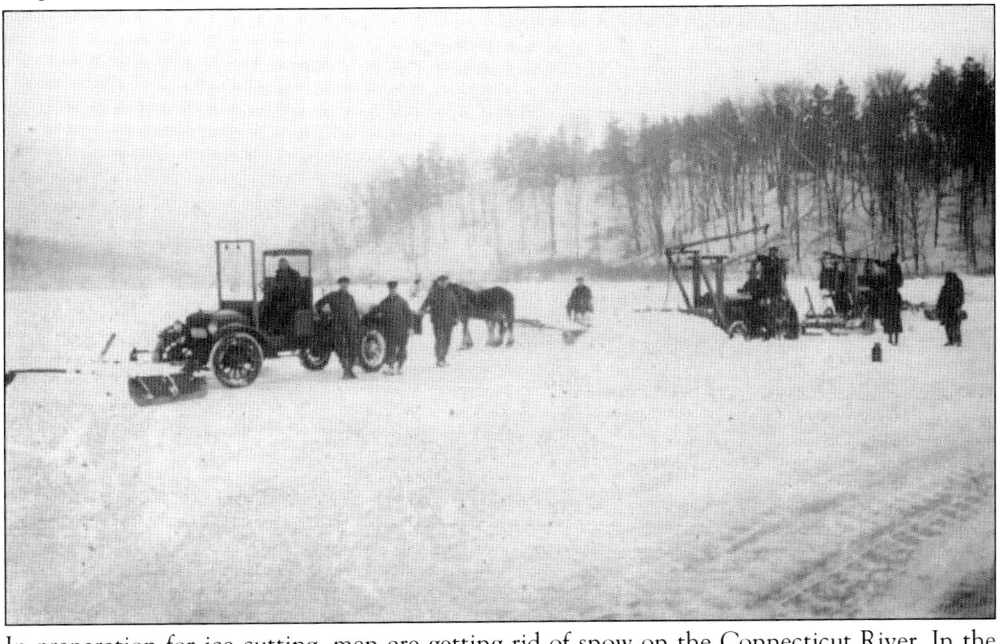

In preparation for ice cutting, men are getting rid of snow on the Connecticut River. In the background is Turners Falls. (Courtesy Gill Historical Society.)

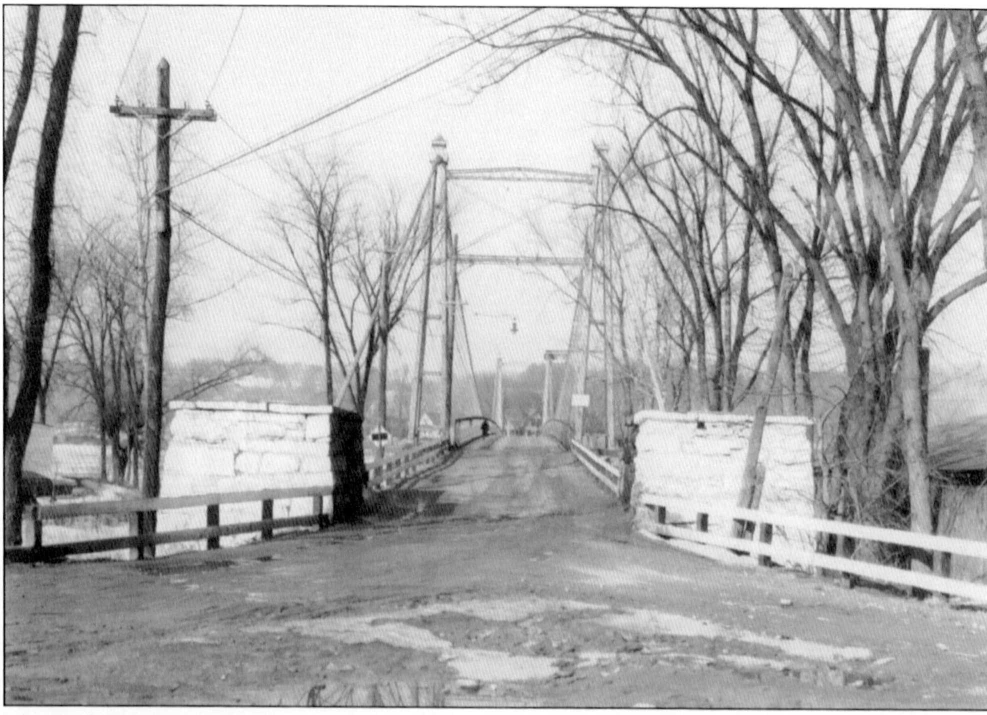

The Red Suspension Bridge was extant from 1878 until 1942. This view was taken from Unity Park, looking toward Riverside Gill. Some of the stones in the piers contain the famous armored mud balls. The bridge was replaced by the present Gill Montague Bridge. The bridge was 563 feet long, cost $42,000, and was damaged in the flood of 1936. It was taken down during World War II for a scrap metal drive. Earlier ferries used to cross the river at this site. On the Turners Falls side of the river, Ferry Road was laid out up the hill from this site. (Photograph by Alex Gamelin; courtesy WMECO.)

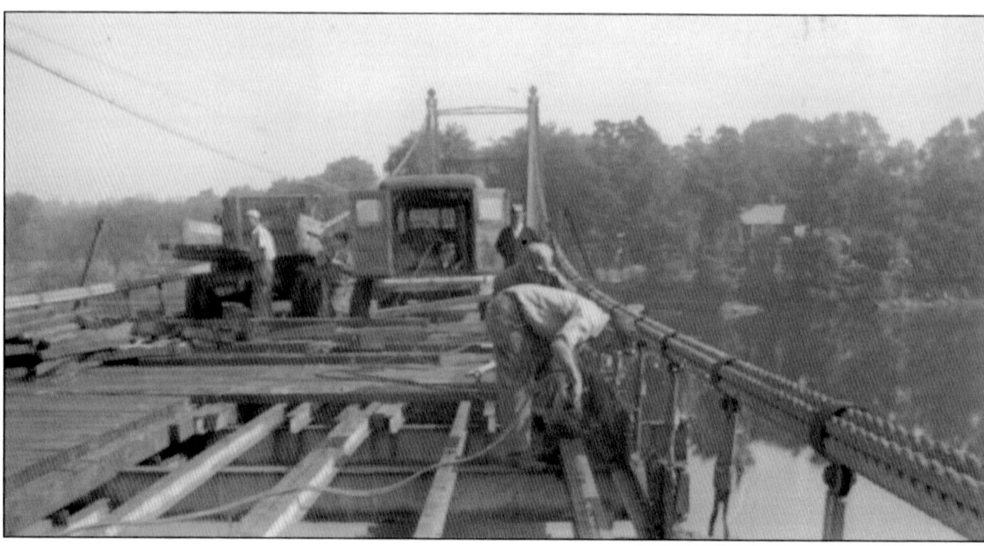

These men are taking down the Red Bridge in 1942. The town of Gill is in the background. (Courtesy Gill Historical Society.)

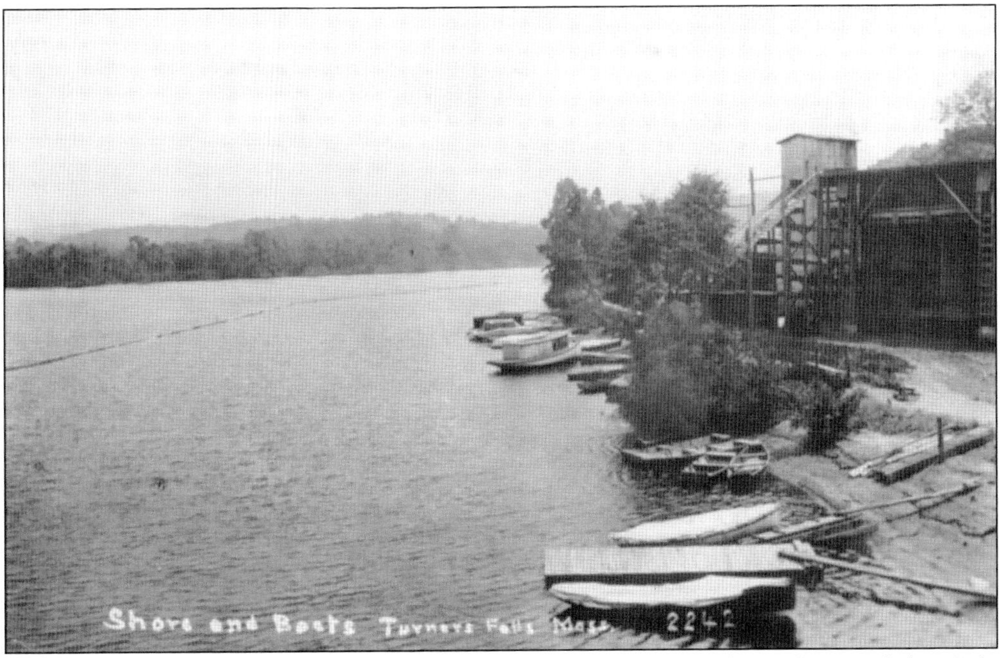

Boats are on the Turners Falls side of the Connecticut River. The icehouse of the C.A. Davis Ice Company is in the background. Note the logging boom to the left of the shoreline. (Courtesy Peter S. Miller.)

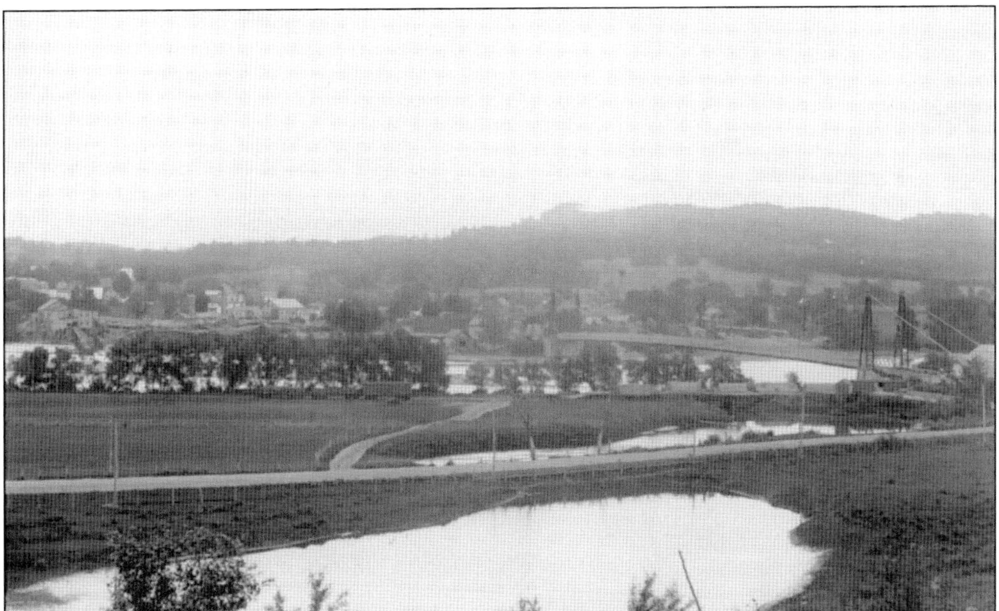
Unity Park is shown before it was filled in with fill from the last widening of the canal in 1912. The Unitarians purchased this land when their church disbanded. The background is the Turners Falls Lumber Company in Riverside, and to the right is the Red Bridge. (Courtesy Turners Falls Library.)

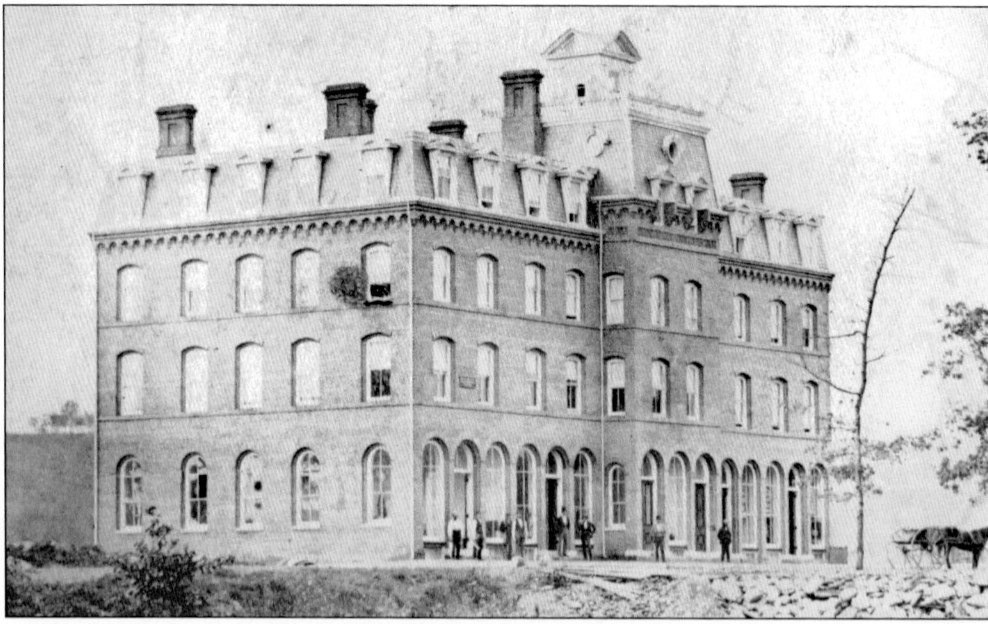

The Farren House was standing from 1874 to the early 1960s. The building was named in honor of Barnard Farren, who owned a brickyard in Montague City. He was a builder and contractor of the Hoosic Tunnel. Farren often summered in Montague City, returning to his native Philadelphia in the winter months. The Farren House was later known as the Grand Trunk Hotel. Some years later, this building contained apartments and town offices. After it was torn down, Cumberland Farms had a convenience store built at the site. The former Cumberland Farms store was taken over by the Commonwealth of Massachusetts for its new visitors center. (Photograph by Charles E. Barton; courtesy Peter S. Miller.)

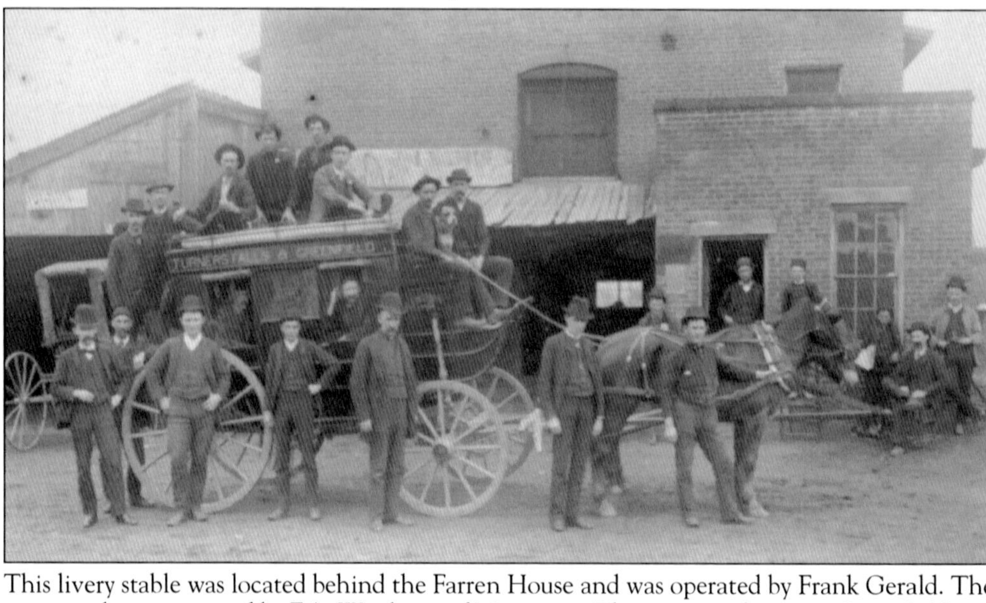

This livery stable was located behind the Farren House and was operated by Frank Gerald. The stagecoach was operated by F.A. Woolman of Montague. The stage ran between Greenfield and Turners Falls. Sometimes the stage carried passengers from Greenfield to attend events at the Collie Opera House. (Photograph by A.W. Howes and Company; courtesy Peter S. Miller.)

St. Anne's Church and Parochial School was on J Street. The school later closed, and the building was turned into condominiums. The church was built in 1885 and the school in 1896 and was known as the French Church. (Courtesy Peter S. Miller.)

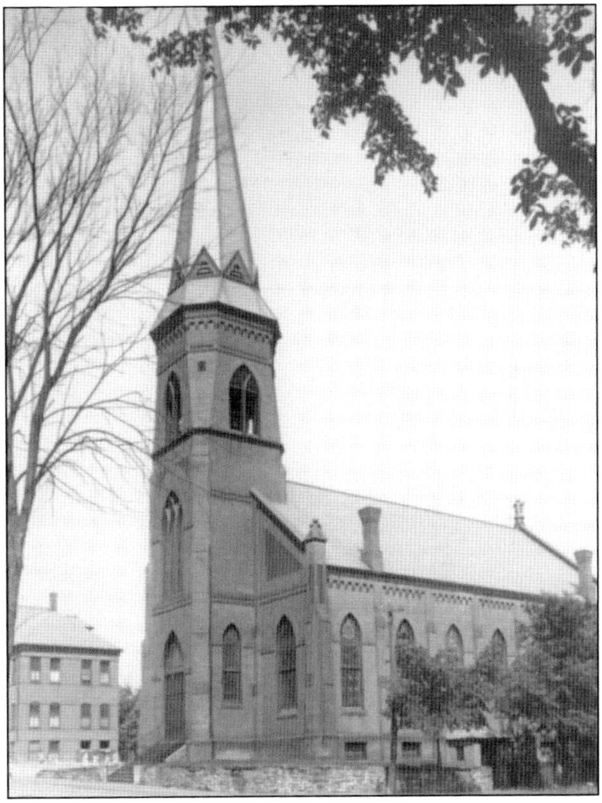

This building still stands at the corners of Avenue A and Second Street. It was the home of the Turners Falls Reporter newspaper, the N.B. Hall Dining Room, and F.H. Brown and Company stationery store. (Photograph E.W. Cook; courtesy Peter S. Miller.)

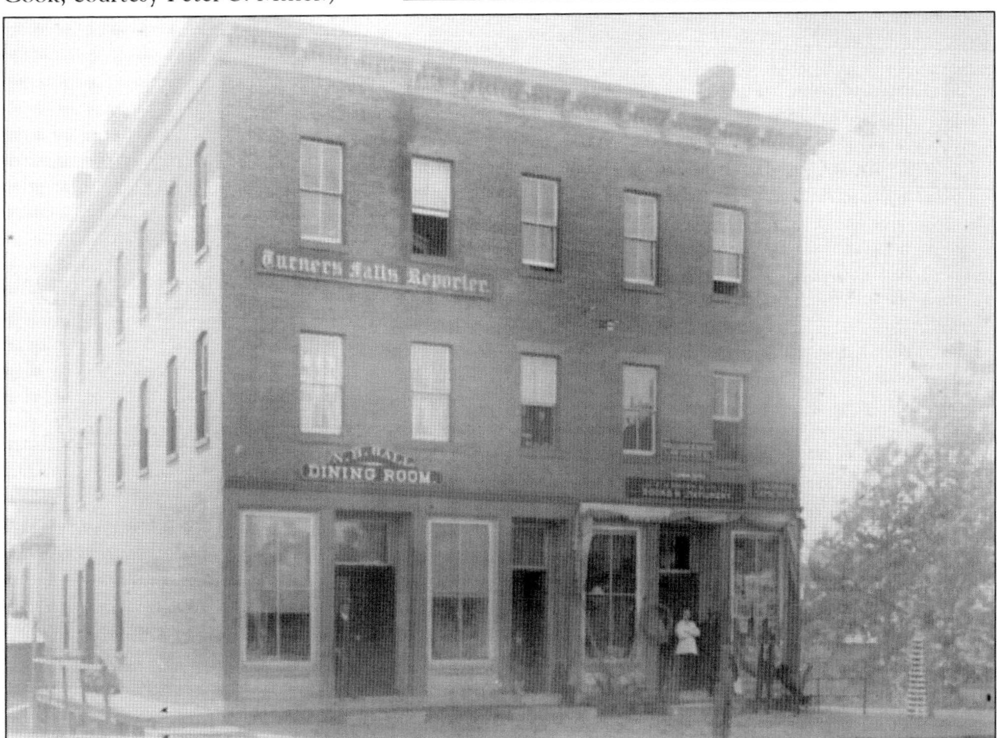

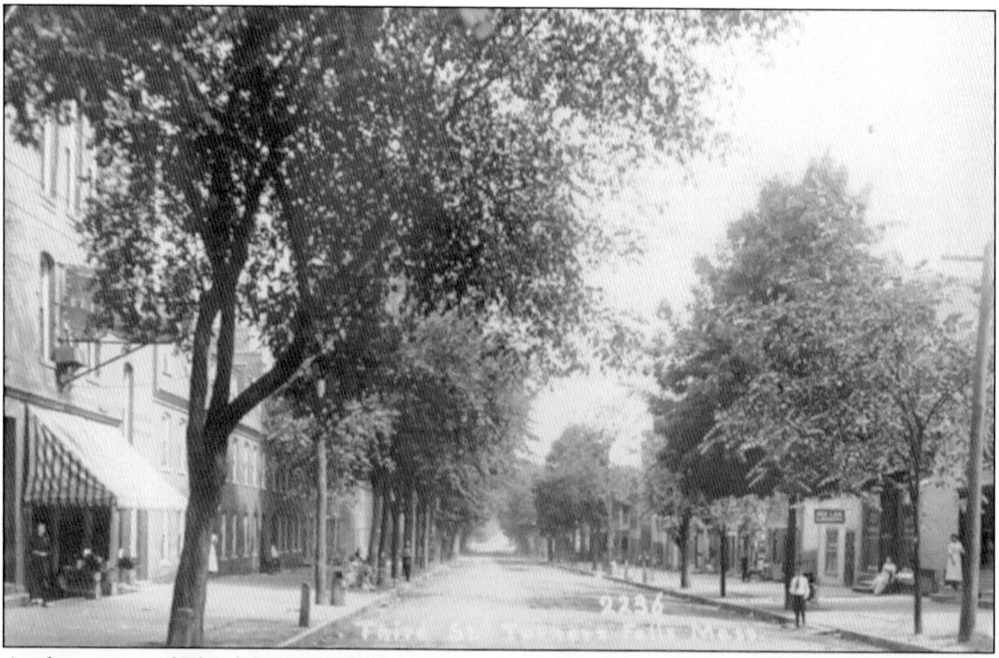

At the corner of Third Street and Avenue A, the Collie Opera House and the Russell Cutlery Housing Block are on the left. On the right, in the background, is Gee Lee Laundry, *c.* 1910. (Courtesy Peter S. Miller.)

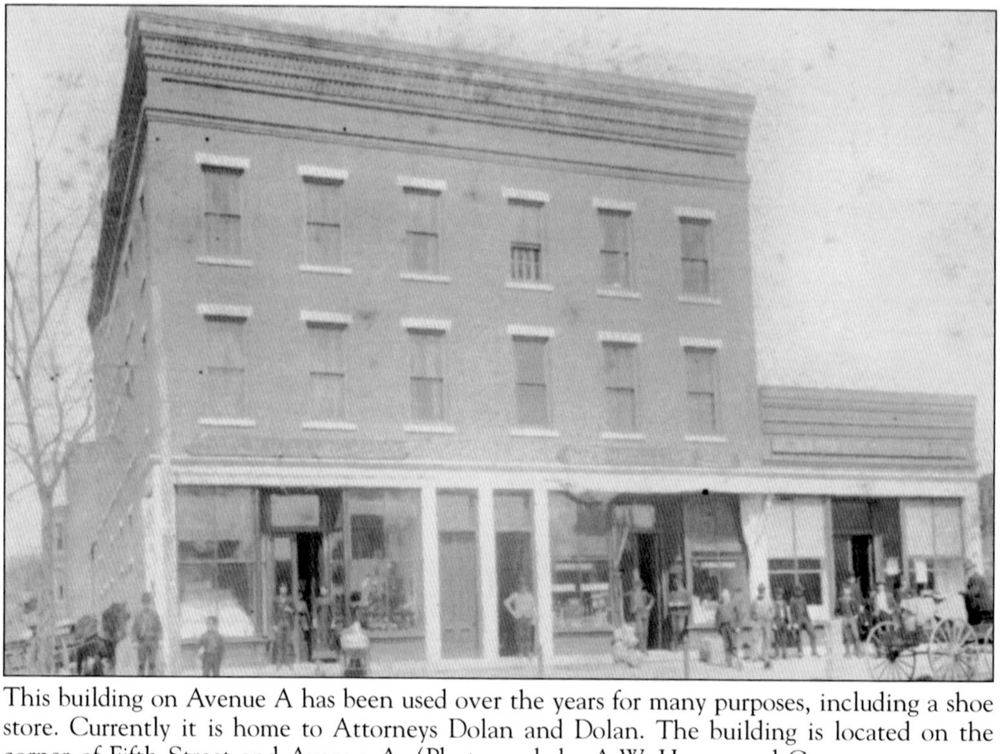

This building on Avenue A has been used over the years for many purposes, including a shoe store. Currently it is home to Attorneys Dolan and Dolan. The building is located on the corner of Fifth Street and Avenue A. (Photograph by A.W. Howes and Company; courtesy Gill Historical Society.)

In the center of this c. 1906 photograph is Dr. Joseph R. Charron with three of his children—Wilfred, Joe Jr., and John. Dr. Charron was a well-known and highly respected Turners Falls physician. He delivered countless children in the area and was often nicknamed "Mr. Stork." His life was one of service to others and devotion to family. He is credited with saving countless lives during the influenza epidemic of World War I. Often seen in a horse and buggy and later in the back seat of his chauffeur-driven car, Dr. Charron would spend countless hours on house calls in the town and surrounding area. Educated in Canada, he was known for his well-mannered way and his wit. Married to Anna Mary Charron, he had 10 children, most of whom were also active medical professionals in this area. (Courtesy Dr. Arthur Charron.)

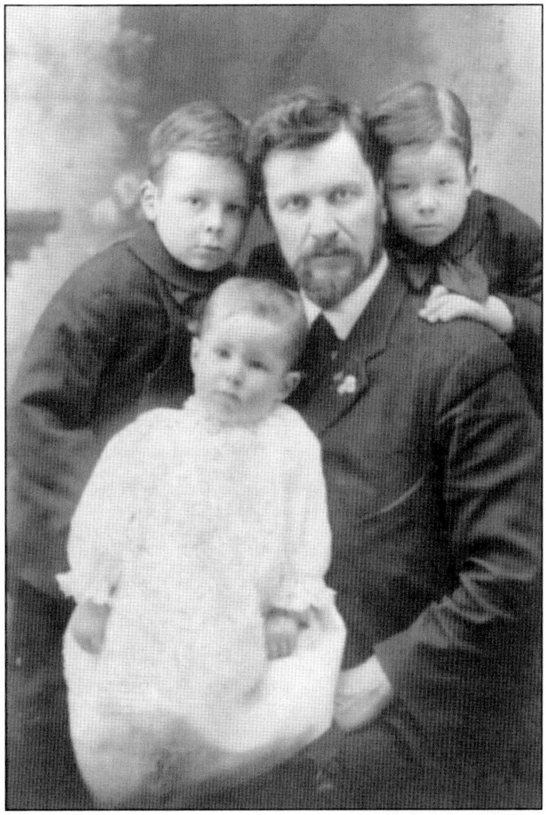

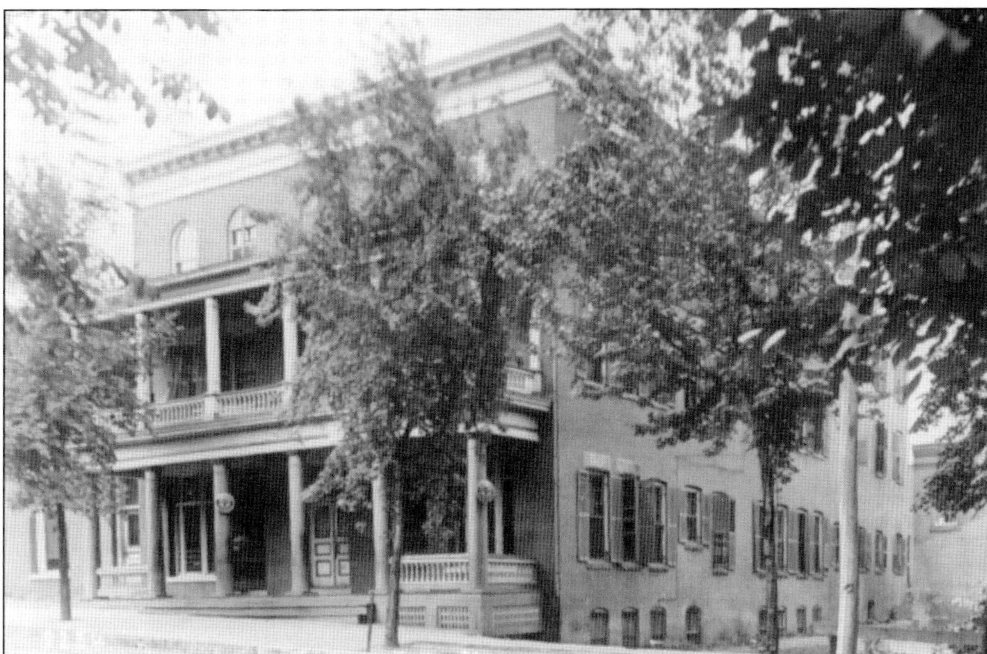

The American House Block at 25 Fourth Street, in 1913, was a well-known building. Built in 1896 by Jermiah C. Collins, it was remodeled in the 1970s. (Courtesy Peter S. Miller.)

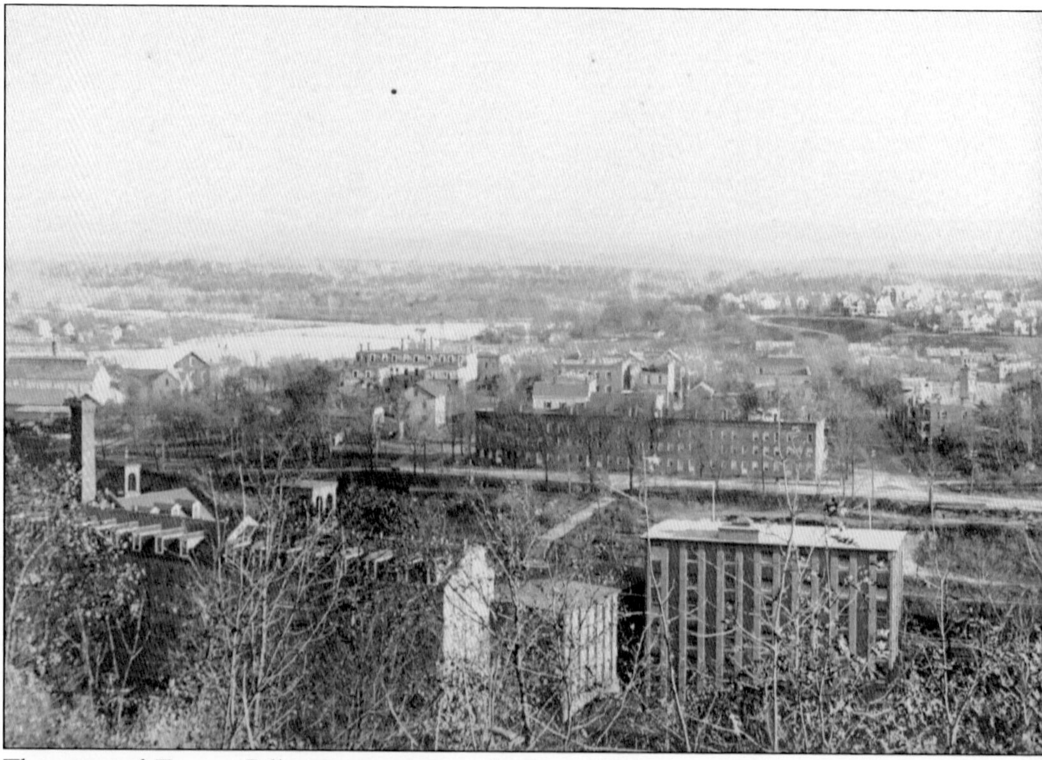

This view of Turners Falls is a composite of two c. 1906 photographic postcards. In the foreground is Russell Cutlery, the Keith and Esleeck Paper Companies, the lower White Suspension Bridge, and the Turners Falls Paper Company. The long building on the other side

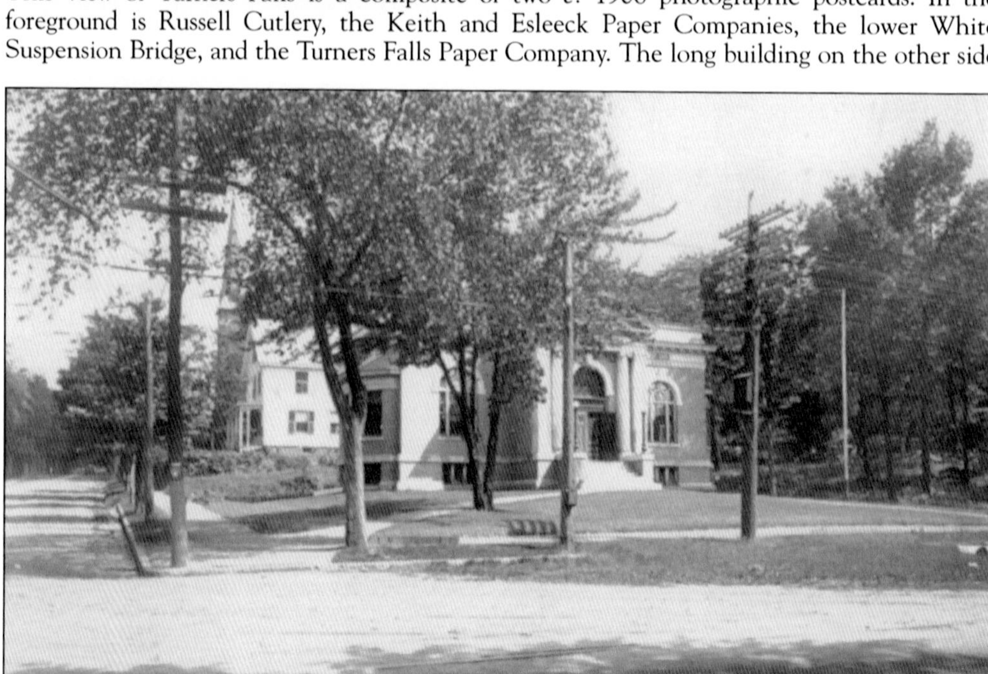

The Carnegie Library was built in 1904 with matching funds donated by the famous industrialist Andrew Carnegie, c. 1912. (Courtesy Peter S. Miller.)

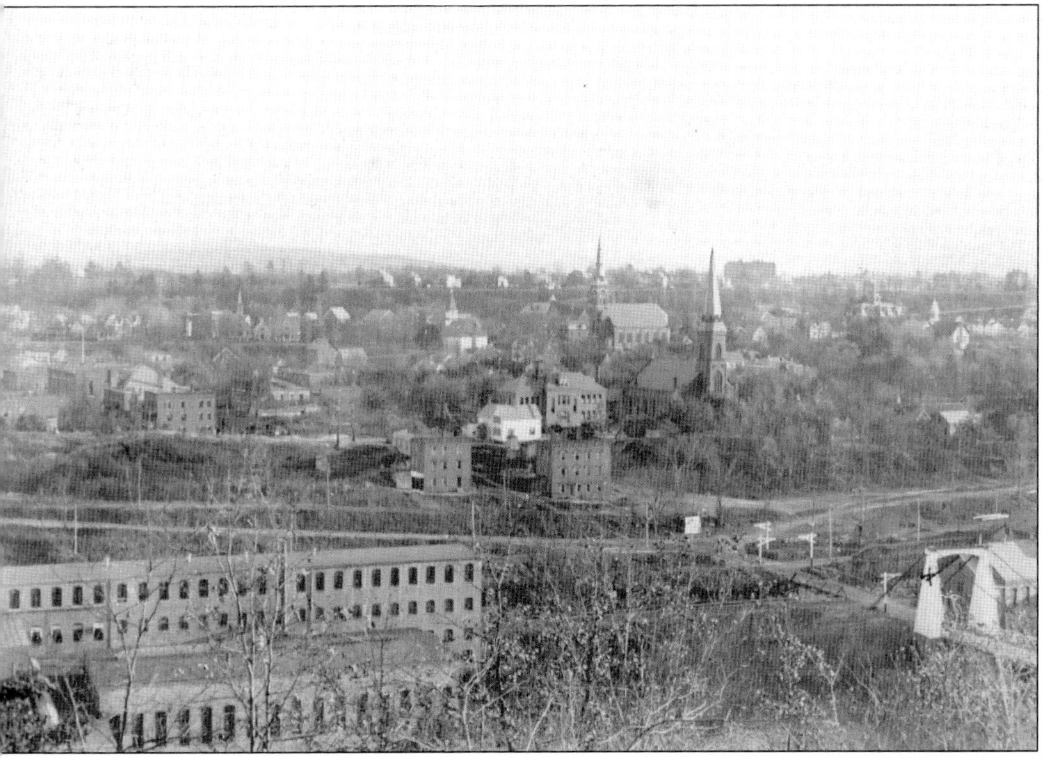

of the canal is the Keith Block, and to the left and above is the Grand Trunk Hotel. To the far left is the Connecticut River. (Courtesy Peter Miller and Kyle Scott.)

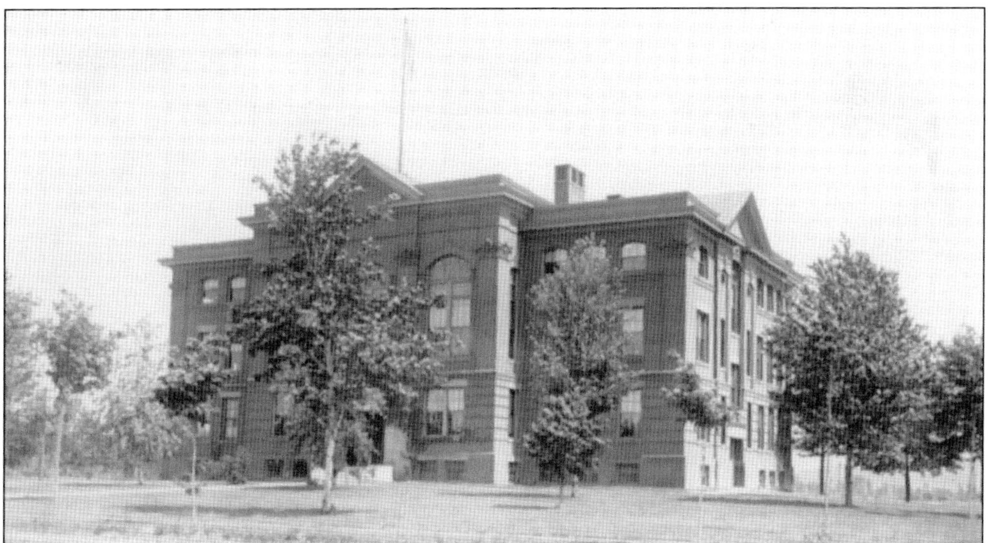

The Turners Falls High School building was destroyed by fire. The Shefield Middle School was later built on the site. For many years, football and baseball games were played behind this building, including the notorious Greenfield and Turners Falls Thanksgiving Day football games. (Courtesy Peter S. Miller.)

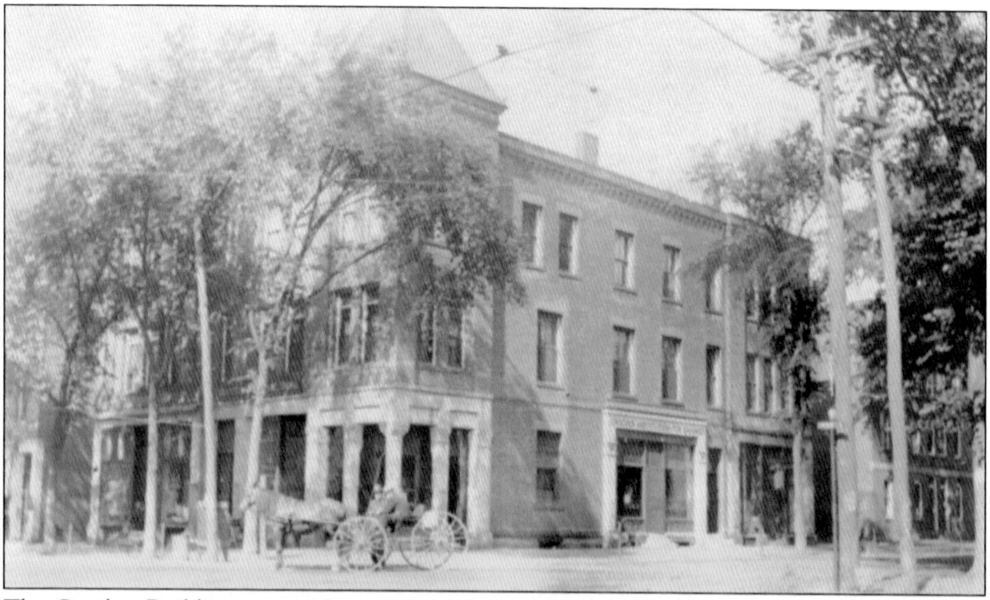

The Crocker Building was at the corner of Second Street and Avenue A. This building once housed both the Crocker National Bank and the Crocker Institution for Savings. The former bank, founded in 1872, was absorbed by the First National Bank and Trust Company of Greenfield and is now Fleet Bank. The Crocker Institution for Savings was founded in 1869 and was later taken over by Greenfield Savings Bank. In 1998, this building was set on fire by vandals and is currently being restored. Both banks were founded by Col. Alvah Crocker. (Photograph *c.* 1912 by T.H. Reynolds; courtesy Peter S. Miller.)

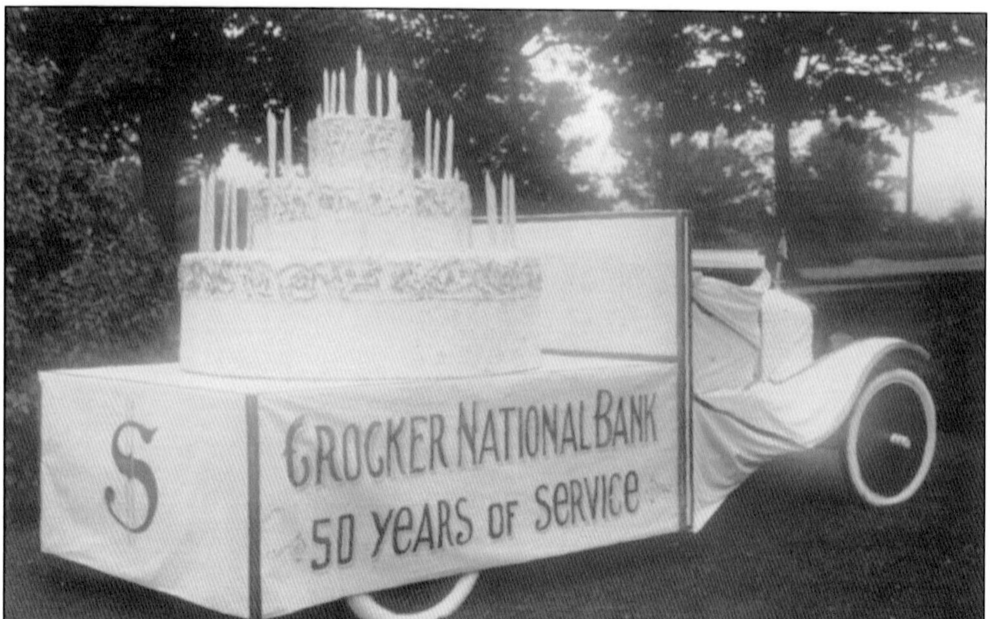

The Crocker National Bank had this float in a local parade, *c.* 1922. (Photograph by T.H. Reynolds; courtesy Peter S. Miller.)

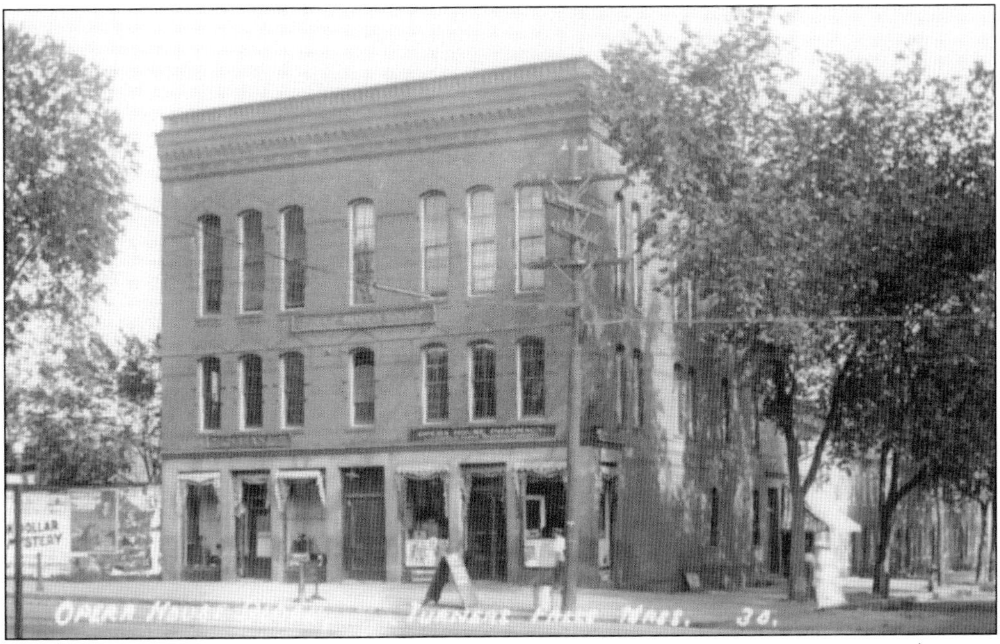

The Collie Opera Block, shown in 1912, was built in 1874 by Marie Collie. It cost $22,000 and seated 1,000. The building was 46 by 74 feet and had two ante rooms, two offices, two tenements, two stores on the street level, and two basement stores. C.E. Gardner of Springfield was the original architect. Dennis J. Shea, a well-known showman and businessman, had a long association with the building. By February 14, 1927, he had completed the Shea Theater Block next-door. After several uses to include a second-floor bowling alley, the Renaissance Community gutted most of the interior and painted part of the outside of the building. Currently, the town is putting the building back into use. (Courtesy of Frank Abbondanzio.)

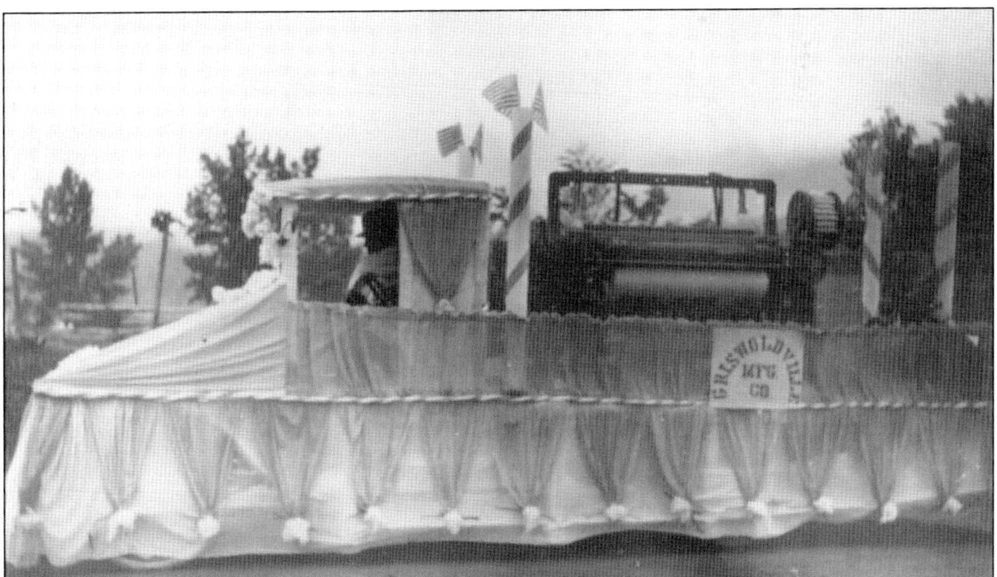

The Griswold Manufacturing Company float is shown in a 1922 parade. (Photograph taken by T.H. Reynolds; courtesy Peter S. Miller.)

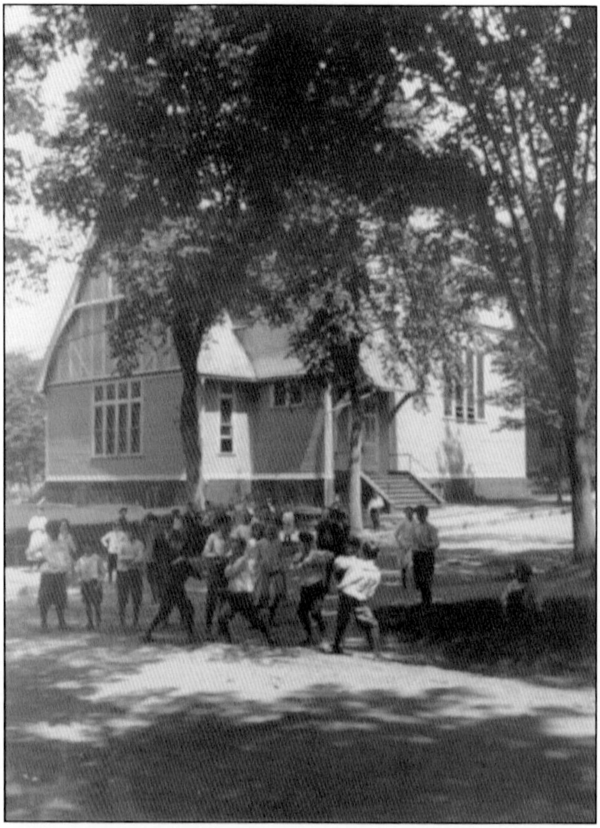

The Unitarian church on upper L Street in Turners Falls was later used as a Catholic church. The building partially burned in 1927. Currently, the building is the home of the Montague Elks. (Photograph taken in 1912; courtesy Peter S. Miller.)

Below is the first trolley to run in Turners Falls. It ran from June 23, 1895, to July 3, 1934. The trolley tracks were removed in 1952. (Photograph taken by C.H. Scofield; courtesy Peter S. Miller.)

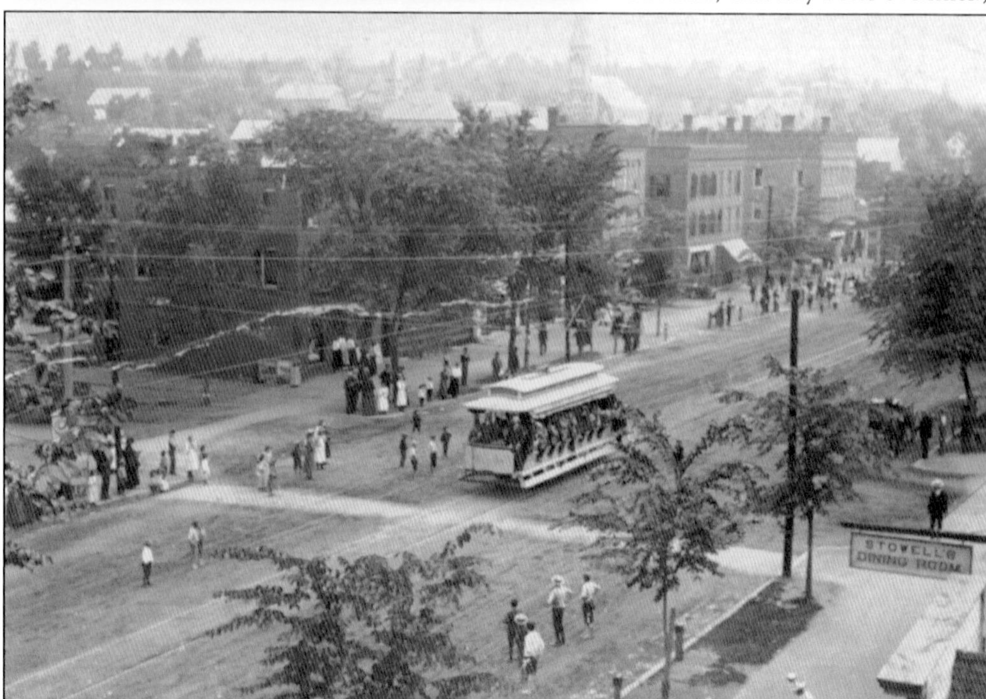

Edward "Red" Hughes was a police officer and served as police chief from 1945 until 1977. (Courtesy Turners Falls Police Department.)

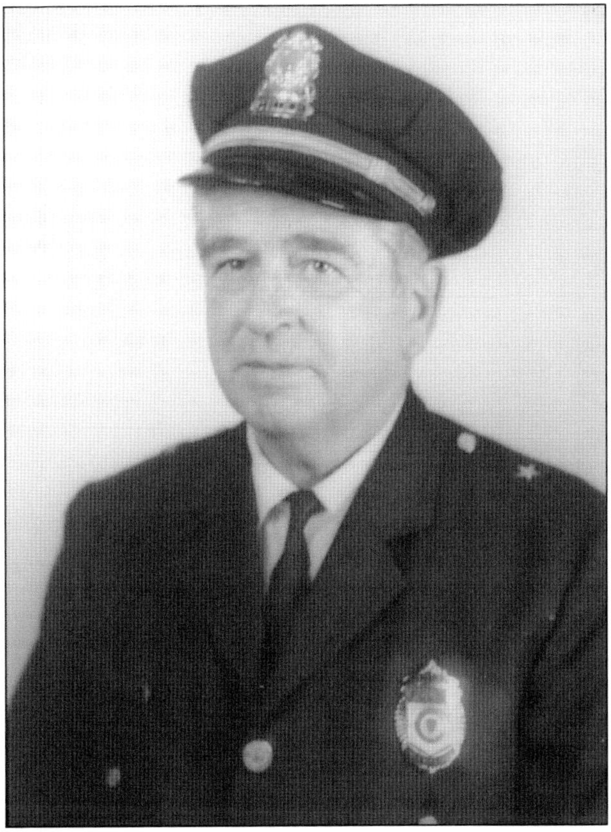

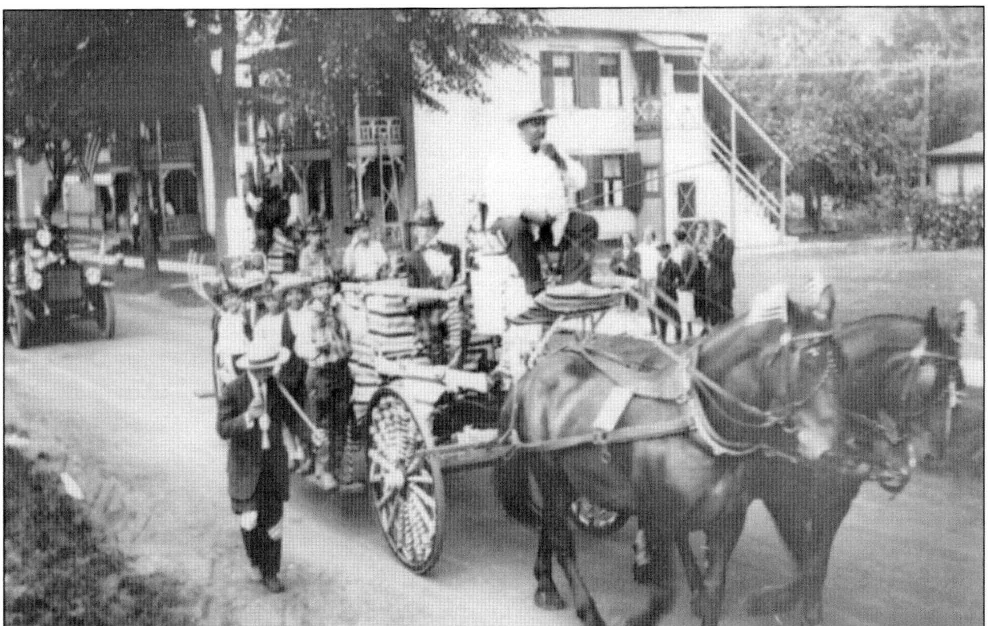

A Turners Falls horse-drawn fire truck is shown during a 1912 parade. (Photograph T.H. Reynolds; courtesy Peter S. Miller.)

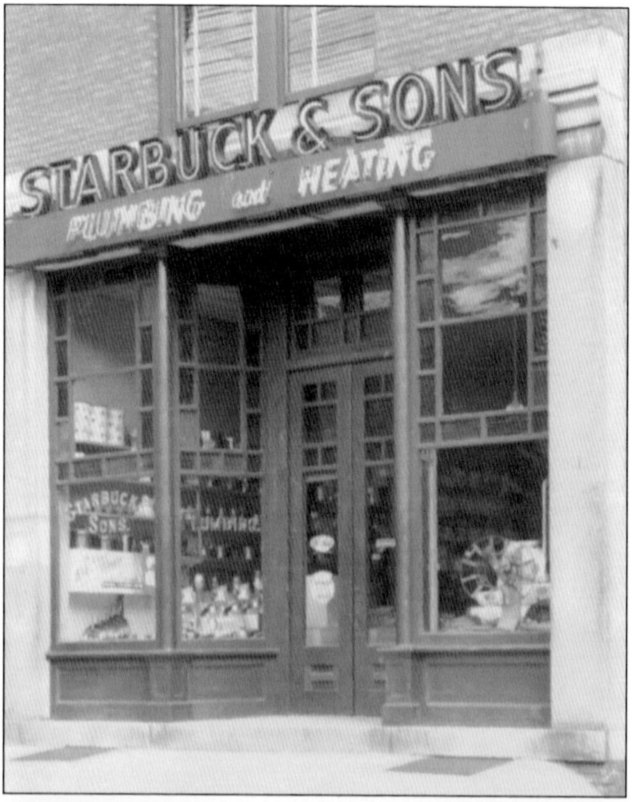

The Starbuck and Sons store was on Avenue A in Turners Falls. George Starbuck built it in 1872 as a plumbing and hardware store. (Courtesy Turners Falls Library.)

A.E. Martel's drugstore was located on Fourth Street in Turners Falls and operated in town for many years. (Courtesy Turners Falls Library.)

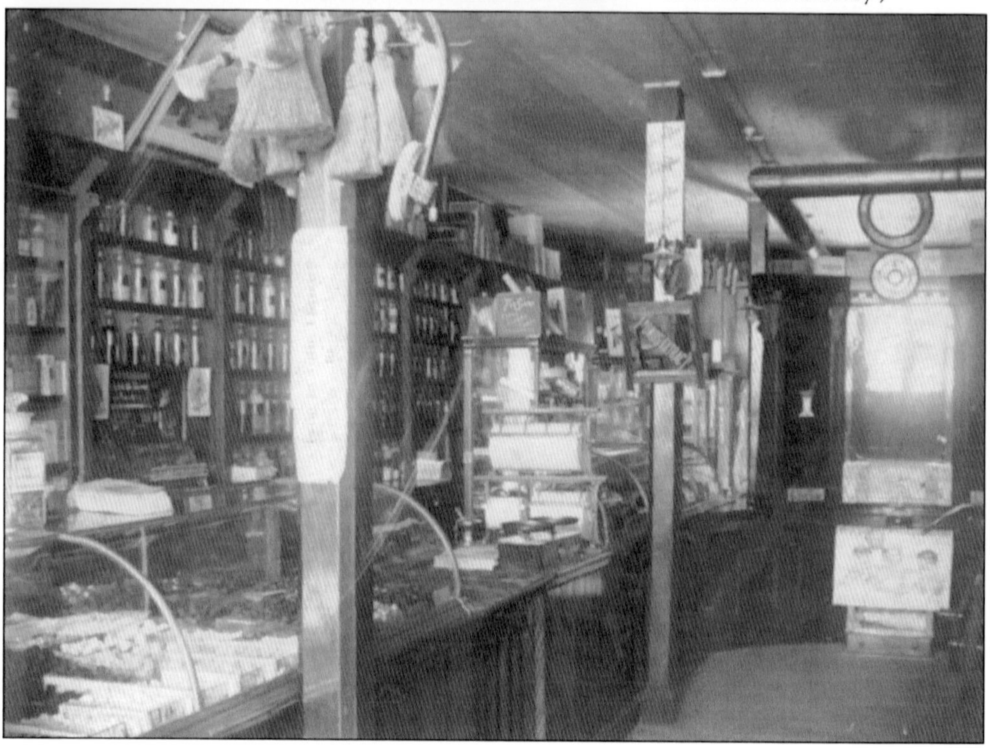

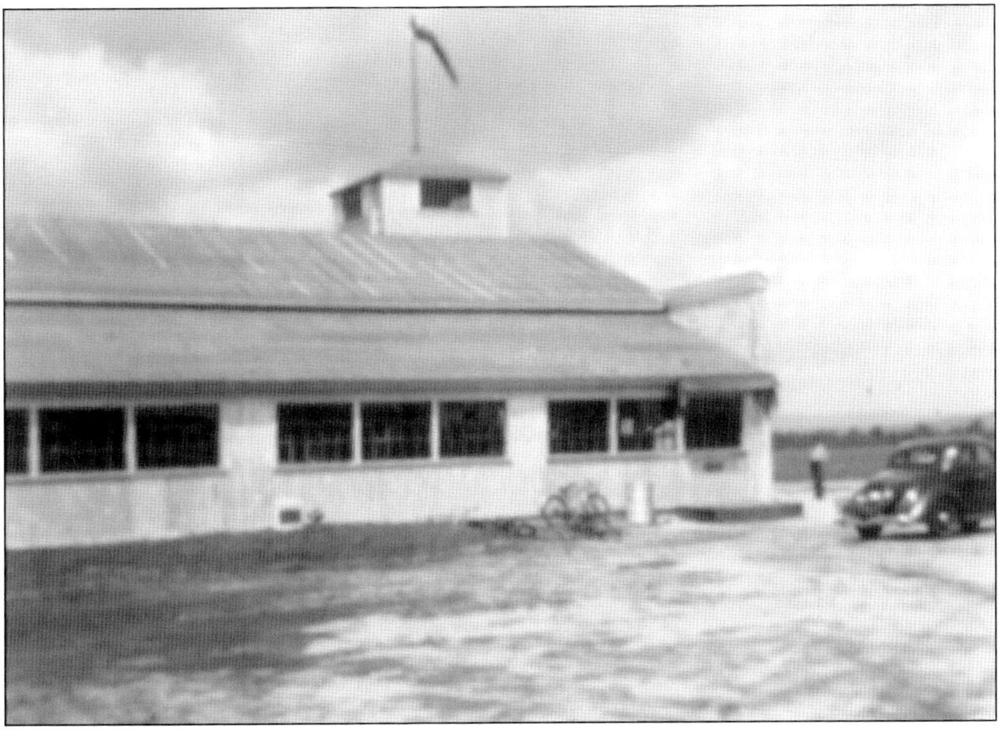

A hanger at Turners Falls Airport and the main tower are shown sometime between 1942 and 1945. This was the era when the likes of Ted Williams, the famous Red Sox baseball player, trained here during World War II. (Courtesy William Peloskey.)

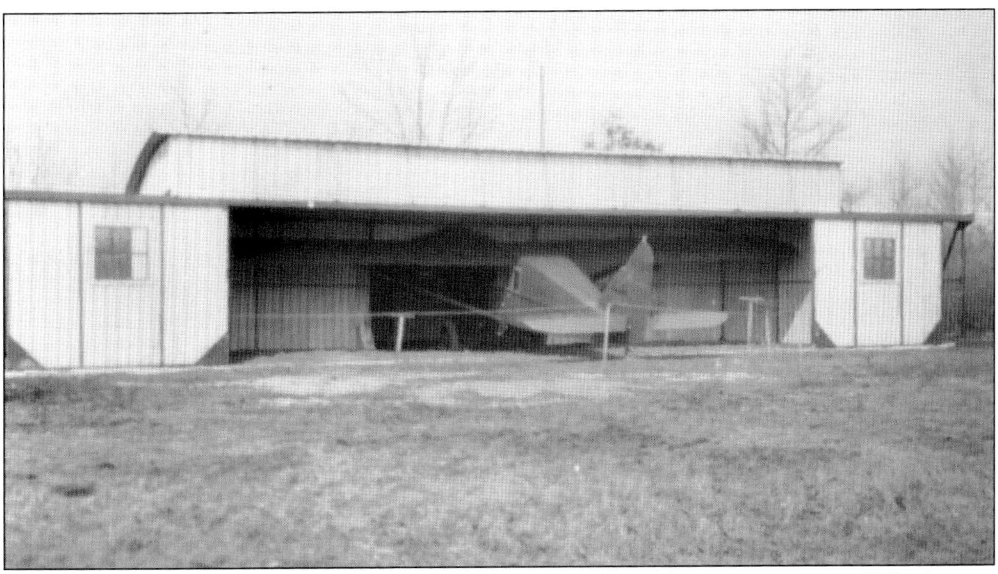

This photograph shows the Greenfield Tap and Die Company hanger at Turners Falls Airport in 1928. The company had its own airplane. (Courtesy William Peloskey.)

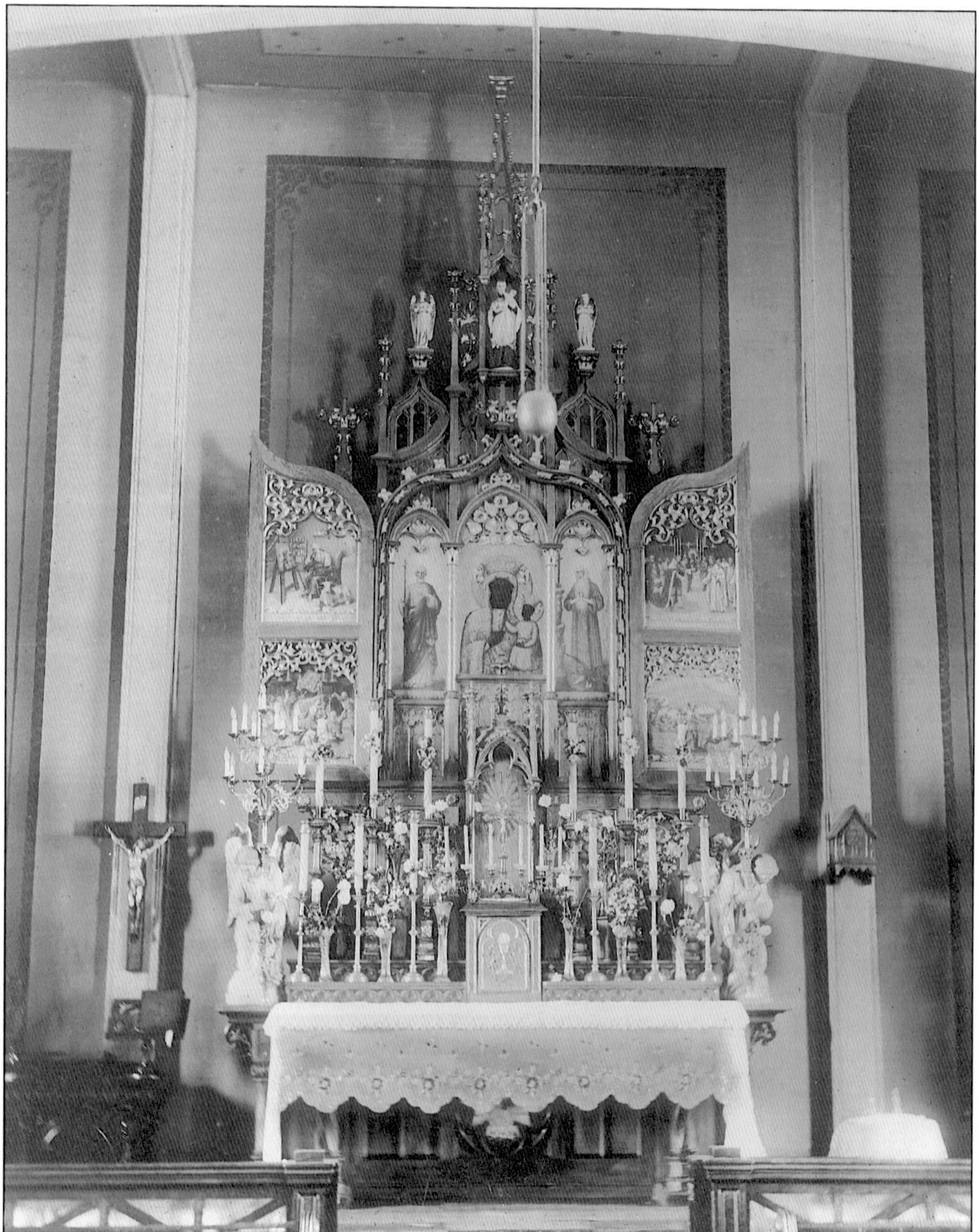

The altar of Our Lady of Czestochowa, a Polish church, is a gem of its type and unique in Franklin County. It was donated by the Holy Rosary Society. The altar was first in the old Unitarian church on L Street and was hand carved by local resident Joseph Schab. The paintings on the altar are from Poland and date to 1914. (Courtesy Our Lady of Czestochowa.)

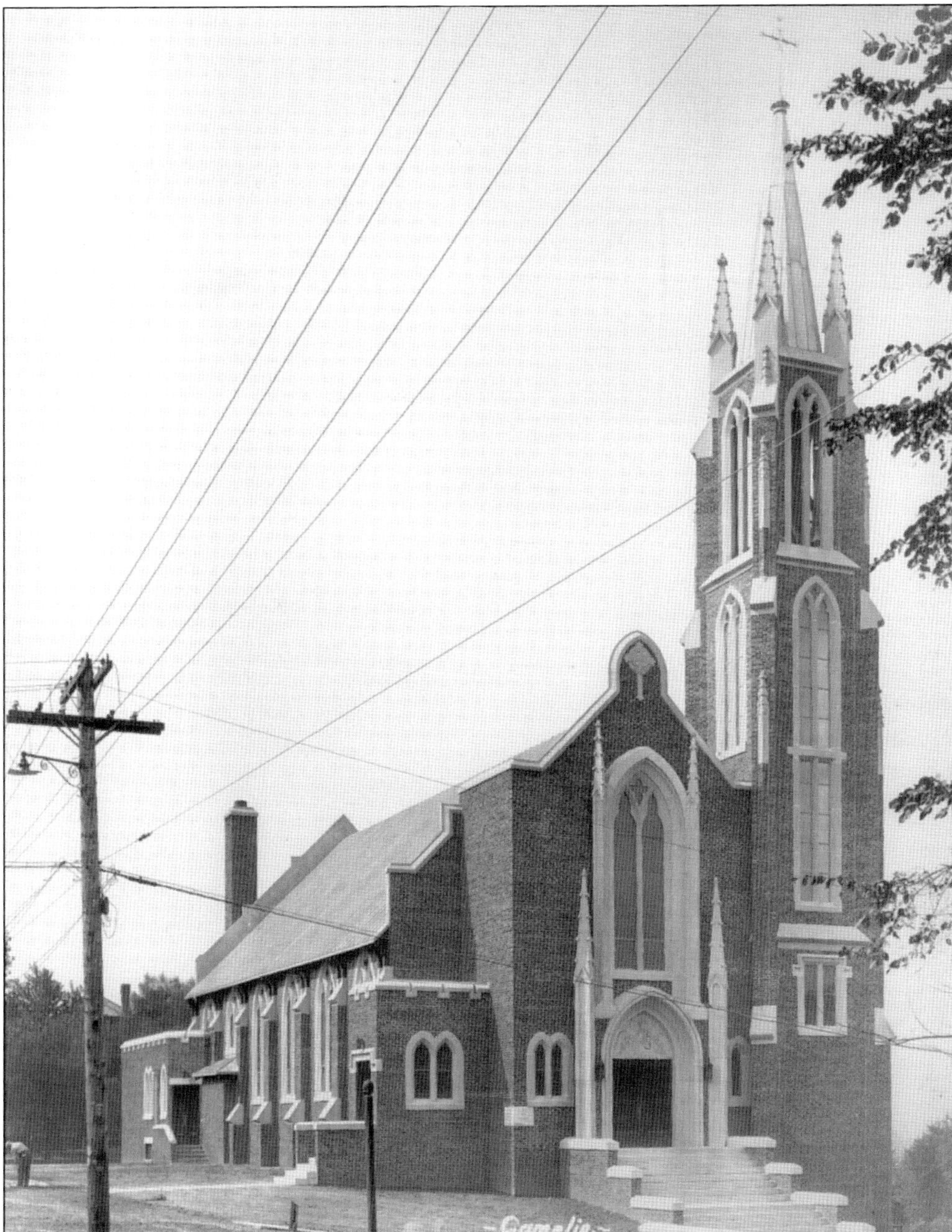

Our Lady of Czestochowa was on K Street in Turners Falls. The church had its groundbreaking on October 7, 1928, with Bishop Thomas O'Leary performing the groundbreaking ceremony. The church was completed in 1929. (Photograph by Alex Gamelin; courtesy Our Lady of Czestochowa.)

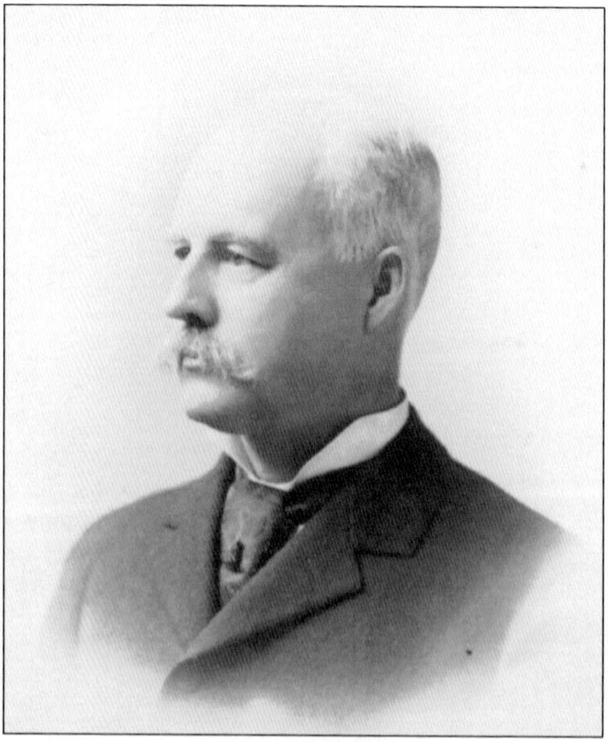

R.N. Oakman, an engineer who relocated in town, was brought to the community to work on the original layout of Turners Falls with Alvah Crocker and others. Originally from Selma, Alabama, he became the First Master of Mechanics Lodge of Freemasons in 1878. (Courtesy Mechanics Lodge of Freemasons.)

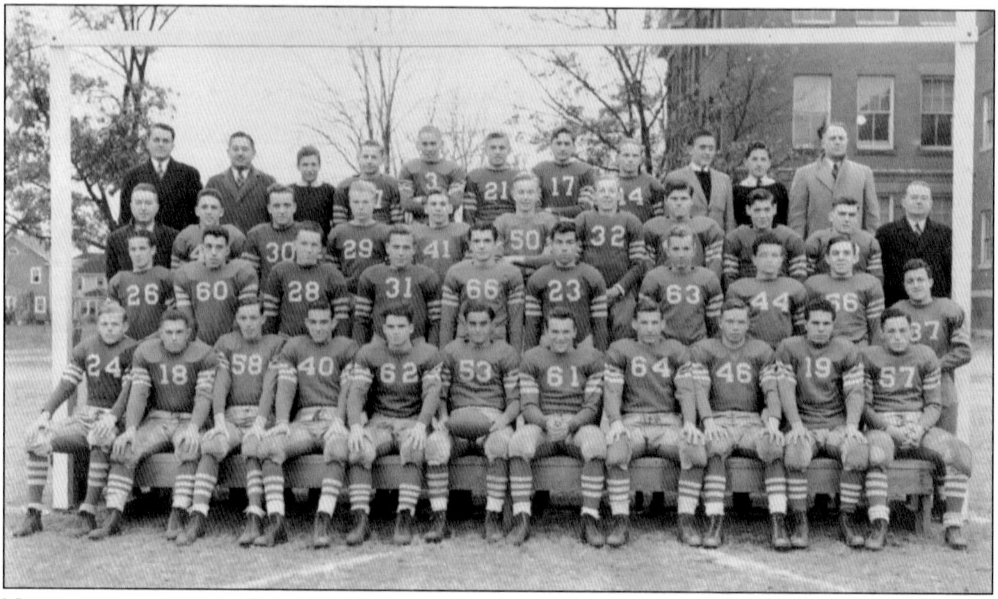

Not everyone is named in this photograph of the 1938 Turner Falls High School football team. The few that are identified are, from left to right, the following: (first row) Simanski, No. 24; Desautels, No.18; Guy, No. 58; Conway, No. 40; LaFrance, No. 62; Ed Borden, No. 53; Skypeck, No. 61; Martin, No. 64; Tremel, No. 46; Bonnette, No. 19; and Shanahan, No. 57; (second row) Beathun, No. 60; Clough, No. 23; Grogan, No. 63; Welcome, No. 40; Whiteman, No. 30; Hoff, number unknown; Emonds, No. 29; LaFrance, No. 41; and Ducharm, Wrightson, Sheff, Martin, Lourden, Bean, and Pitrock, numbers unknown. (Courtesy Kyle J. Scott.)

The photograph shows 39 Third Street in Turners Falls, the Desautels Second Hand Store. This store was owned and operated for many years by George "Buttnut" Desautels and later by his son, Alfred G. Desautels, who operated the store until January 2000. Prior to the Desautels family taking ownership of the building, the property was used for a plumber's workshop. (Courtesy Town of Montague.)

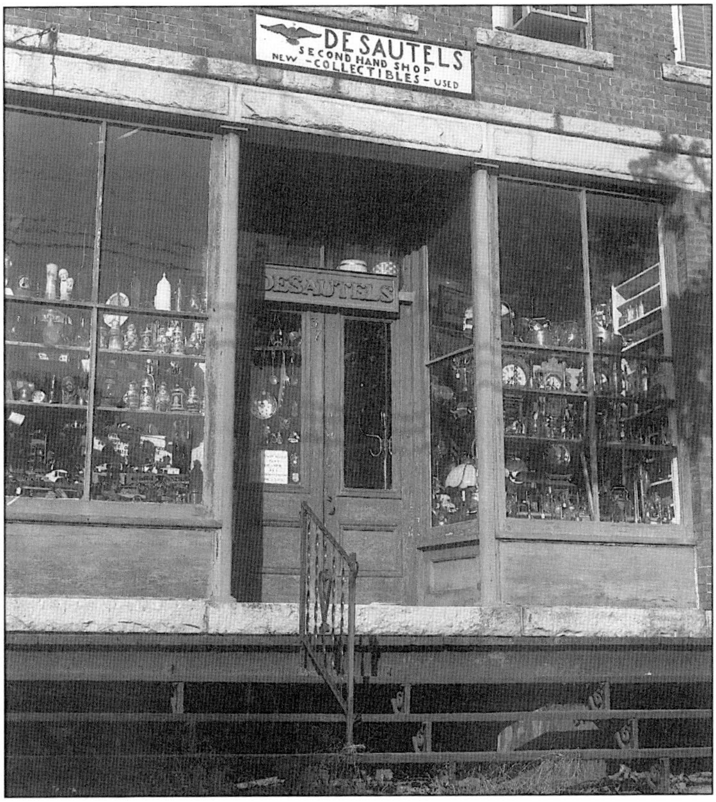

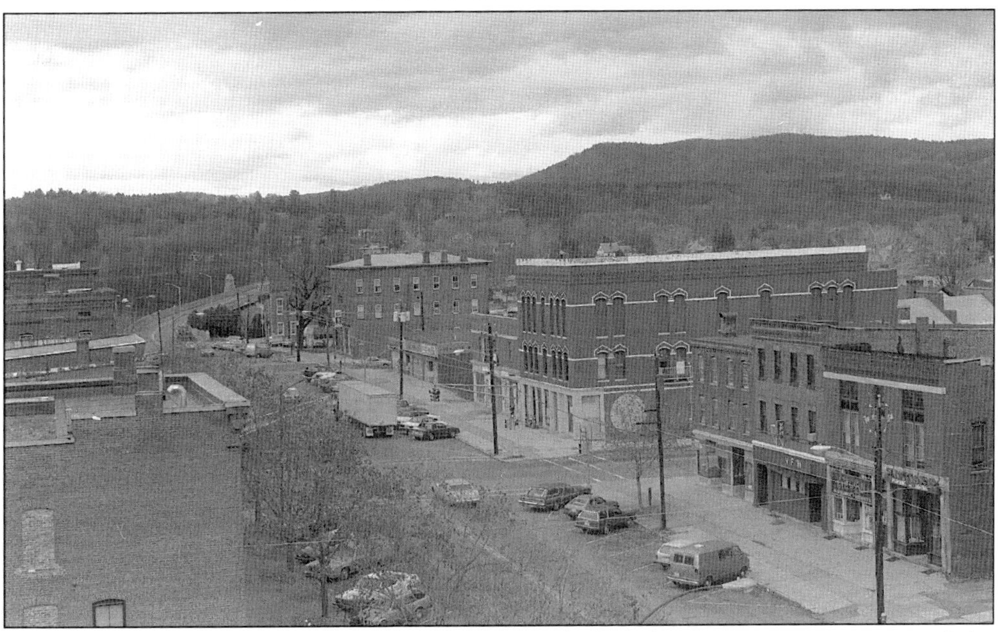

This photograph of Avenue A was taken *c.* 1980, before the reconstruction project of the street. Shown are the Collie Opera House, the Veterans of Foreign Wars building, Melan's Store, Starbuck and Sons, Montague Town Hall, and the Bridge Cafe. (Photograph by Judith Radebaugh; courtesy Town of Montague.)

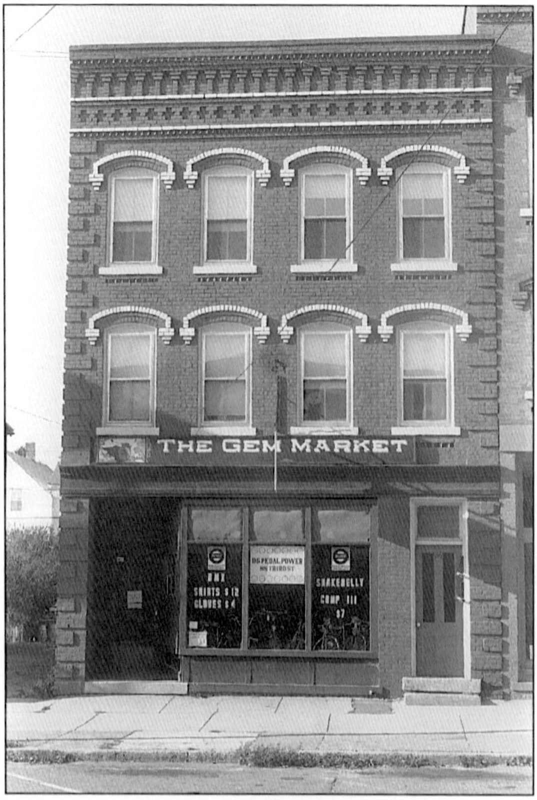

The Gem Market building at 88 Third Street in Turners Falls is shown here sometime in the early 1980s. (Photograph by Judith Radebaugh; courtesy Town of Montague.)

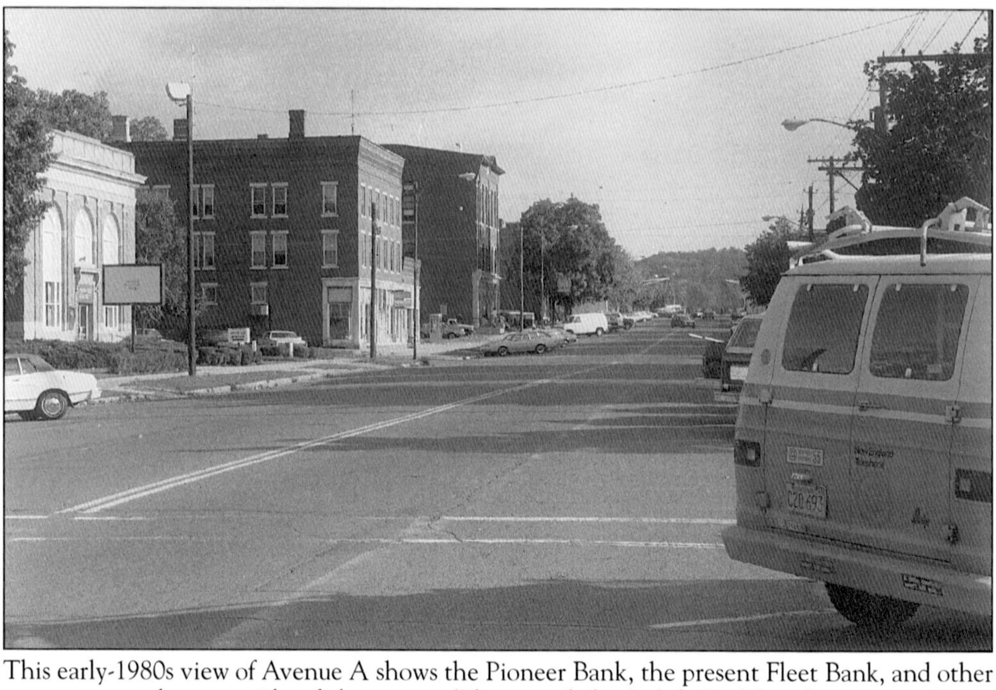

This early-1980s view of Avenue A shows the Pioneer Bank, the present Fleet Bank, and other structures on the west side of the street. (Photograph by Judith Radebaugh; courtesy Town of Montague.)

Shown is the rear of the Collie Opera House from a Third Street point of view. Taken in the early 1980s, the picture shows Silver Screen Design, a silk screening business that operated from that location for some time. (Photograph by Judith Radebaugh; courtesy Town of Montague.)

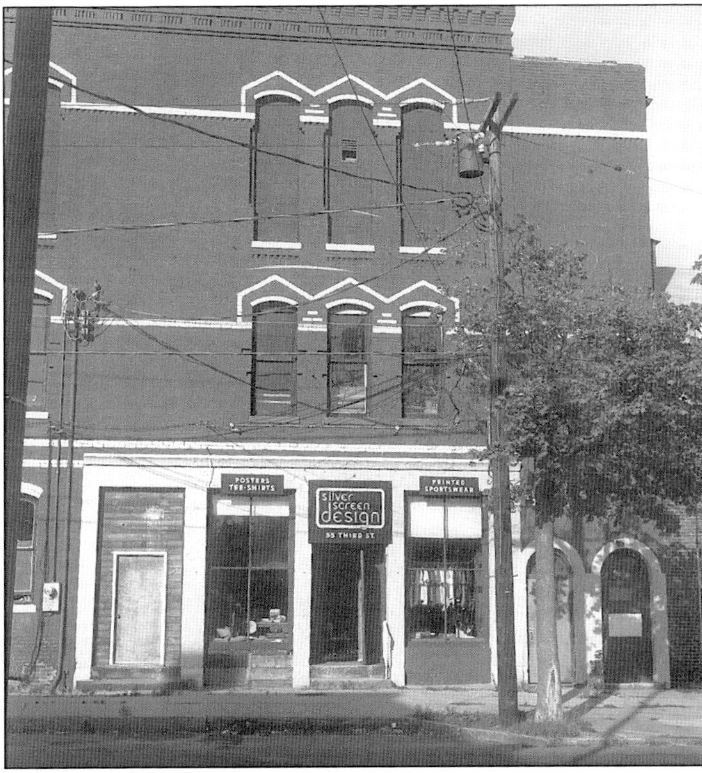

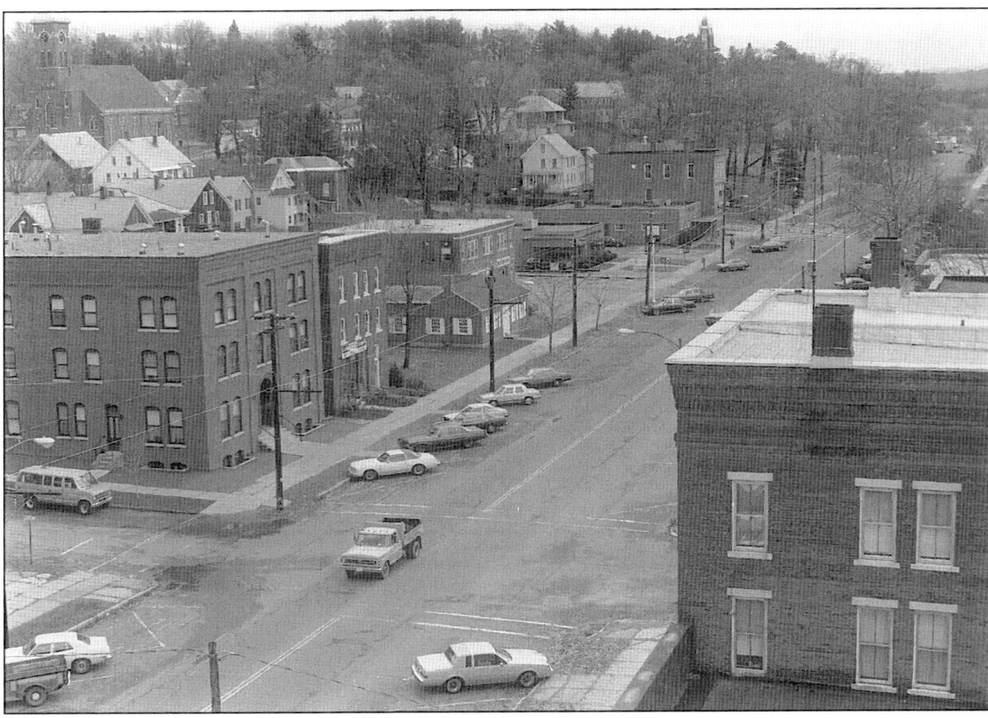

This photograph of Avenue A, looking toward Seventh Street, was taken sometime in the early 1980s. (Photograph by Judith Radebaugh; courtesy Town of Montague.)

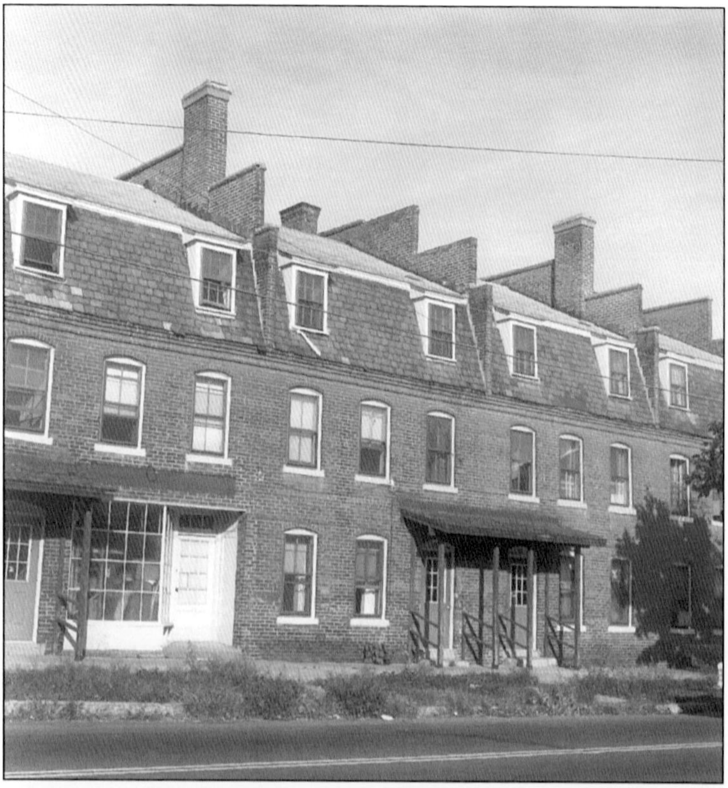

This photograph of the Cutlery Block on Third Street in Turners Falls was taken sometime in the early 1980s. Built originally to house workers of the John Russell Cutlery Company, the building at the time the photograph was taken had some 60 apartments providing housing to Turners Falls renters. (Photograph by Judith Radebaugh; courtesy Town of Montague.)

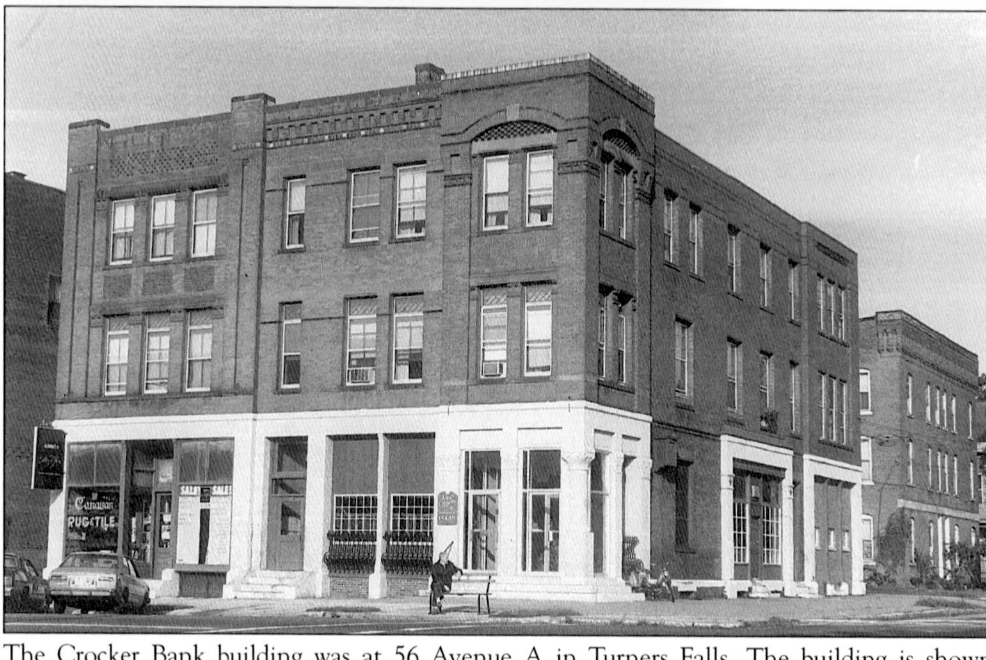

The Crocker Bank building was at 56 Avenue A in Turners Falls. The building is shown sometime in the early 1980s with the Dolan and Dolan law offices and a rug and tile shop occupying the storefronts. The other floors were used as a boardinghouse. (Photograph by Judith Radebaugh; courtesy Town of Montague.)

This 1960s photograph shows the Crocker Institution for Savings at 56 Avenue A. After the bank was moved out of the block, the clock was removed. Supposedly, the clock (or just the faces of the clock) was obtained by Walter Jones of Amherst. After his death, the parts were sold at auction. (Courtesy Town of Montague.)

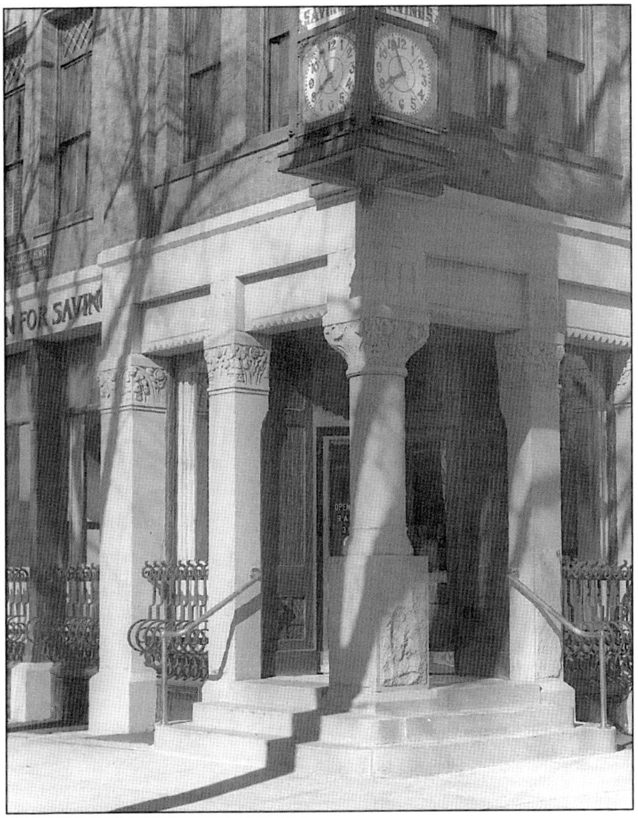

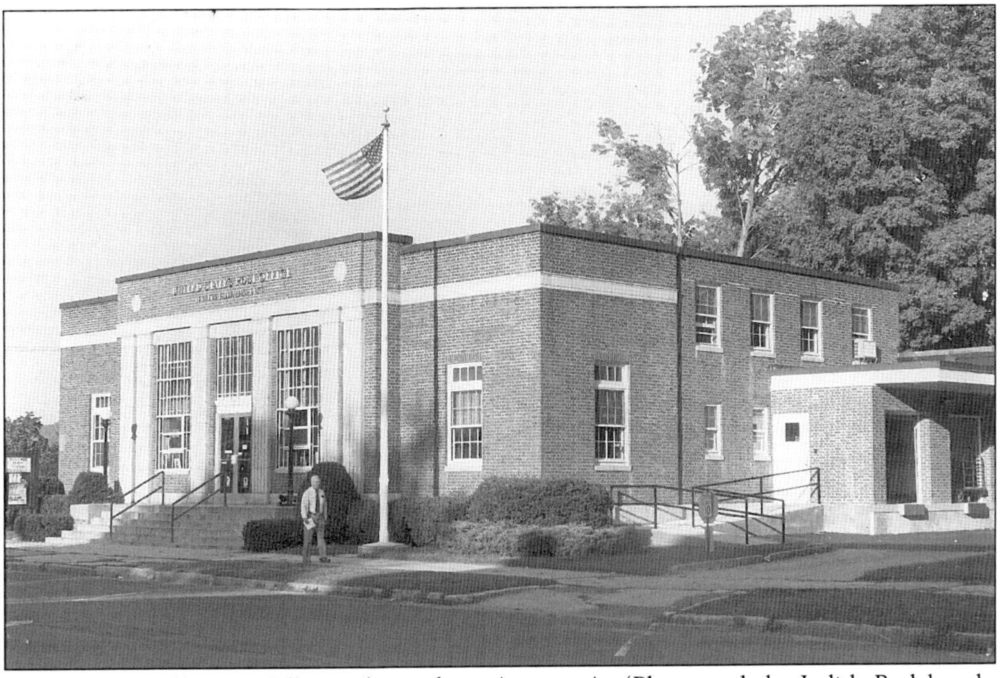

The Turners Falls Post Office is located on Avenue A. (Photograph by Judith Radebaugh; courtesy Town of Montague.)

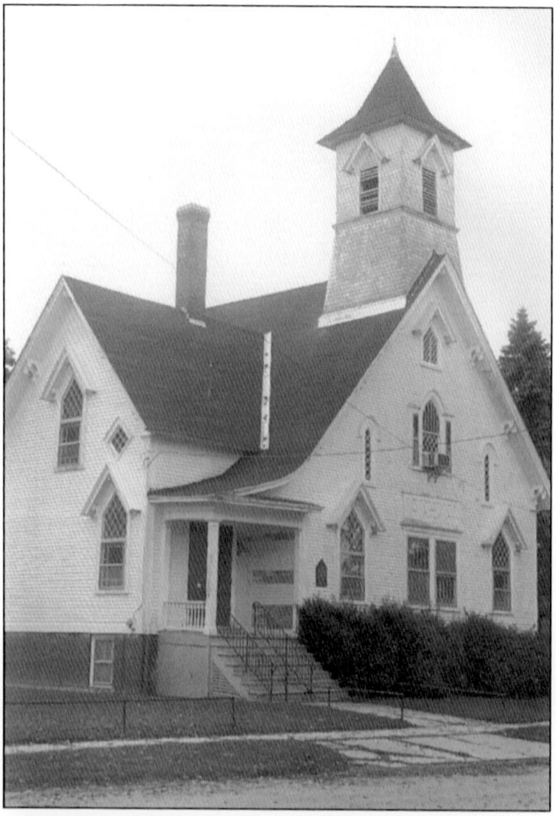

The First Baptist church stands at 10 Prospect Street. (Photograph by Judith Radebaugh; courtesy Town of Montague.)

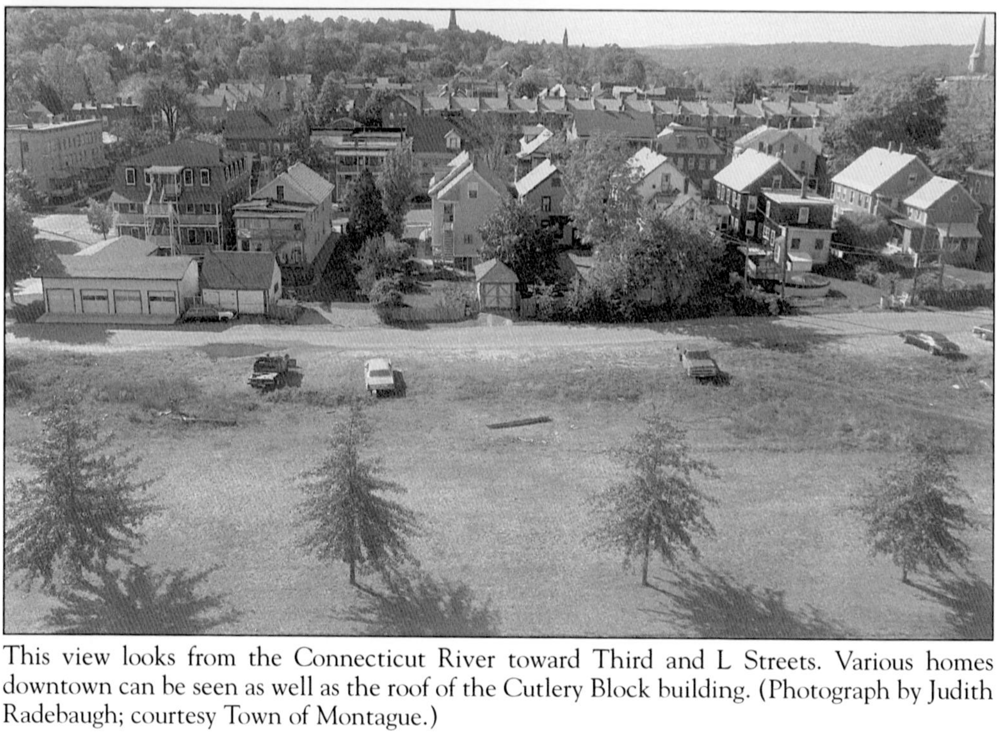

This view looks from the Connecticut River toward Third and L Streets. Various homes downtown can be seen as well as the roof of the Cutlery Block building. (Photograph by Judith Radebaugh; courtesy Town of Montague.)

Two

MILLERS FALLS

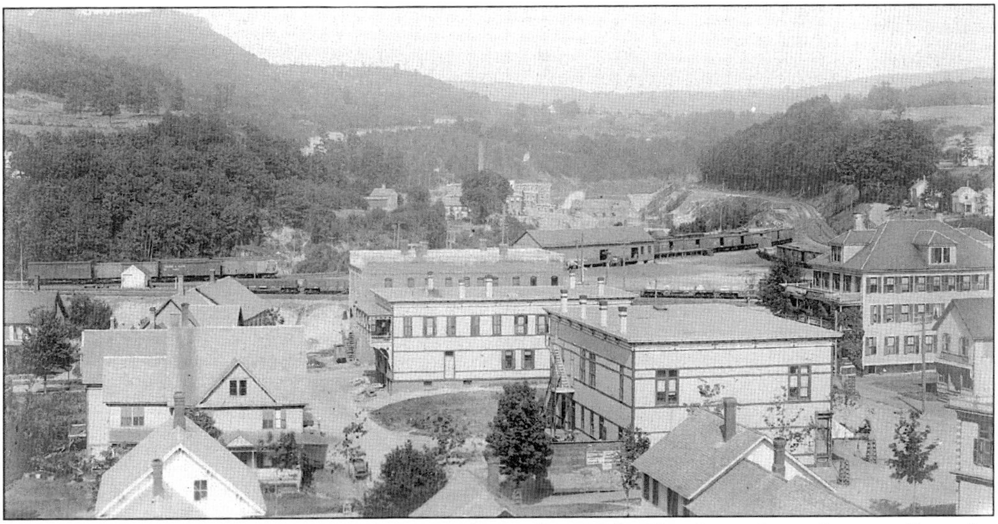

In this c. 1910 view of Millers Falls, note the Millers Falls Hotel on the right as well as the freight house with cars pulling up to it. (Courtesy Peter S. Miller.)

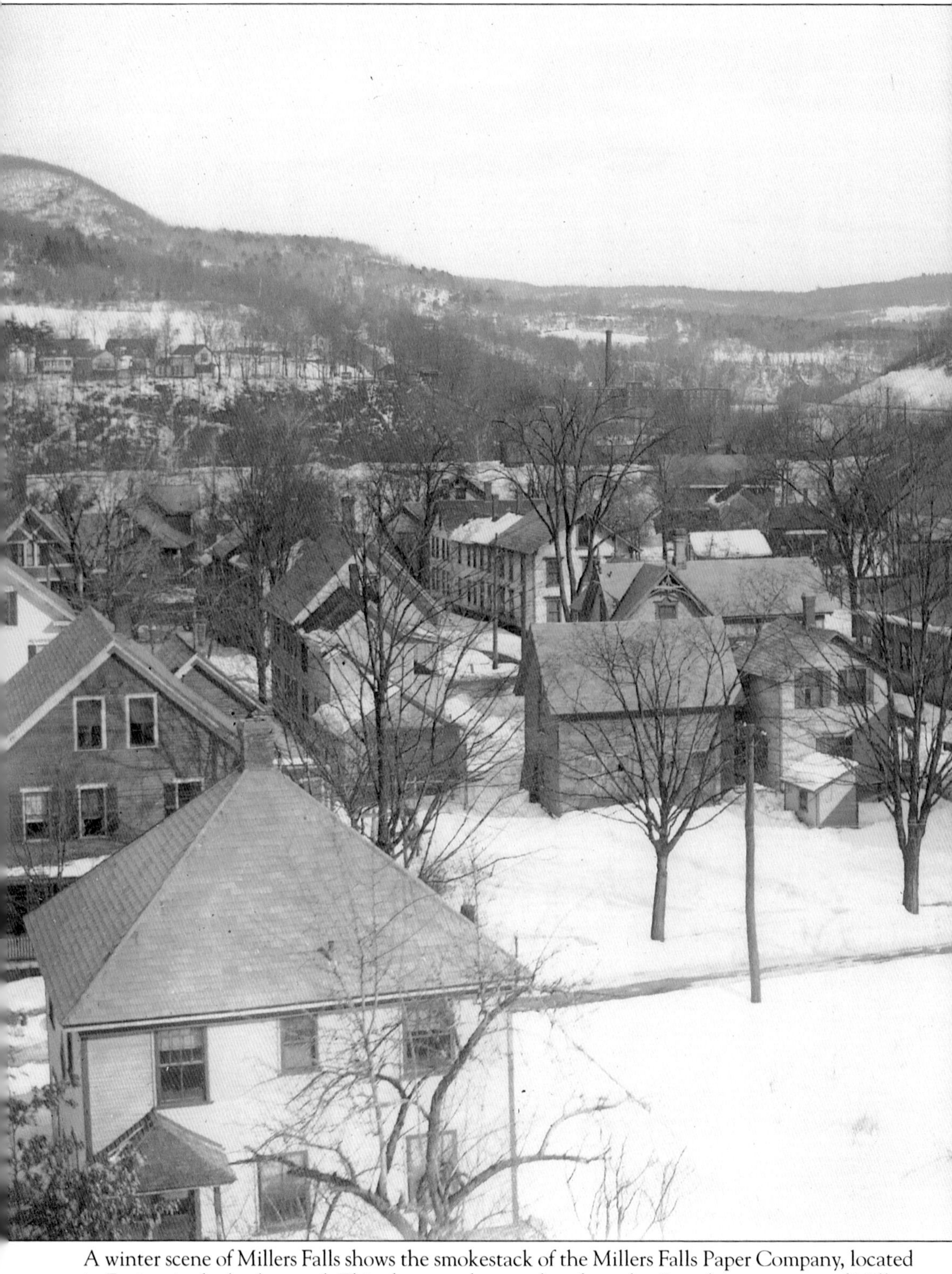

A winter scene of Millers Falls shows the smokestack of the Millers Falls Paper Company, located in Erving, in the background. This photograph was taken from the Grand Avenue area of Millers

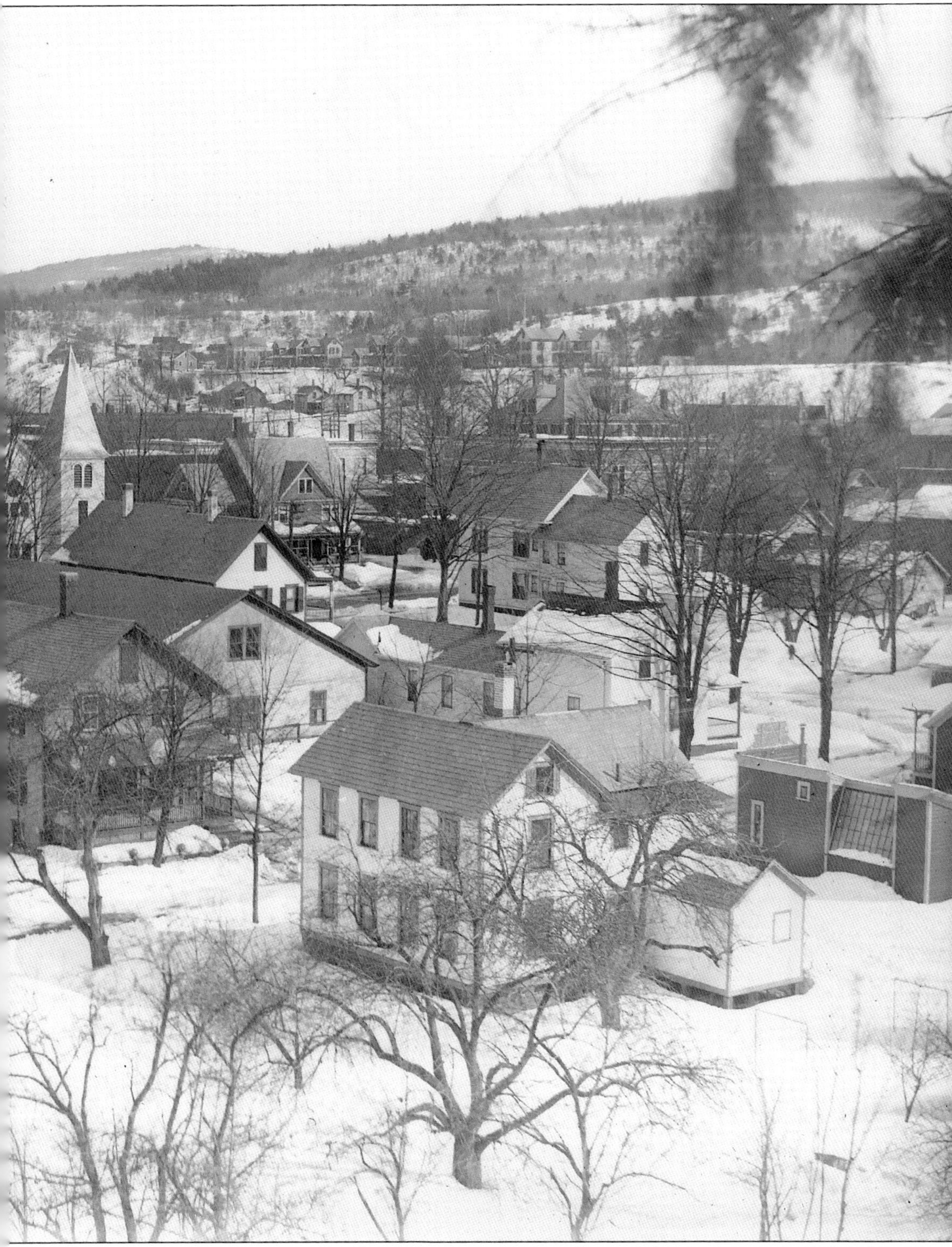

Falls *c.* 1915. The Scott photography studio is on the far right, and the Congregational church, which later burned, is in the center. (Courtesy Millers Falls Library.)

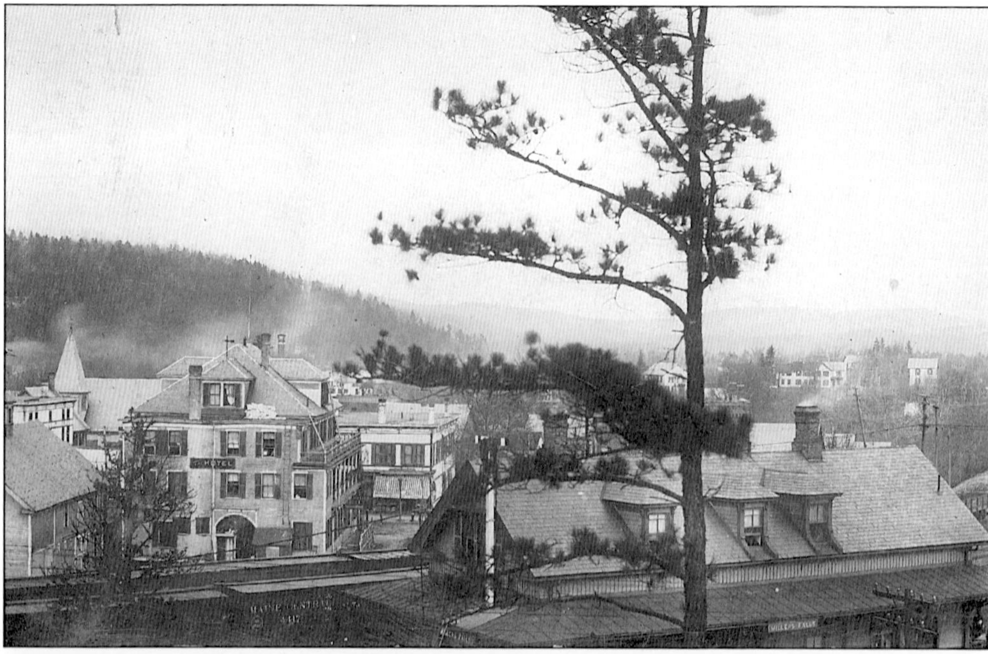

This 1906 photograph shows the Millers Falls Hotel still standing and the railroad line running past it. Note the boxcars and station in the foreground. (Courtesy Peter S. Miller.)

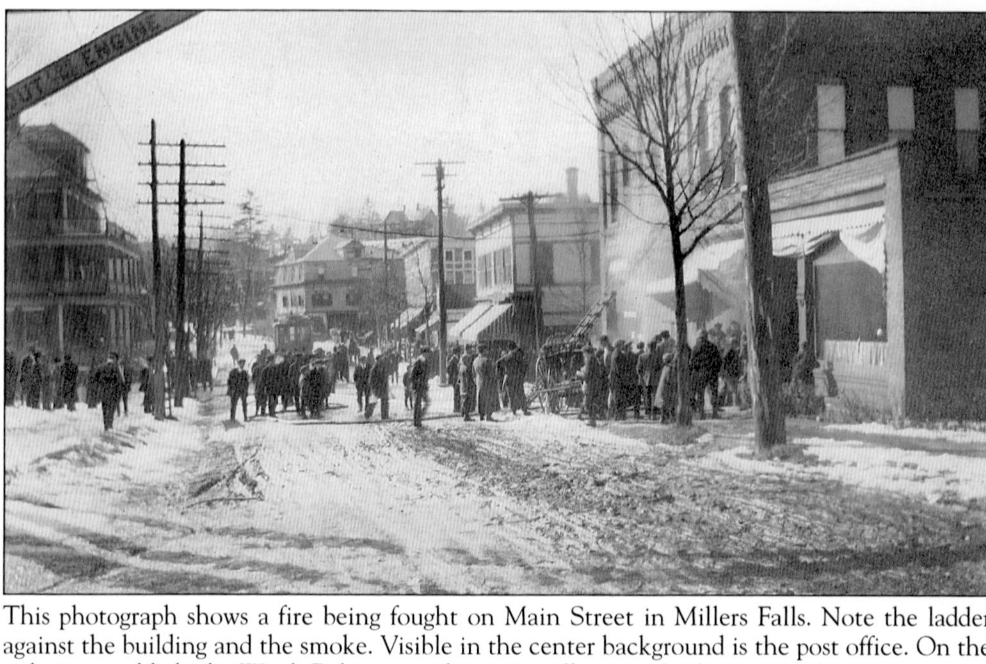

This photograph shows a fire being fought on Main Street in Millers Falls. Note the ladder against the building and the smoke. Visible in the center background is the post office. On the right is most likely the Wards Bakery storefront. A trolley can also be seen in the center among the passers-by. (Courtesy Peter S. Miller.)

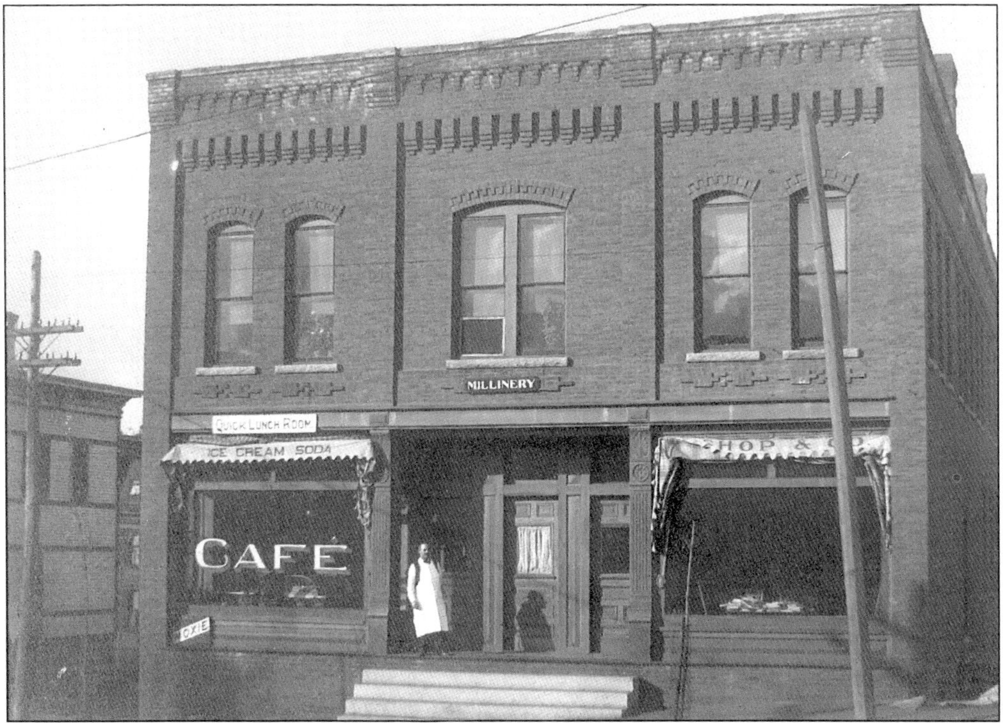

The Quick Lunch Room, a local eatery of the early 1900s, was close to the railroad crossing in Millers Falls. Note the sign for a millinery upstairs. This brick structure still stands today. (Courtesy Peter S. Miller.)

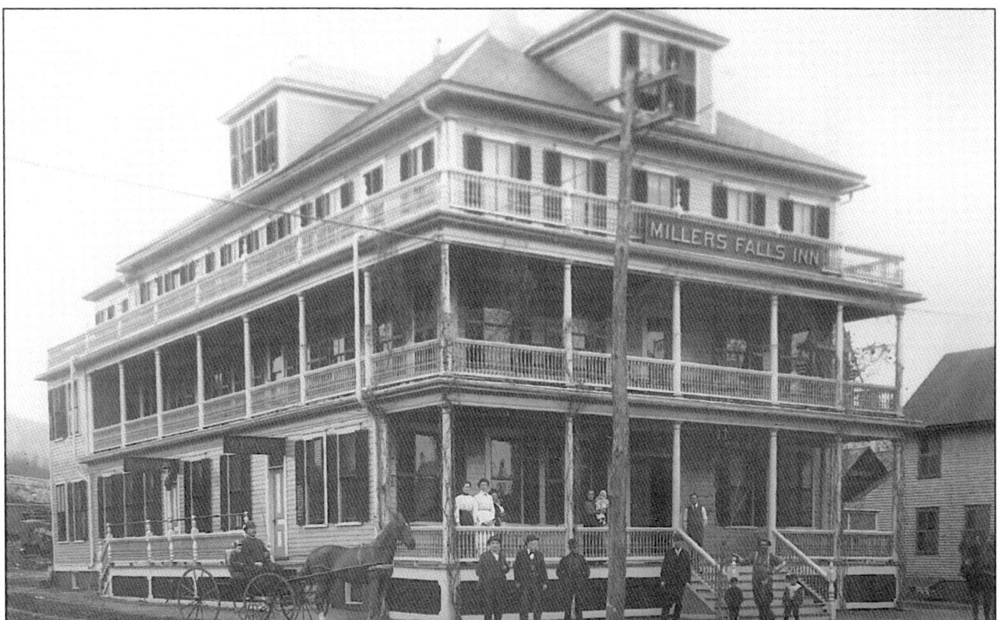

At the Millers Falls Inn and Hotel, note the well-dressed patrons and the horse and buggy on the left of this *c.* 1910 photograph. The many porches were later removed. (Courtesy Millers Falls Library.)

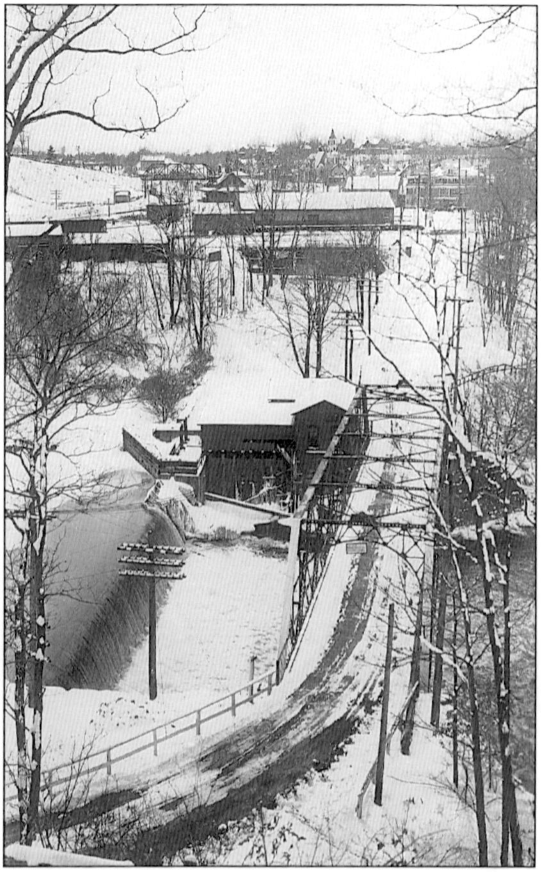

This view shows the bridge from across the Millers Falls River going to the Millers Falls Paper Company in Erving, Massachusetts. Visible are the small dam and the powerhouse. (Courtesy Millers Falls Library.)

The Millers Falls River divides the village of Millers Falls in half, each half in a different town. This photograph of the early bridge was taken from the Erving side of the river. Also visible is the sign for the Millers Falls Tool Company, also located in Erving. (Courtesy Millers Falls Library.)

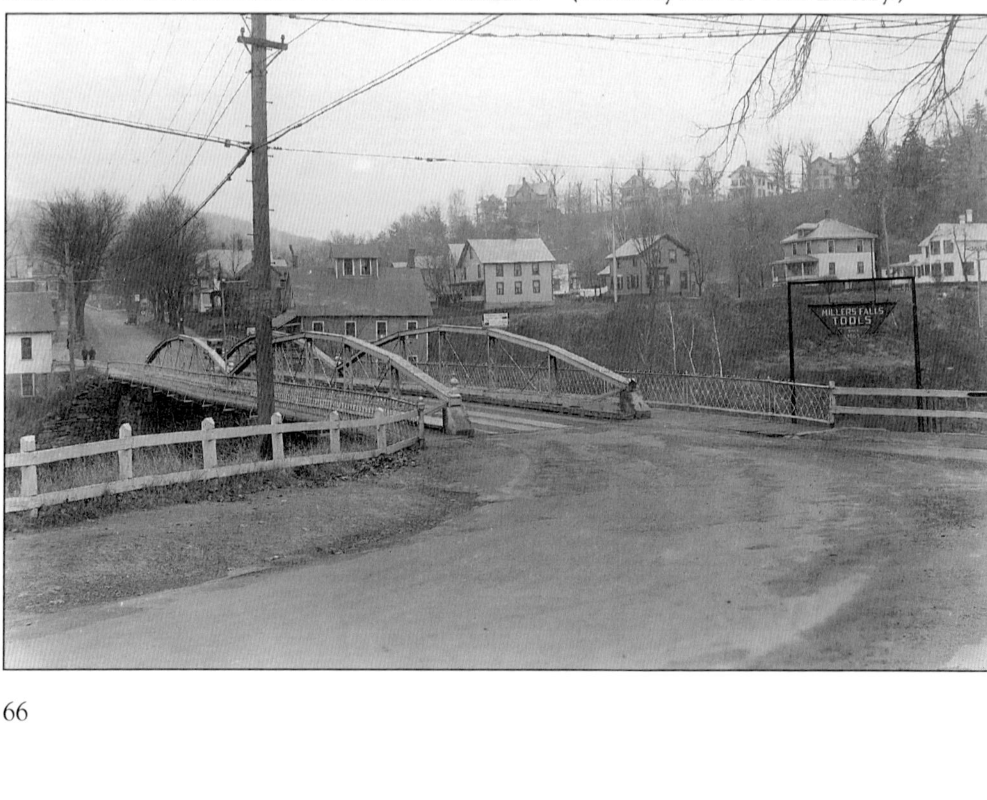

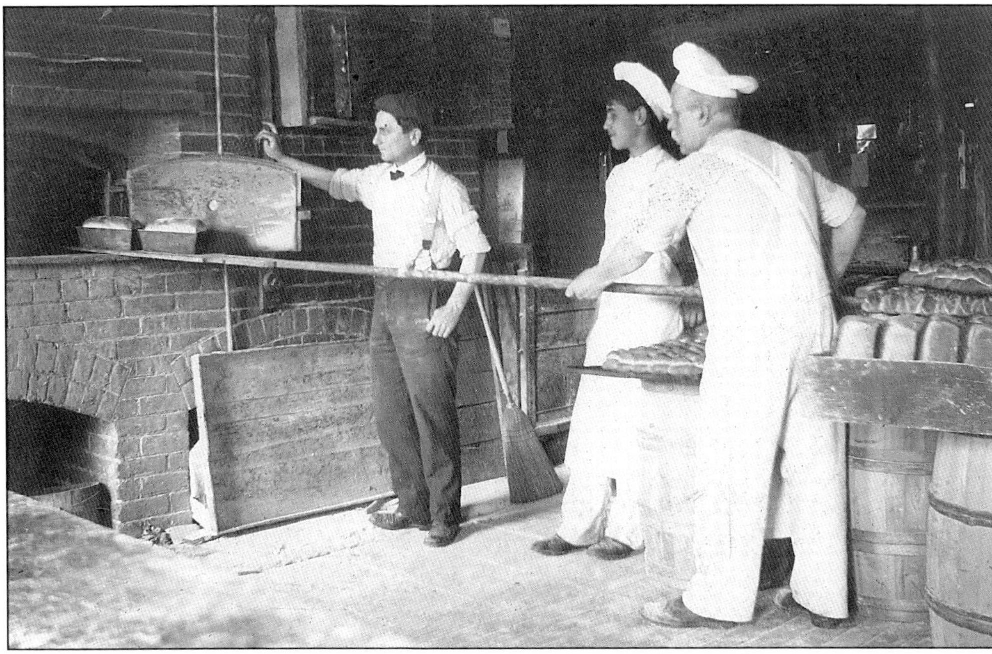

This 1903 photograph shows the bakers of Wards Bakery making their product. Present are H.J Ward, wearing the baker's hat, Raymond Gould, center, and I. Forrest. Note the loaves of bread in pans and on the barrels at the right. (Photograph by Adrian Savage; courtesy Millers Falls Library.)

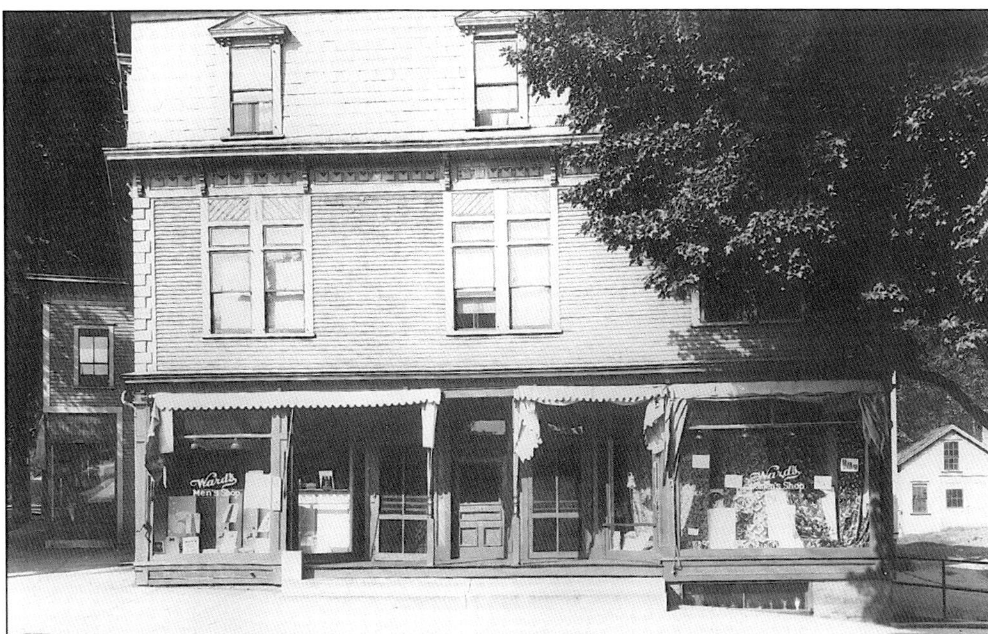

The Wards, an enterprising Millers Falls family, also owned the Wards Men's Shop as well as the Wards Women's Shop. Baking was done below street level. (Photograph by Adrian Savage; courtesy Millers Falls Library.)

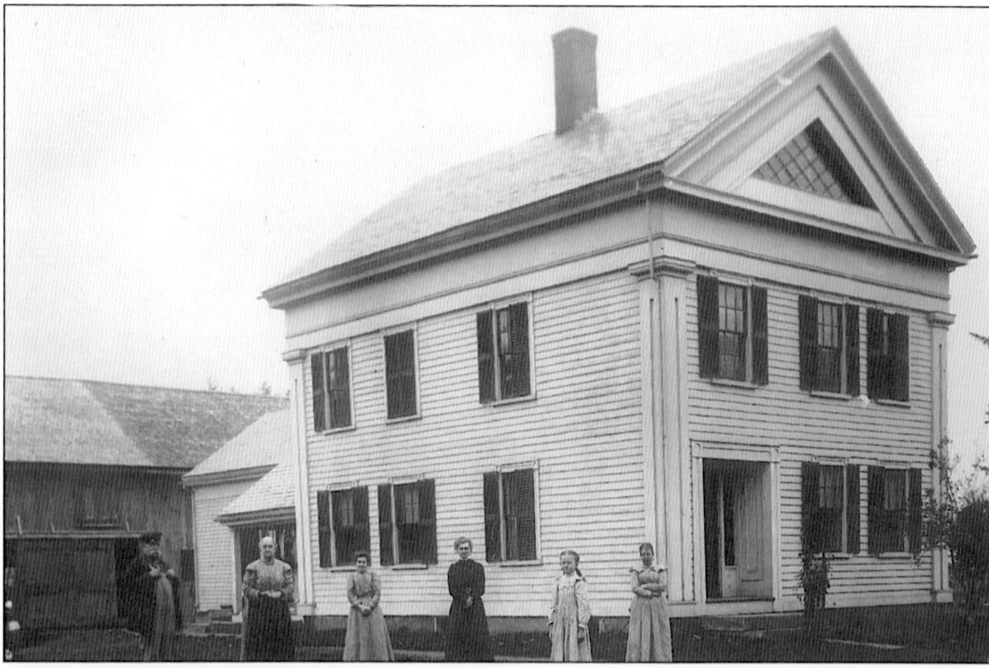

Shown in this undated image of the Martin Grout house in Millers Falls are, from left to right, Alden Grout, Charlotte Stone Grout, Lula Stockweel, an unidentified person, and Florence Giles. (Courtesy Millers Falls Library.)

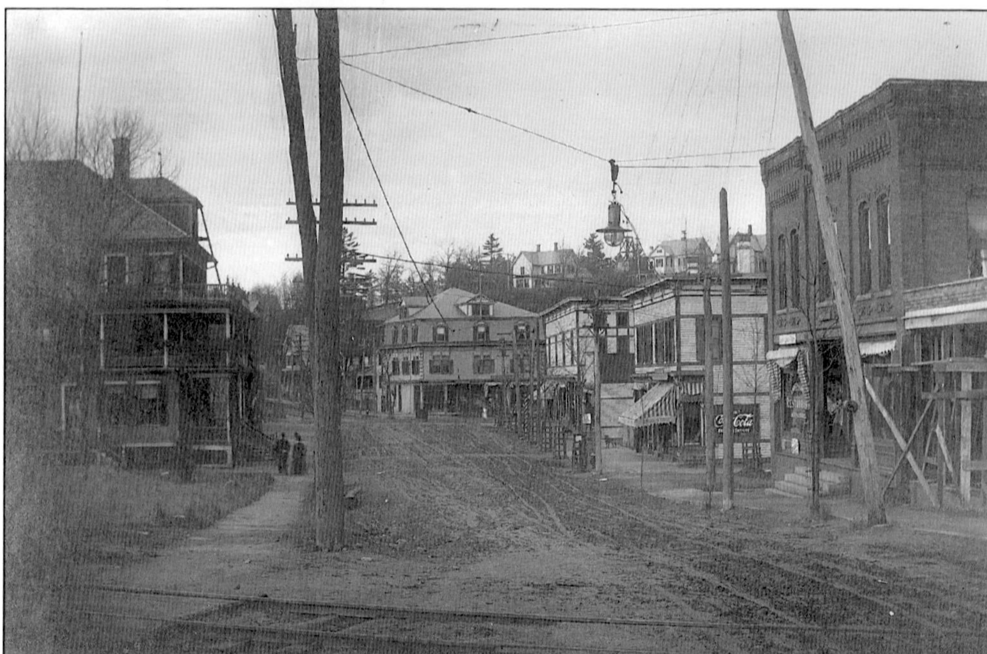

The Millers Falls Hotel is at the left front of this *c.* 1905 photograph, taken from close to the railroad tracks. Directly across the street is the local eatery. The building that today houses Carrolls Market is the next in line on the same side of the street, with the canopy and cola sign. Note the homes above Main Street on Grand Avenue. (Courtesy Millers Falls Library.)

George L. Scott (1868–1952), a Millers Falls photographer, was trained in photography by his maternal uncle, the famous George Rockwood of New York City. From his business, Scott Studios, George L. Scott photographed many of the events and people of the area as well as surrounding areas. Adrian M. Savage, another local photographer, got his start in the Scott Studios in Millers Falls. (Photograph taken by Adrian M. Savage; courtesy Millers Falls Library.)

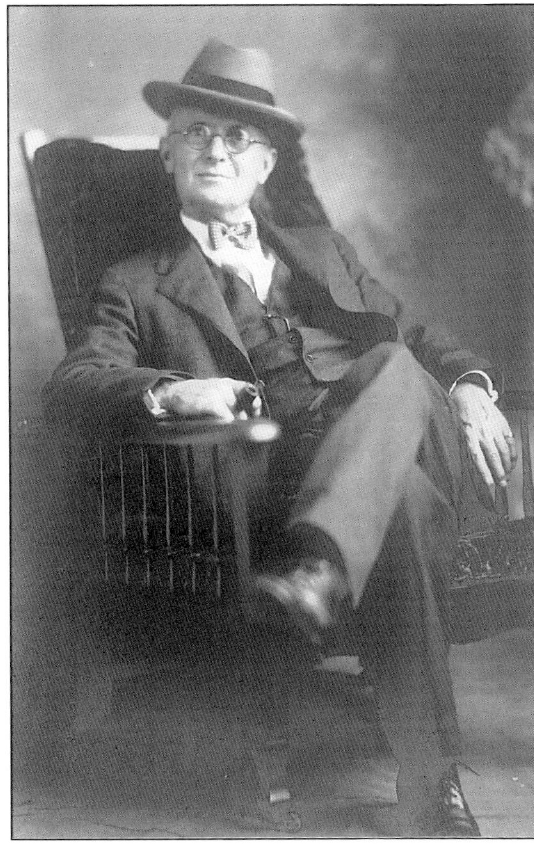

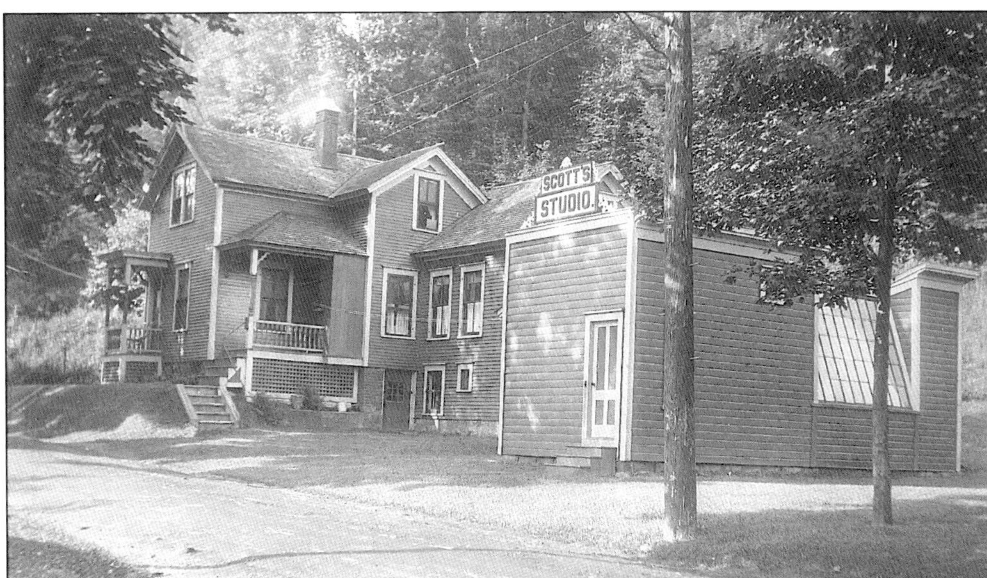

George L. Scott's photography studio was located in Millers Falls. Adrain Savage (1907–1999), who took over his business, lived almost across the street on Cresent Street. (Courtesy Millers Falls Library.)

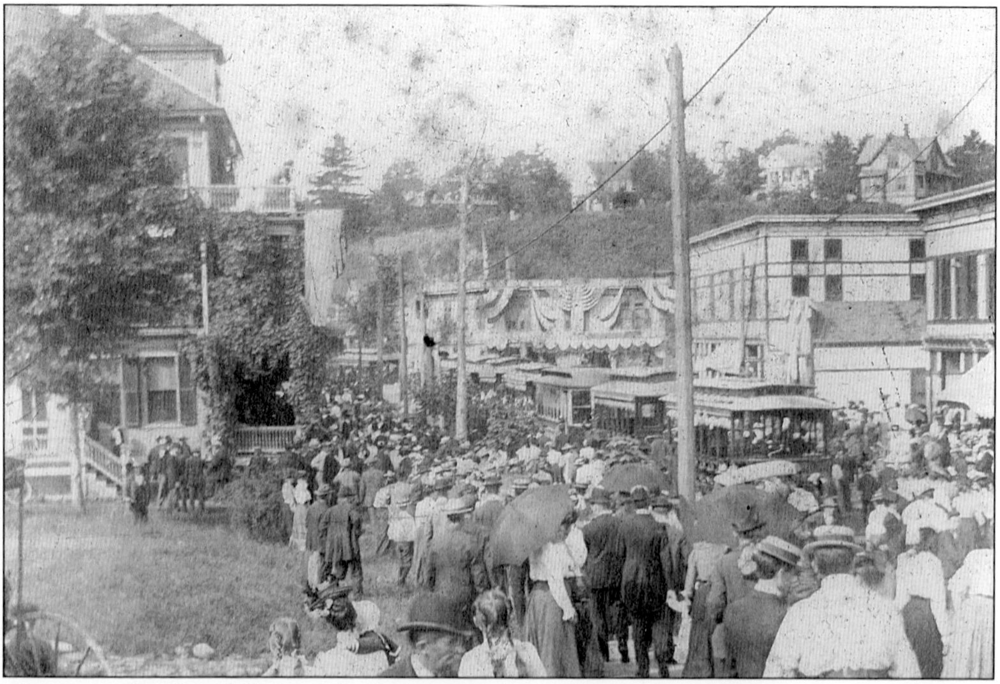

This view of Millers Falls was taken on September 2, 1902, when Teddy Roosevelt visited the village of Millers Falls. Note the people standing about in the styles of the day and the trolley cars carrying Roosevelt. (Courtesy Millers Falls Library.)

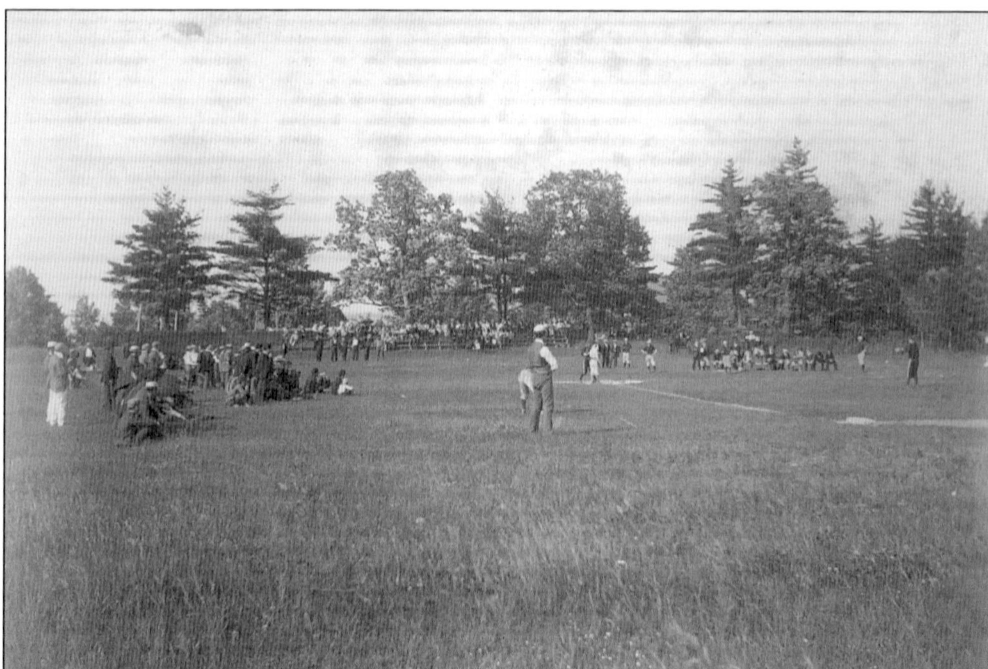

This 1902 photograph was taken in the Highland Park area of Millers Falls. Note the well-dressed players and spectators. (Courtesy Millers Falls Library.)

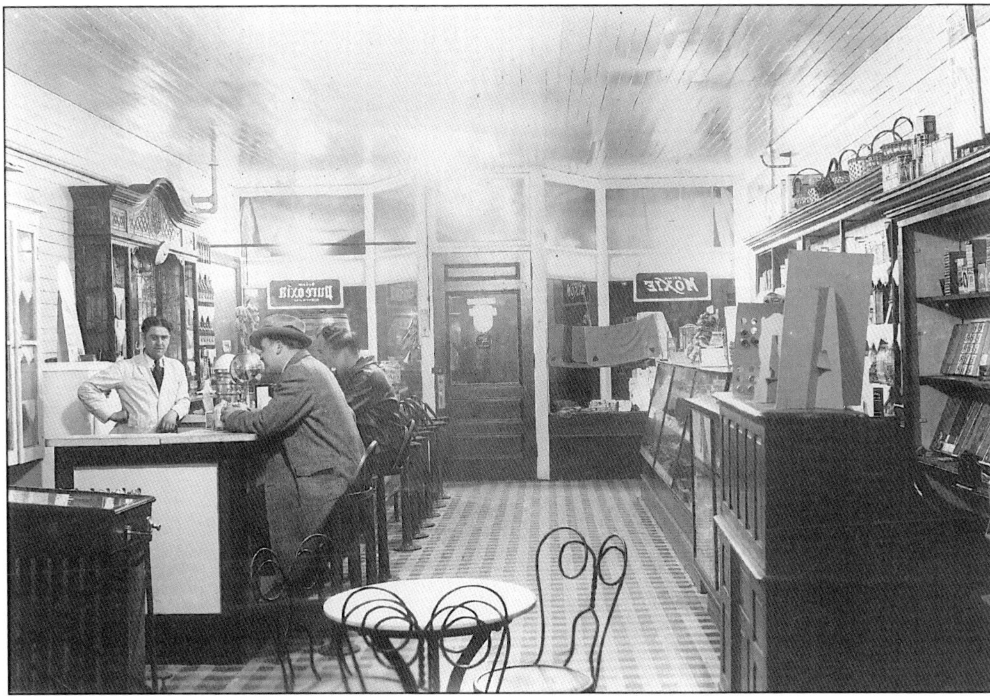

Shown is the interior of Equi's Store with customers being served at the counter. (Courtesy Miller Falls Library.)

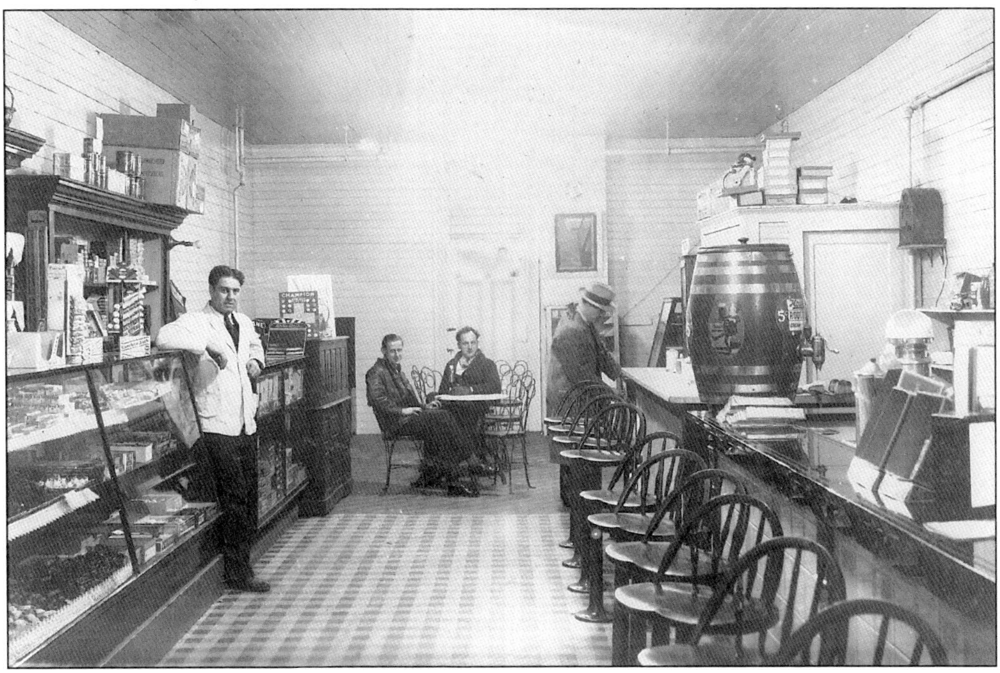

At the rear portion of Equi's Store, candy, lunch, soda, or ice cream could be served as well as products purchased to go. Note the clerk leaning against a candy counter fully stocked on the left. On the right is a large root beer barrel, with a sign giving the price: 5¢ for a glass. (Courtesy Millers Falls Library.)

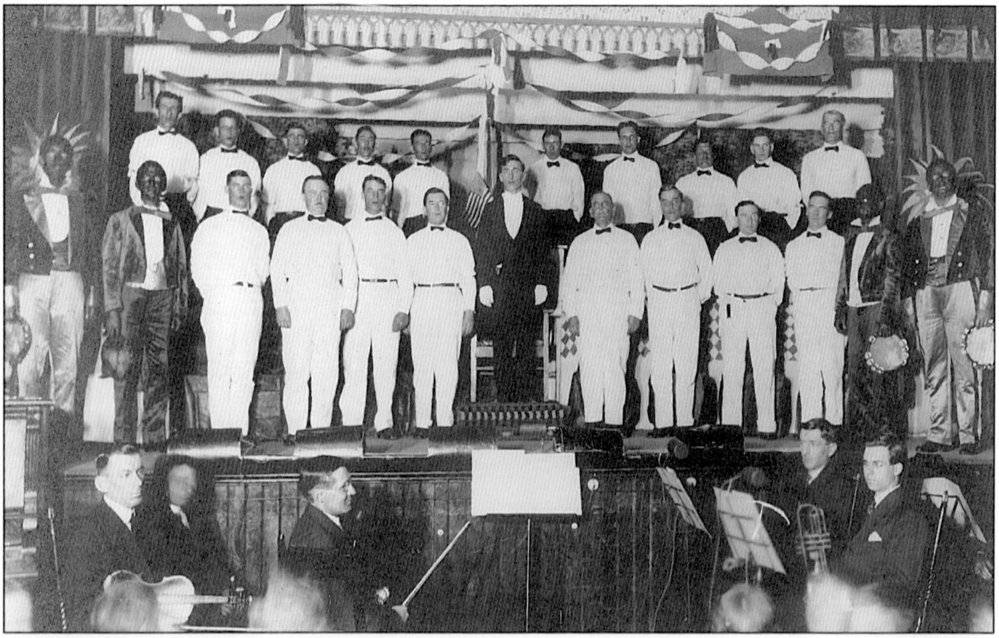

The Red Men's Hall of Millers Falls, later the Millers Falls Veterans of Foreign Wars, was located in this building. Note the orchestra in the pit below the stage. Nolan Maynard is in the front row, fifth from the left. Daniel Donahue is in the center in the black suit, and to his right is William Parsons. Charles Bickford, Henry Morrissey, and Raymond Gould are in the orchestra. (Courtesy Millers Falls Library.)

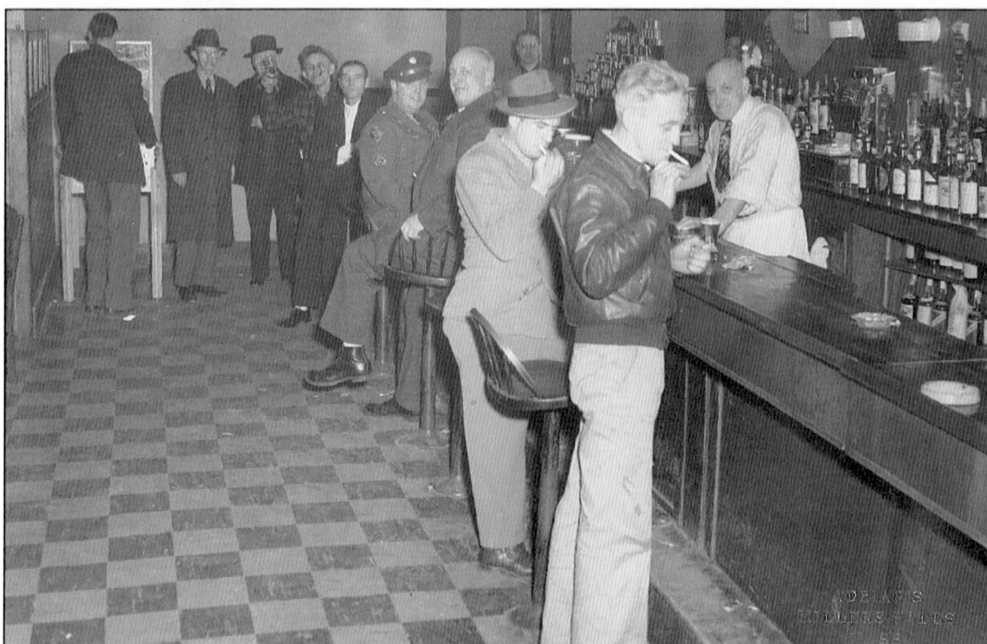

This photograph, probably taken in the 1940s shows, from left to right, Ted Aibin, Francis Lenard, John Bane, Abe Smith, Joe R. Tobin, Buck Morse, Brownie Mackanewicz, Bunty Garnecki, Louis Equi, and Elmer Merriot.

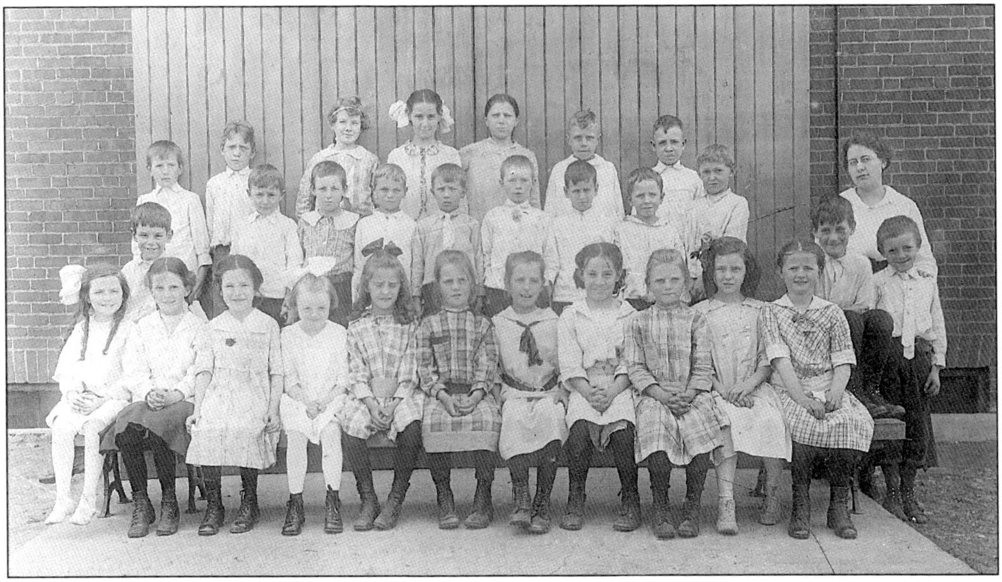

This 1913 photograph of the fourth- and fifth-grade class of old Highland School, East Main Street in Millers Falls, shows large bows in the girls' hair and the boys wearing neckties. (Photograph by Scott Studios of Millers Falls; courtesy Millers Falls Library.)

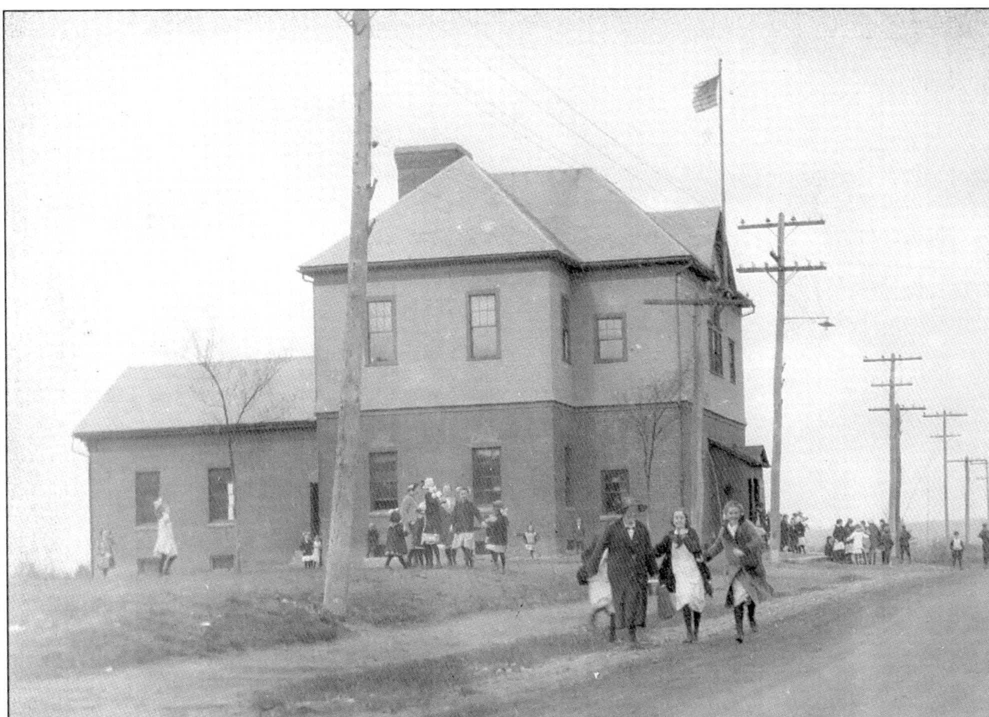

This photograph shows the old Highland School on East Main Street in Millers Falls in 1913. (Photograph by Adrian Savage; courtesy Millers Falls Library.)

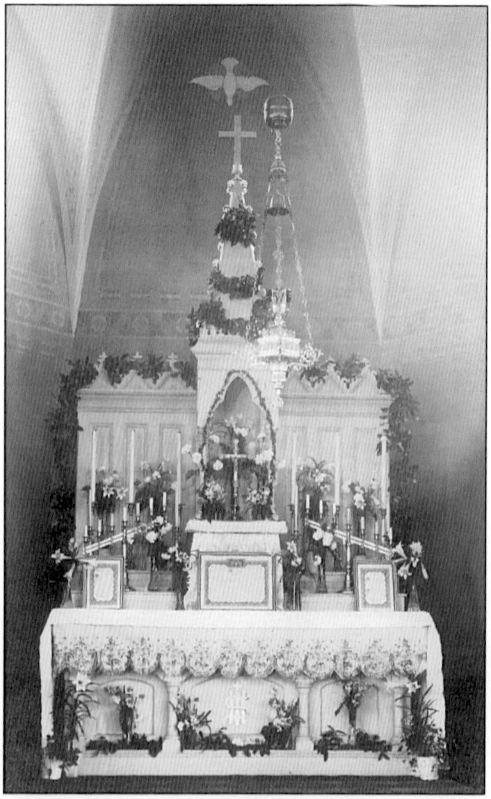

Shown is the altar at St. John's church in Millers Falls. (Courtesy Millers Falls Library.)

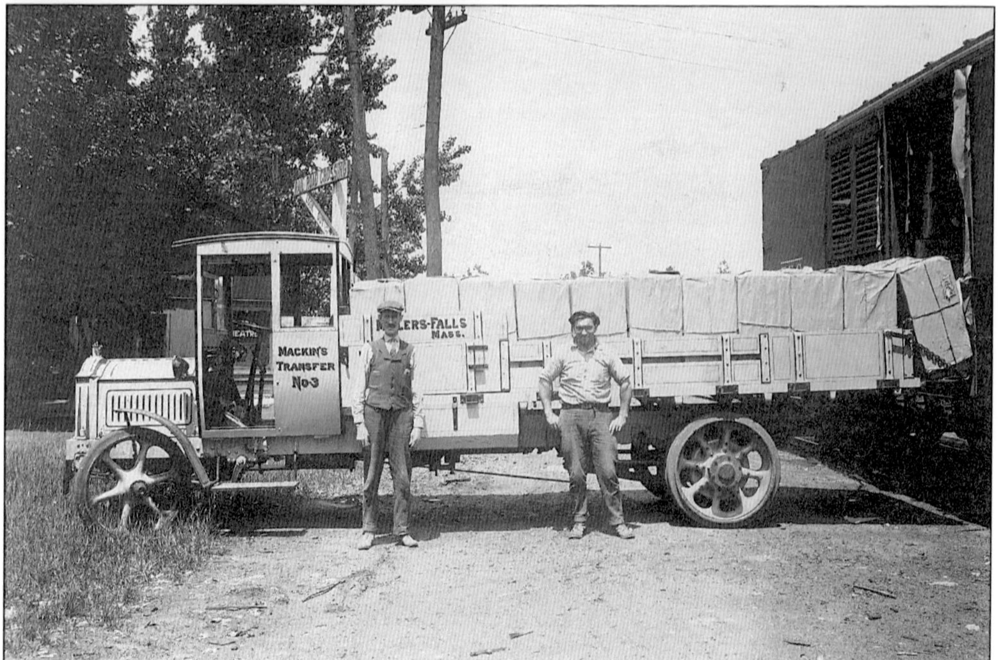

An early Mackin's truck of Millers Falls No. 3 is shown in this c. 1912 photograph. Posing are Patrick Mackin (left) and Bob Bacon. (Courtesy Montague Historical Society.)

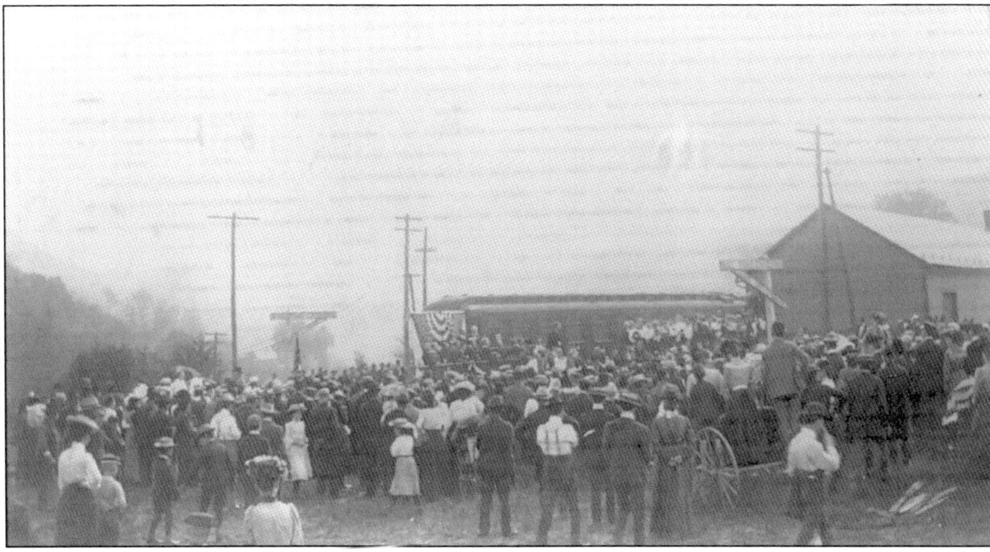

Teddy Roosevelt speaks at the Millers Falls freight yard in 1902. (Courtesy Millers Falls Library.)

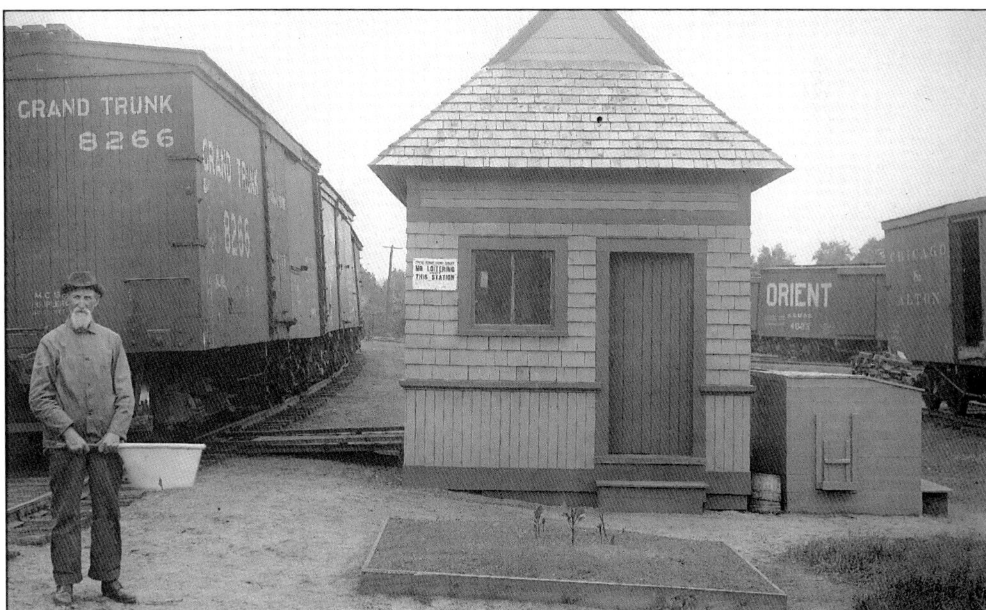

The railroad crossing in Millers Falls is shown with crossing tender Joseph Verville on duty, c. 1910. (Courtesy Millers Falls Library.)

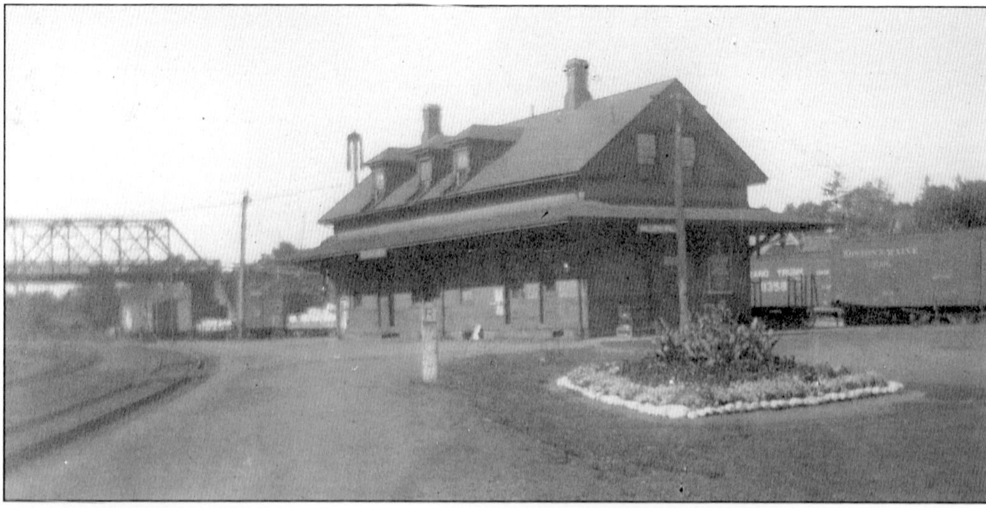

The Millers Falls train station is shown in 1910. (Courtesy Peter S. Miller.)

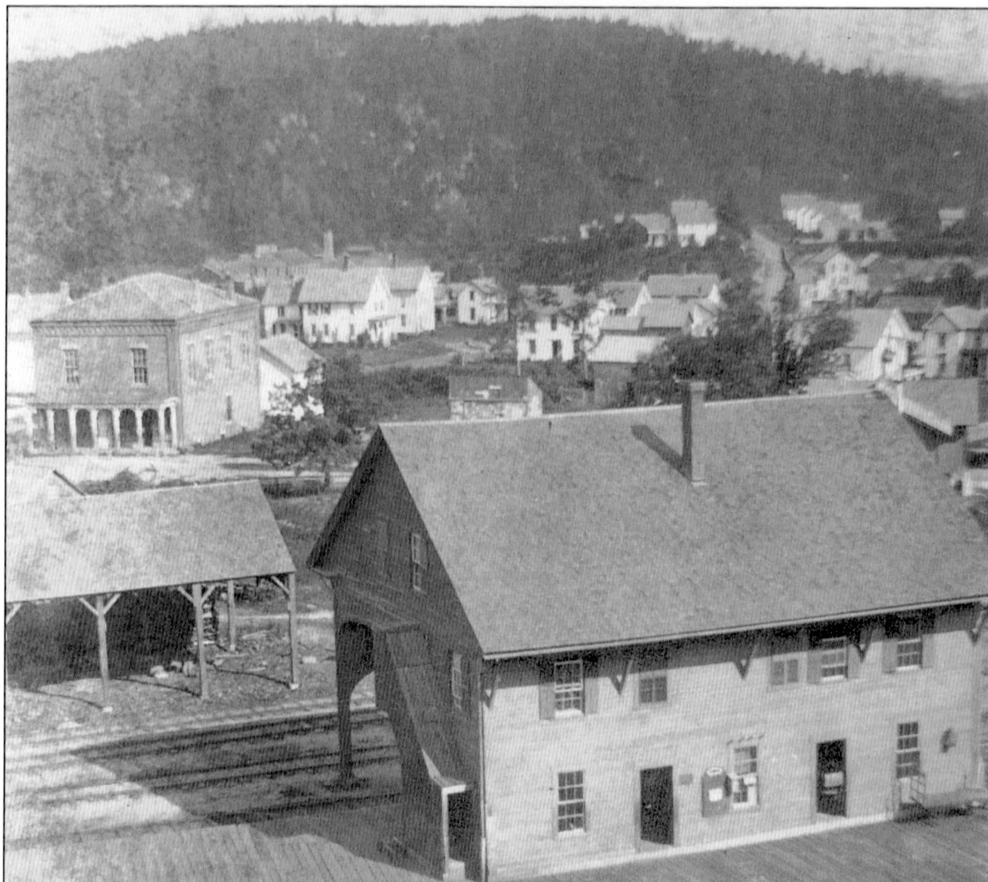

This *c.* 1875 photograph shows the Millers Falls train depot. The fire of October 30, 1895, destroyed many of the buildings in the picture. (Photograph by C.H. Wells; courtesy Peter S. Miller.)

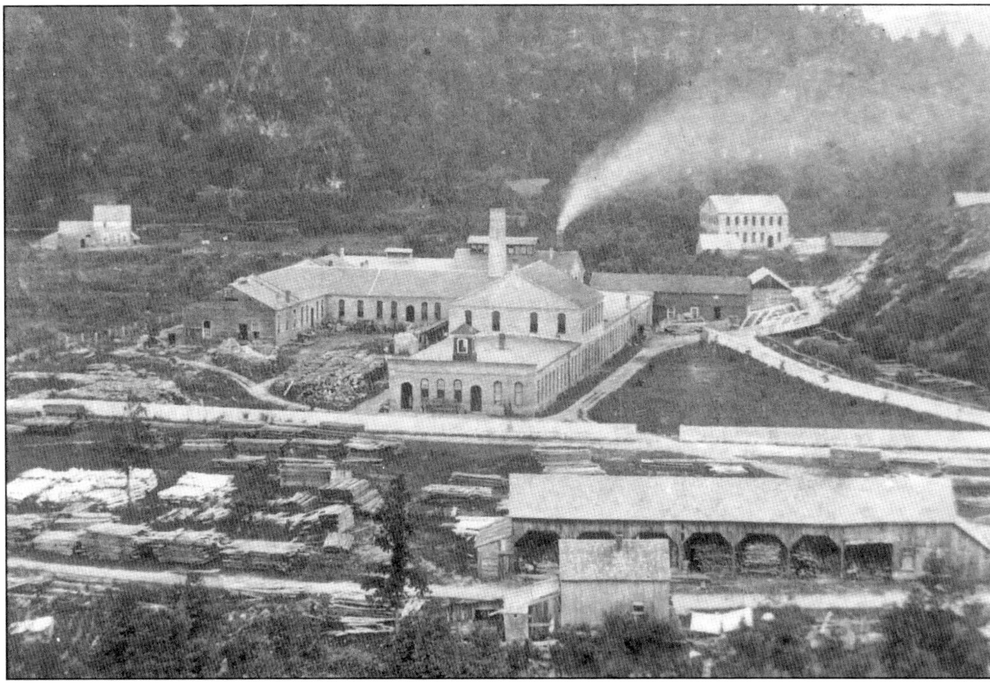

The Millers Falls Tool Company, shown *c.* 1875, was a world-renowned company, but was actually located on the Millers Falls side of Erving. (Courtesy Millers Falls Library.)

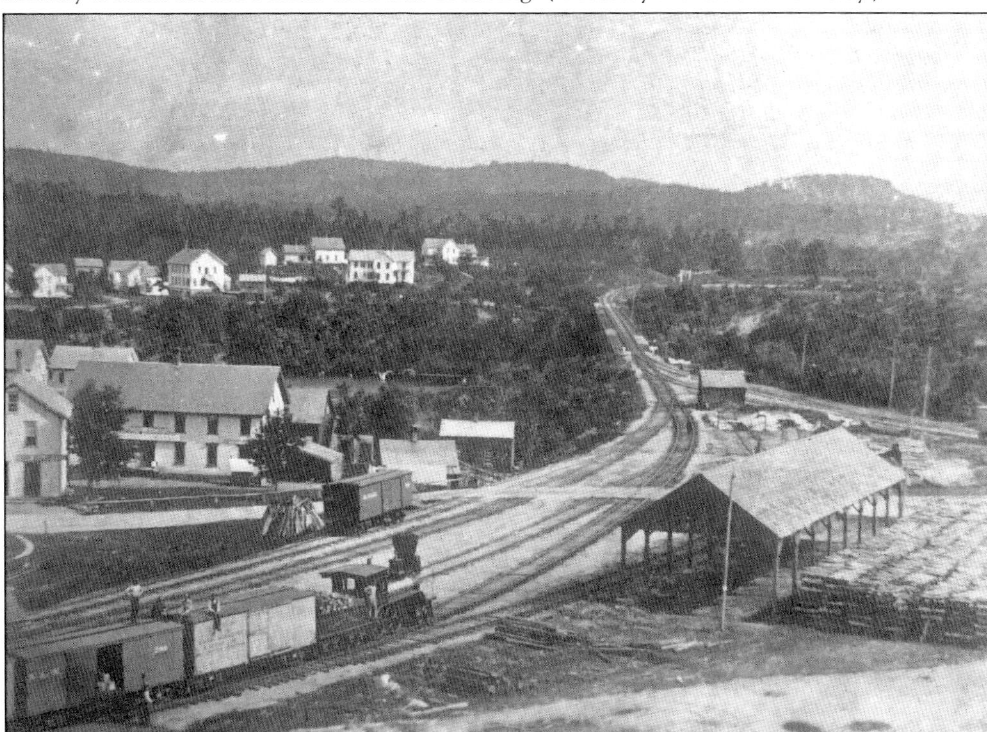

A steam engine pulls cars along the tracks, *c.* 1875, at the railroad and depot in Millers Falls. (Courtesy Millers Falls Library.)

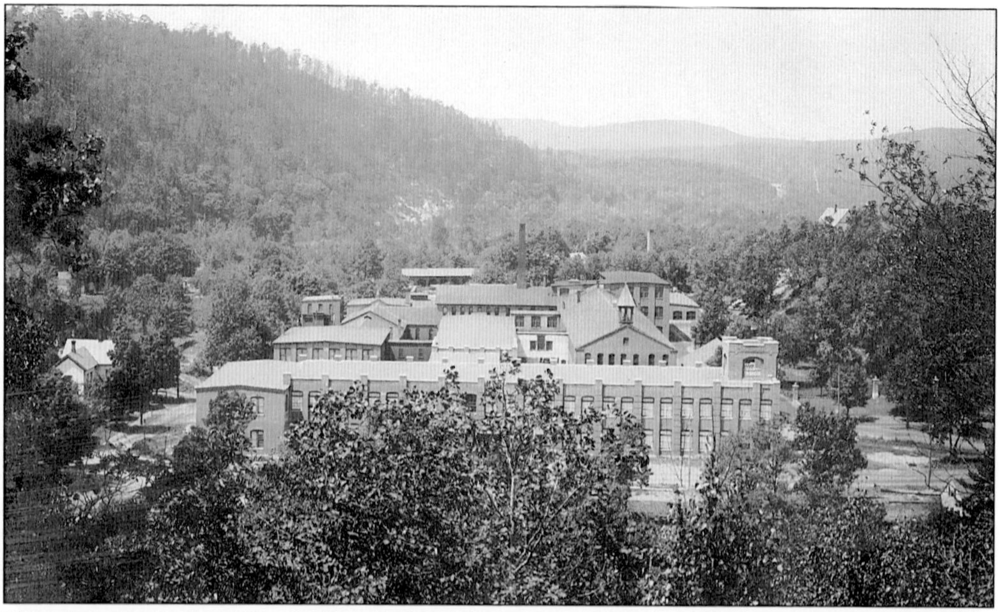

This photograph shows the Millers Falls Tool Company in 1913. (Courtesy Peter S. Miller.)

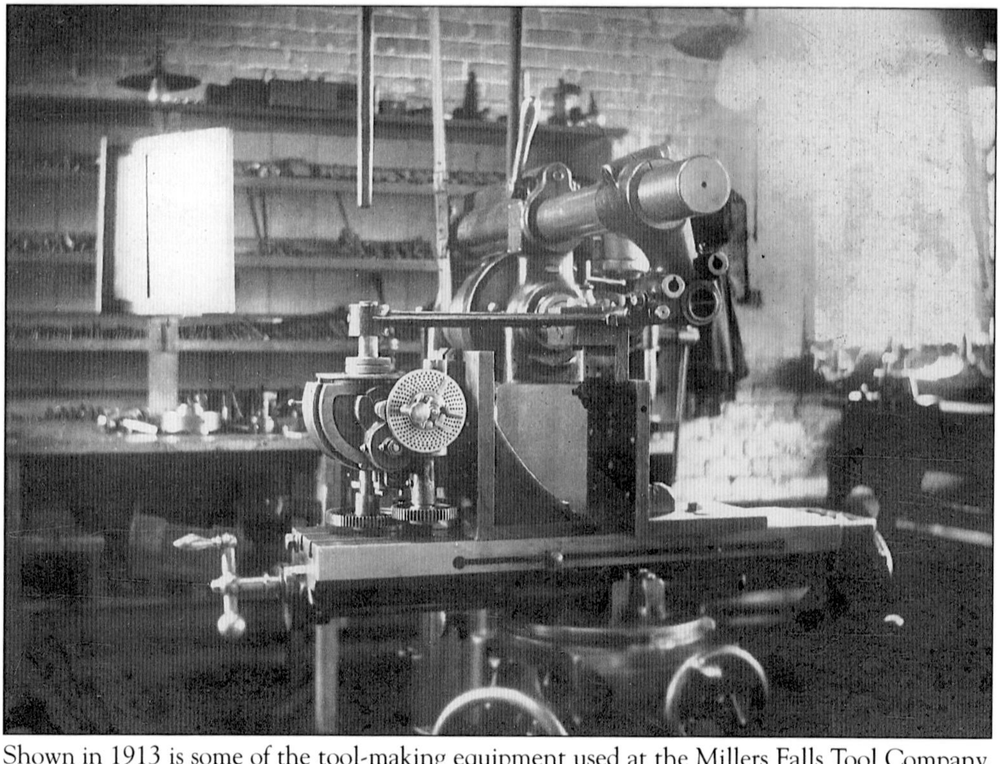

Shown in 1913 is some of the tool-making equipment used at the Millers Falls Tool Company. (Courtesy Peter S. Miller.)

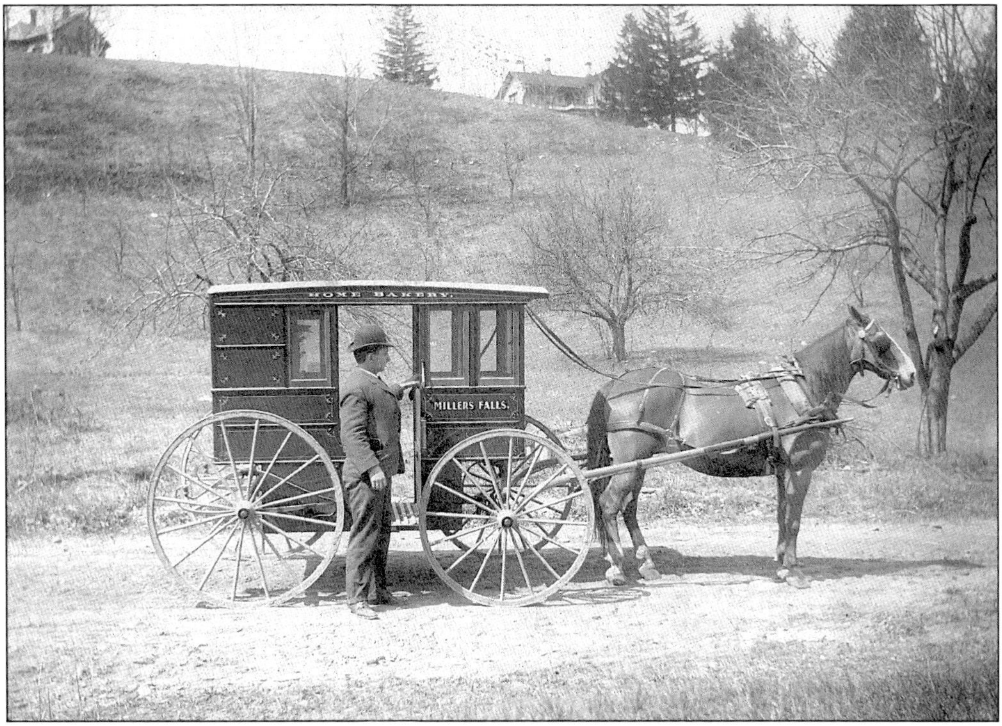

A bakery wagon from Wards Bakery is pictured *c.* 1900 on Front Street in Millers Falls. Owned and operated by Herbert J. Ward, the bakery served local residents for many years. (Courtesy Millers Falls Library.)

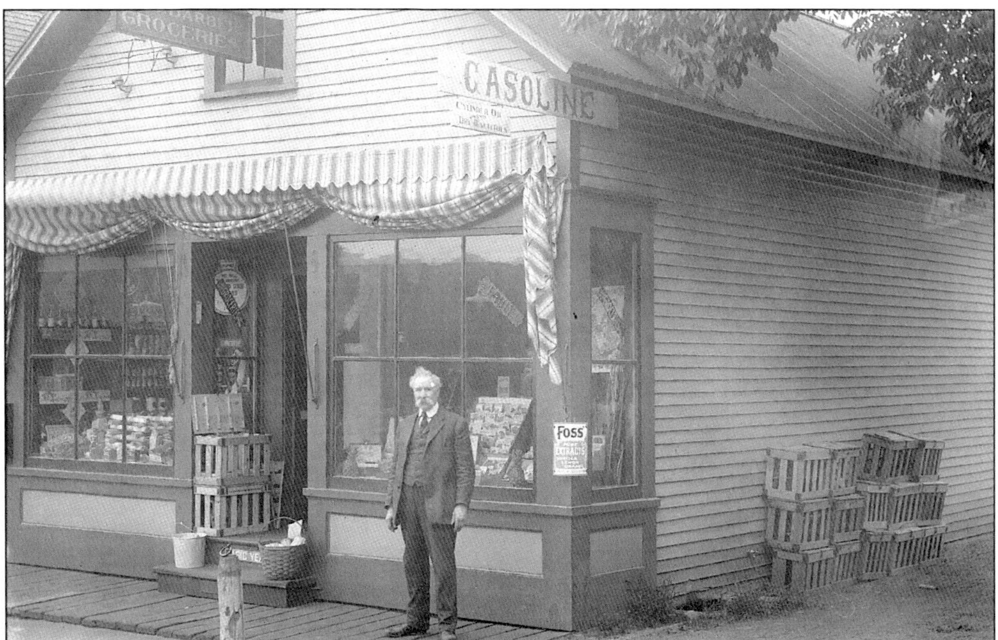

The Millers Falls Grocery Store was owned by C.H. Barber. (Courtesy Peter S. Miller.)

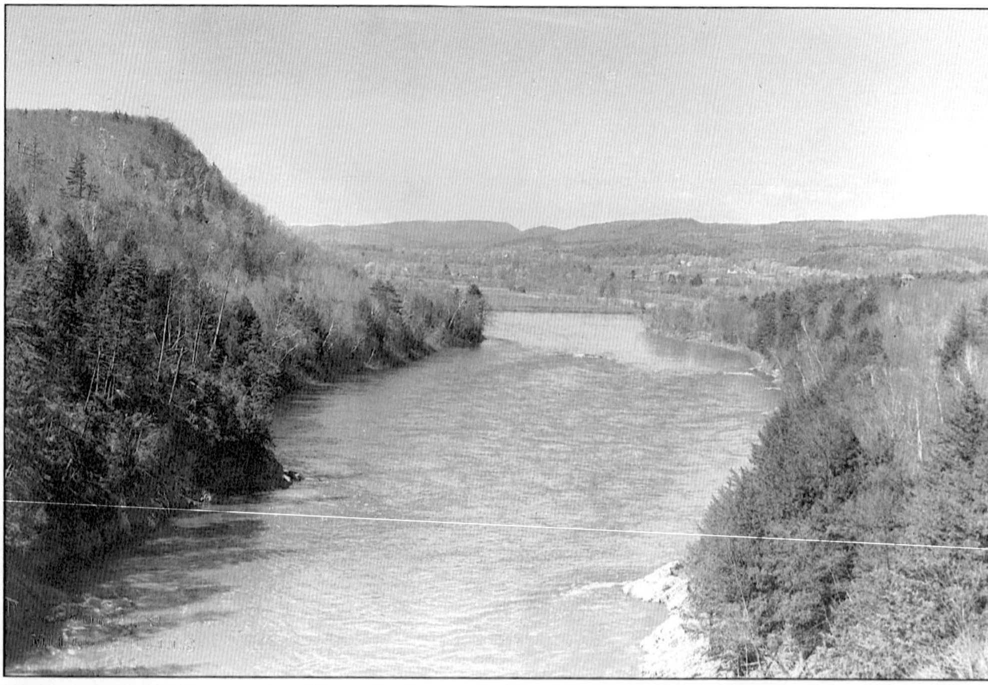

This view of the Connecticut River looks north from the French King Bridge. (Courtesy Millers Falls Library.)

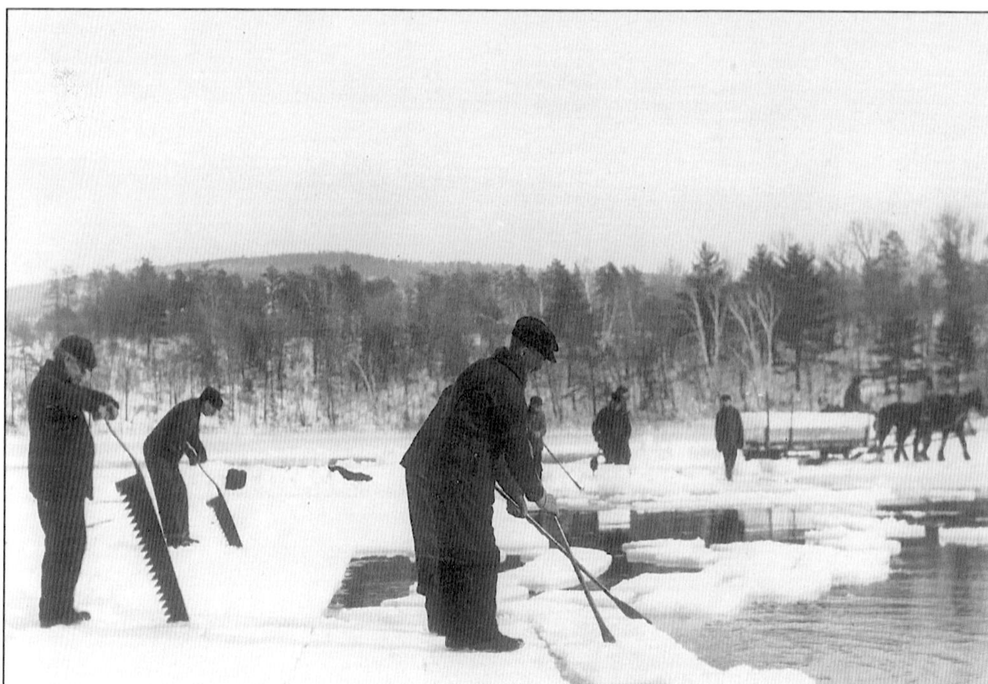

Men cut the ice on Green Pond with the large saws, while others move the ice to be taken away by horse and wagon, *c.* 1910. (Courtesy Millers Falls Library.)

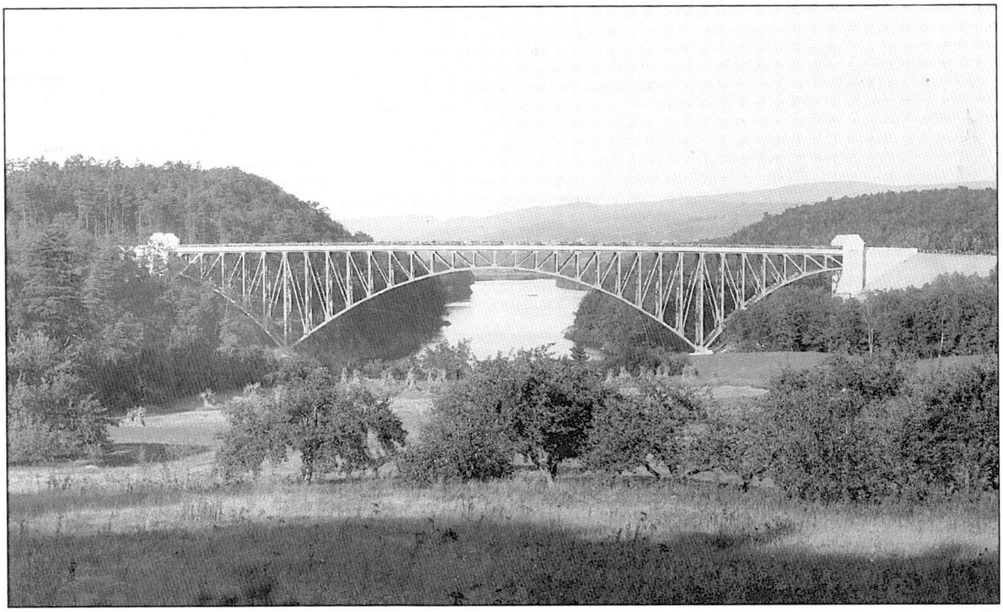

In 1934, the French King Bridge spanned the Connecticut River from Erving to Gill, Massachusetts. Route 2 goes over the bridge. (Courtesy Millers Falls Library.)

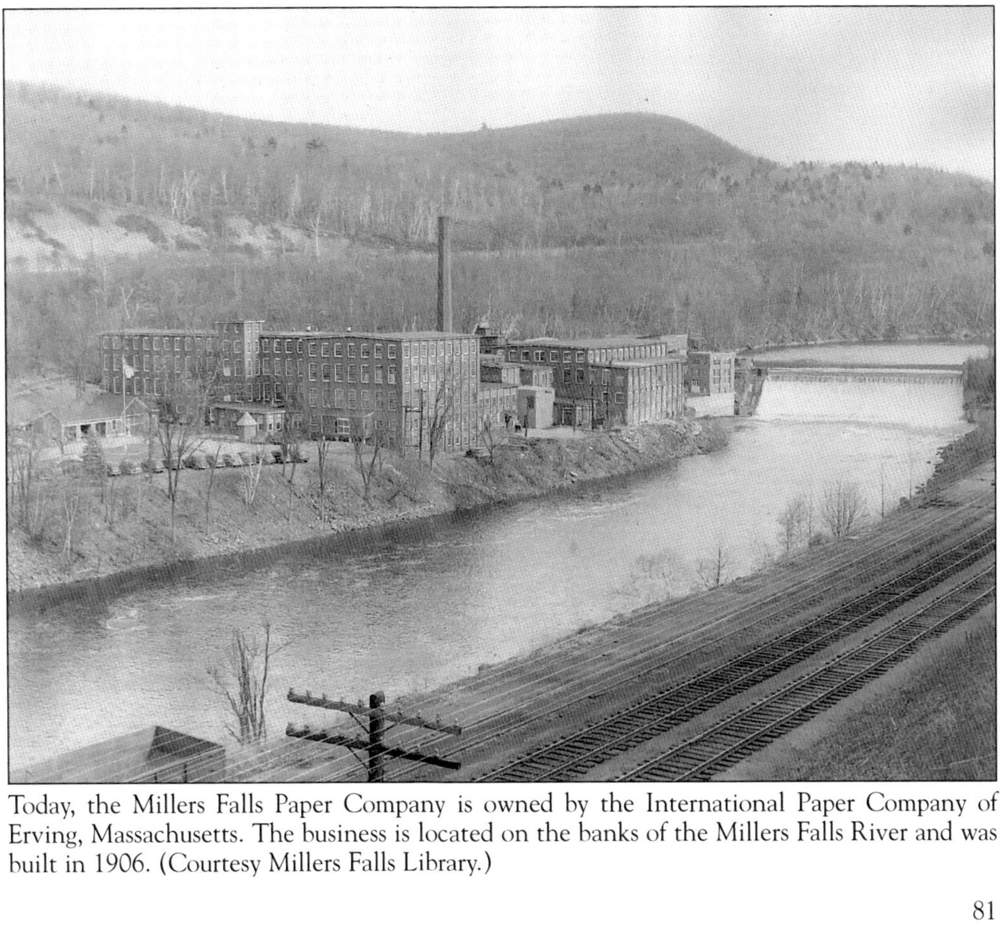

Today, the Millers Falls Paper Company is owned by the International Paper Company of Erving, Massachusetts. The business is located on the banks of the Millers Falls River and was built in 1906. (Courtesy Millers Falls Library.)

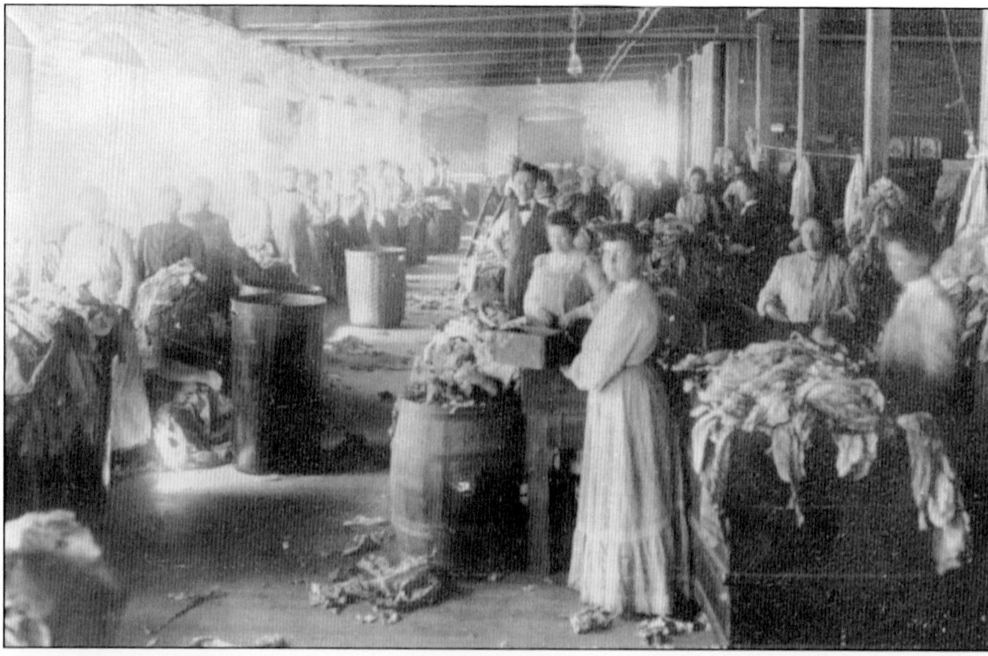

This 1908 view of the rag room of the Millers Falls Paper Company shows rags being sorted for use in making pulp for paper manufacturing. Note the long dresses of the women working and the bow tie of the man. (Courtesy Millers Falls Paper Company.)

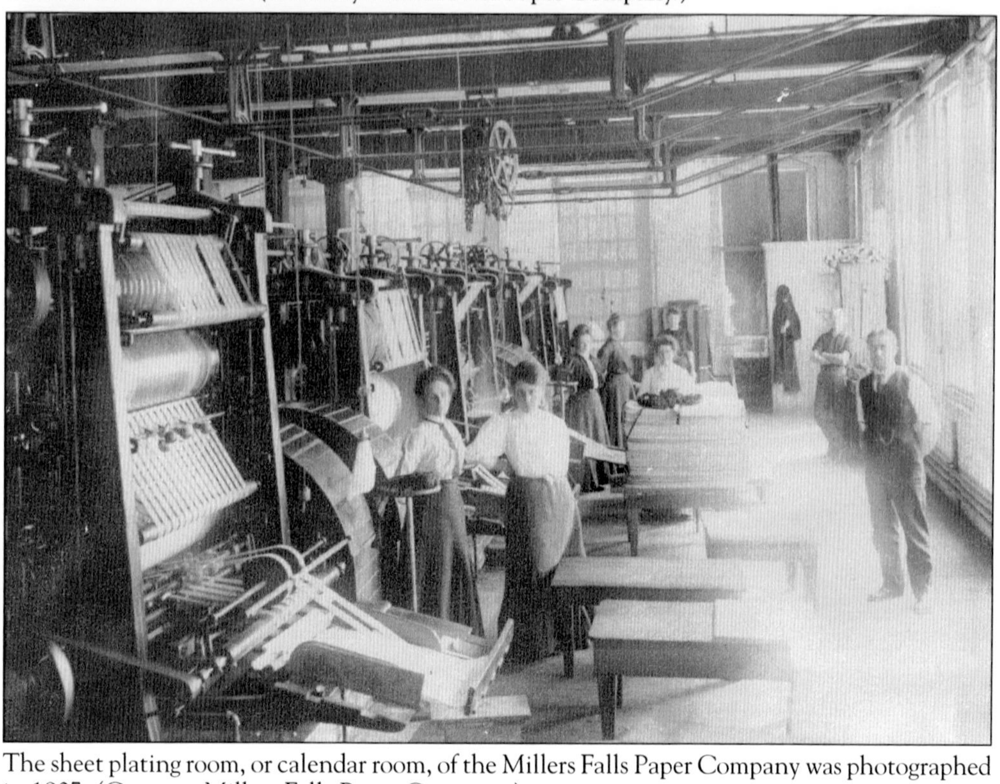

The sheet plating room, or calendar room, of the Millers Falls Paper Company was photographed in 1907. (Courtesy Millers Falls Paper Company.)

Three

Montague Center

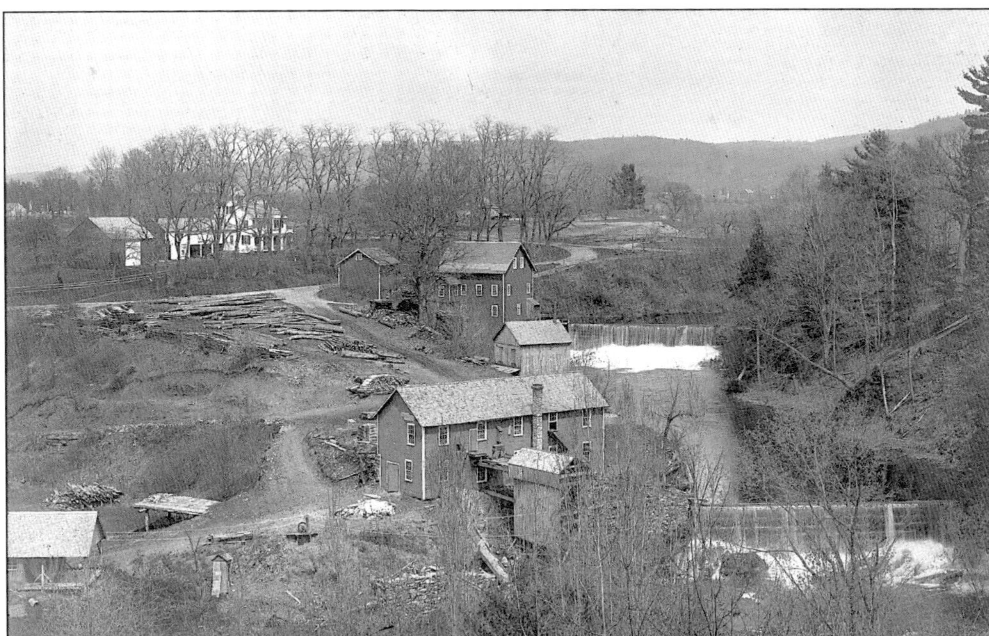

The Sawmill River figures prominently in this great *c.* 1880 scene of the Montague Center area. The large white home in the background is the Sheldon House. The gristmill and the sawmill are also visible. Note the various uses of the Sawmill River. The upper mill later contained the Martin Machine Shop. (Courtesy Montague Historical Society.)

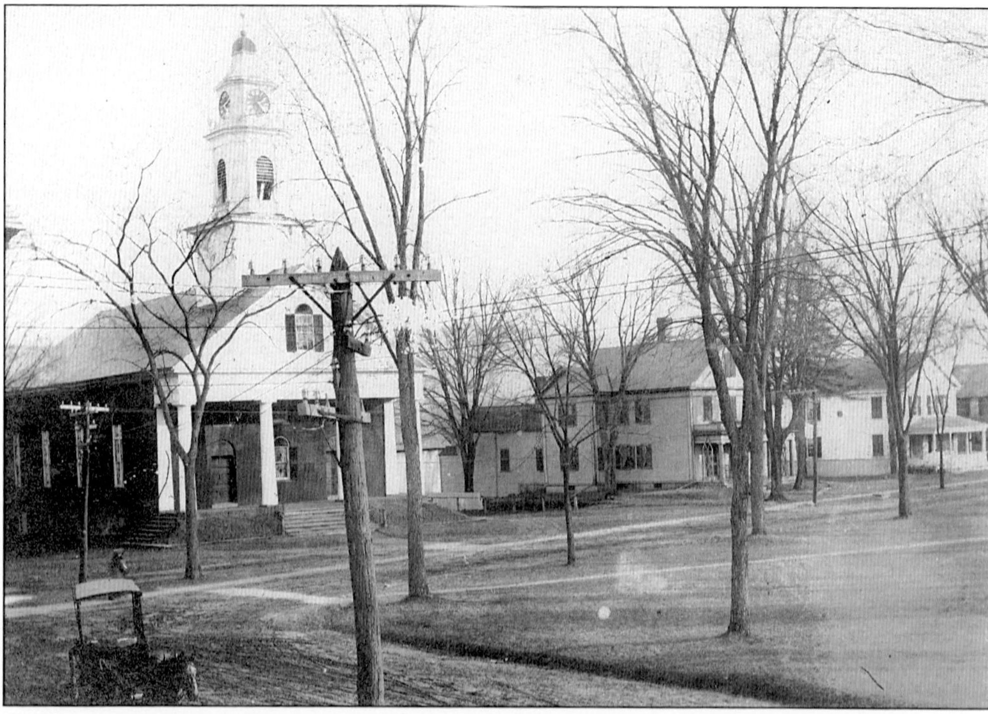

The Montague Center Congregational church and some houses can be seen to the left in this photograph of the Montague Center Common area, c. 1910. (Courtesy Kyle J. Scott.)

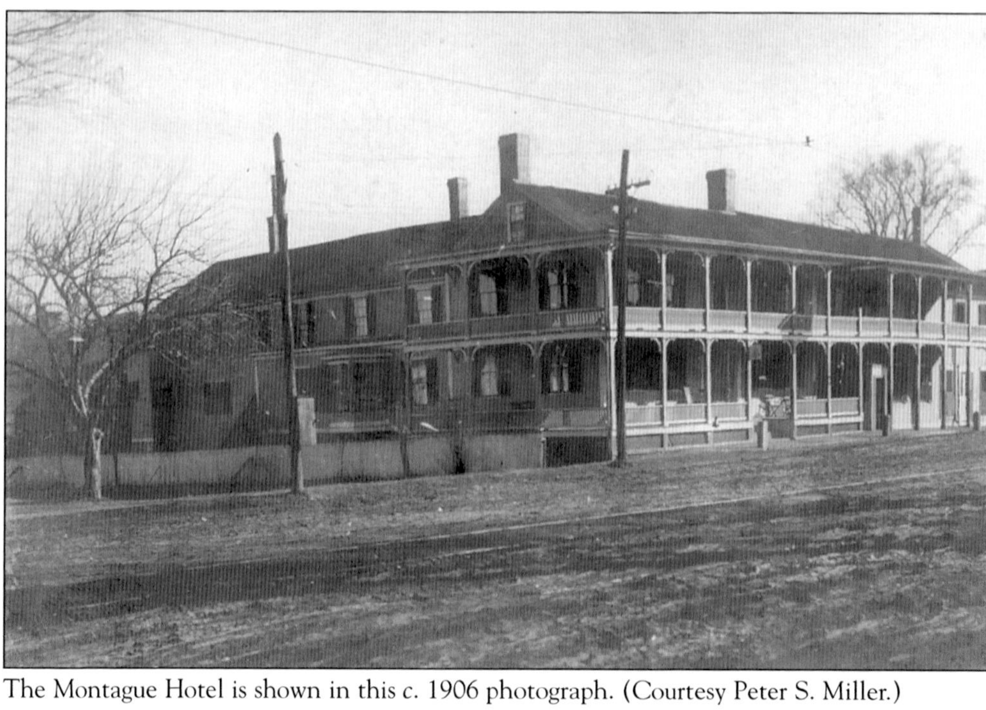

The Montague Hotel is shown in this c. 1906 photograph. (Courtesy Peter S. Miller.)

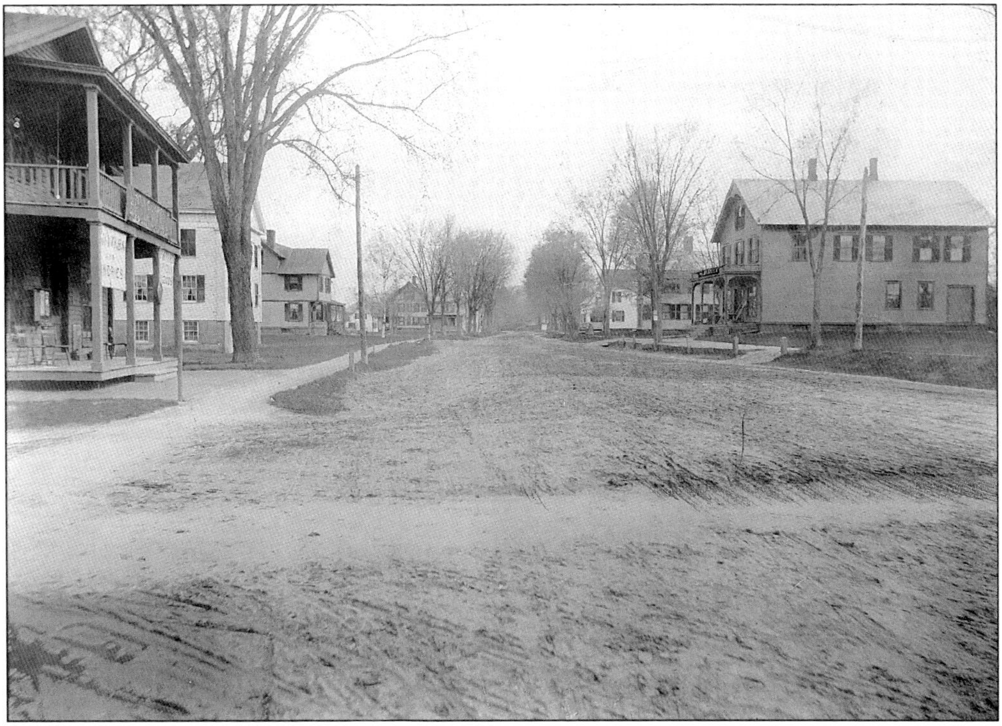

This view of Main Street in Monatgue Center was taken after the Rugg Company fire in 1889, but prior to 1898, when electric cars went into service in this section of town. (Courtesy Montague Historical Society.)

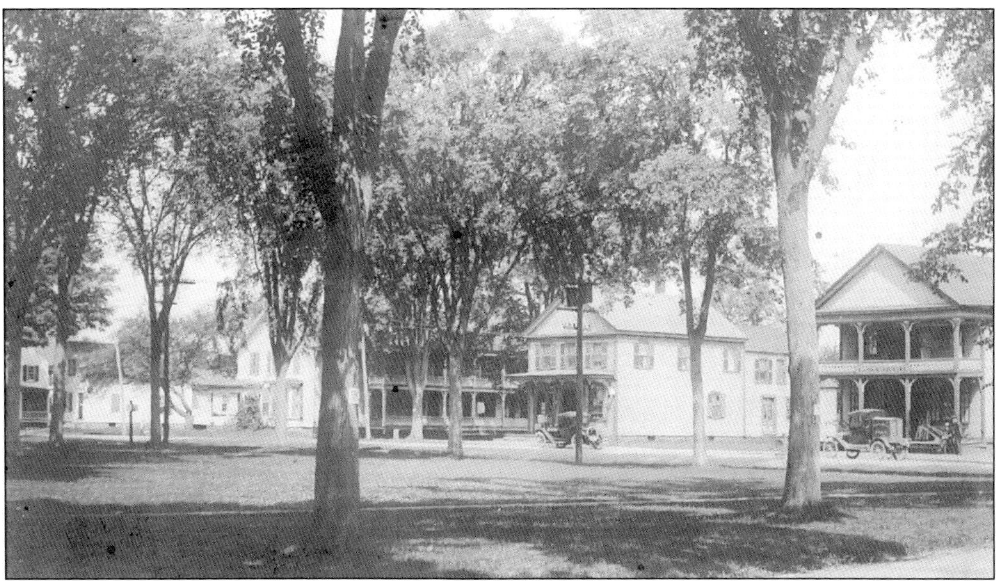

The Montague Center Common is shown here in 1926. Note the vintage automobiles along the street. (Courtesy Peter S. Miller.)

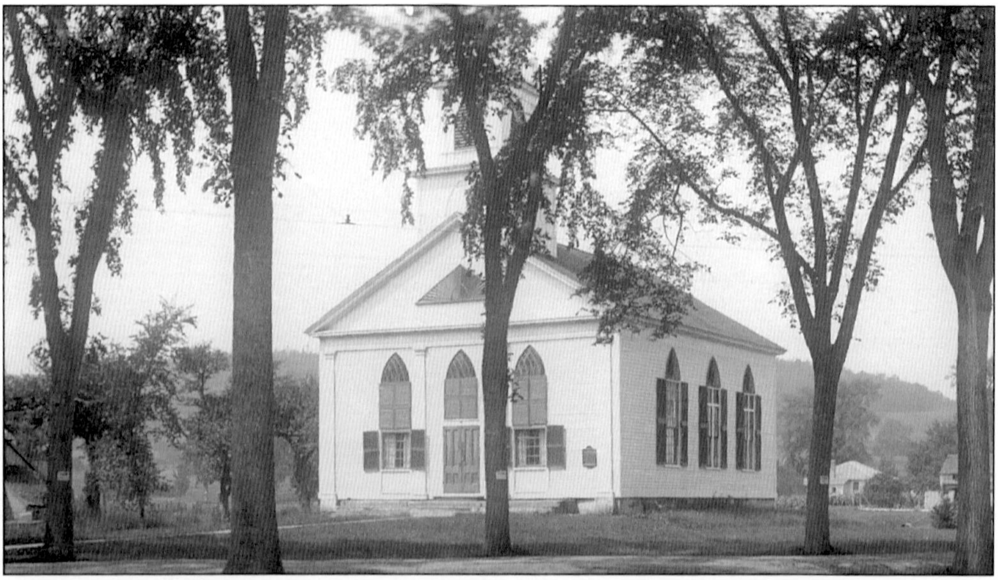

The Unitarian church, built in 1834 by the Unitarian and Episcopalian denominations, still stands and is now the home of the Montague Grange. (Courtesy Kyle J. Scott.)

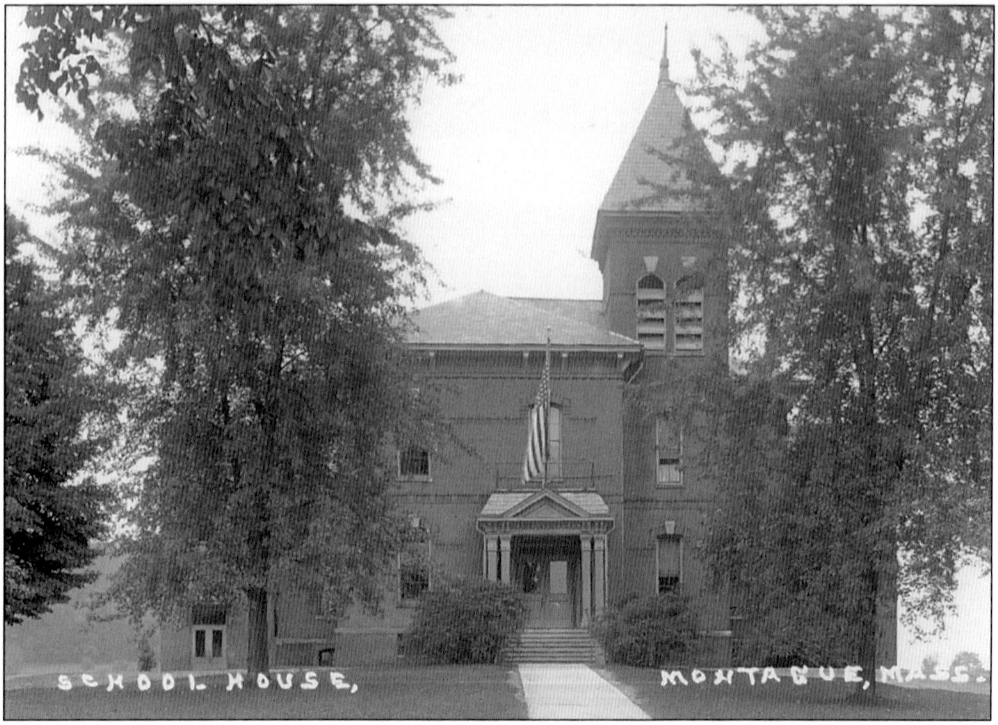

In 1875, classes for all grades, including high school, were held in one building. This was the first consolidated school in America. (Courtesy Peter S. Miller.)

The Montague Congregational church, built in 1834 by two of the towns farmers, Henry and Zabina Taylor, is a sharp-looking structure with a prominent steeple and clock as well as front columns. The church is still in use today. (Courtesy Peter S. Miller.)

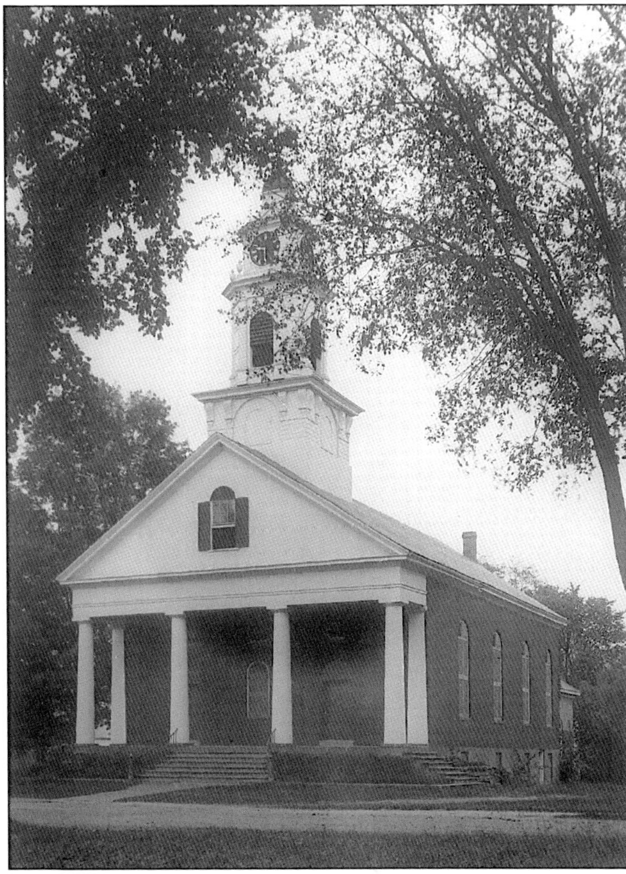

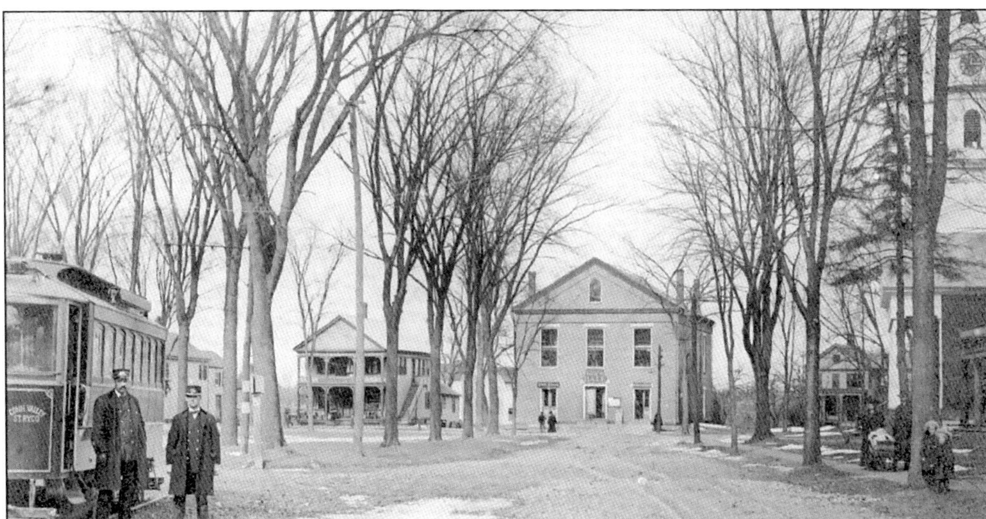

Montague trolley service celebrated its inaugural service on July 4, 1899, with a trip to Lake Pleasant. Note the trolley and conductors at the far left, the Congregational church at the right, and the town hall at the center right near the library. (Courtesy Peter S. Miller.)

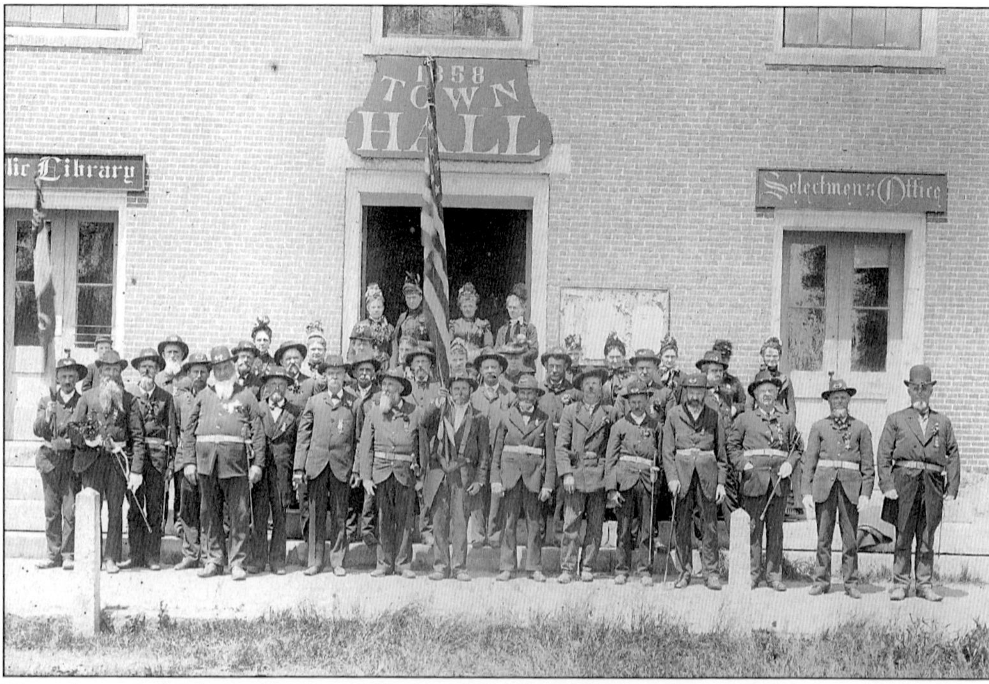

This photograph shows the Grand Army of the Republic standing outside town hall and the library right off the Montague Center Common. (Courtesy Montague Historical Society.)

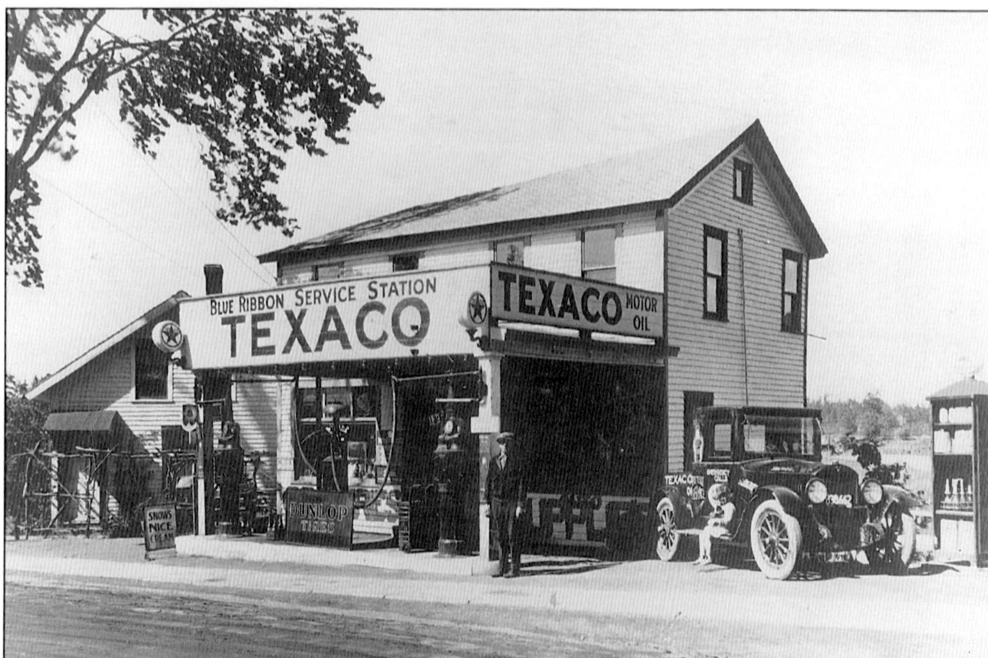

This image of the Texaco station, located at Bridge Street in Montague Center, includes a vintage service truck at the far right. The station also displays a sign shown at the left, selling the popular local favorite, Snows ice cream. (Courtesy Montague Historical Society.)

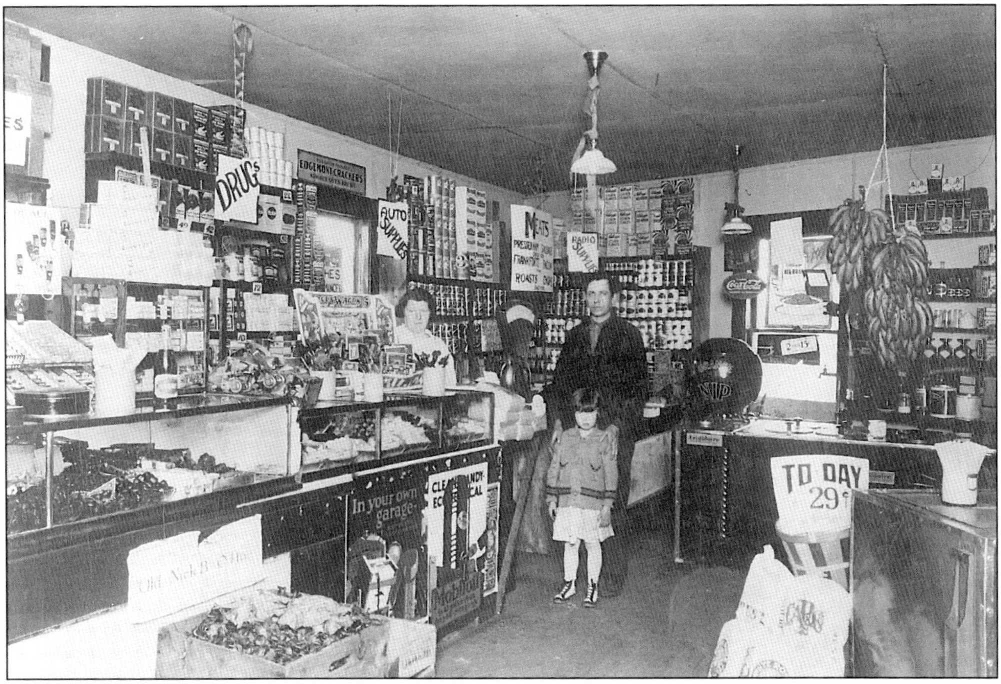

James Bartley was the proprietor of Bartley's Store in Montague Center. The fully supplied store had drugs, auto supplies, meats, radio supplies, and even fresh bananas. It was fully stocked and ready to serve local residents or passers-by. (Courtesy Montague Historical Society.)

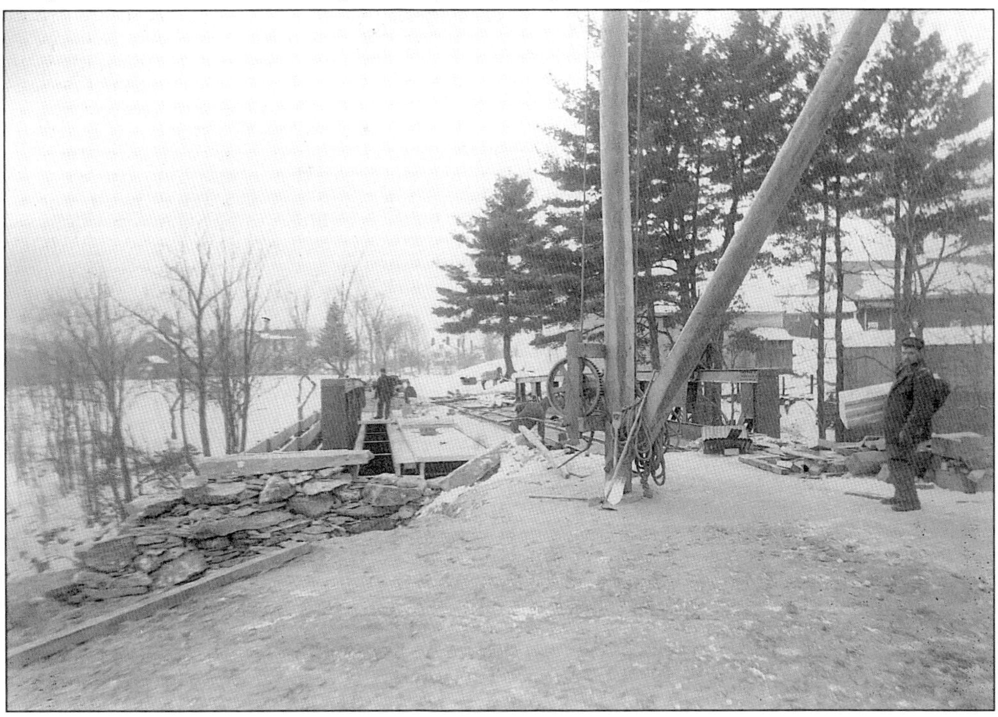

The Berlin Iron Bridge Company installs the Montague Center Bridge in this 1895 photograph. (Photograph by O.C. Leonard; courtesy Montague Historical Society.)

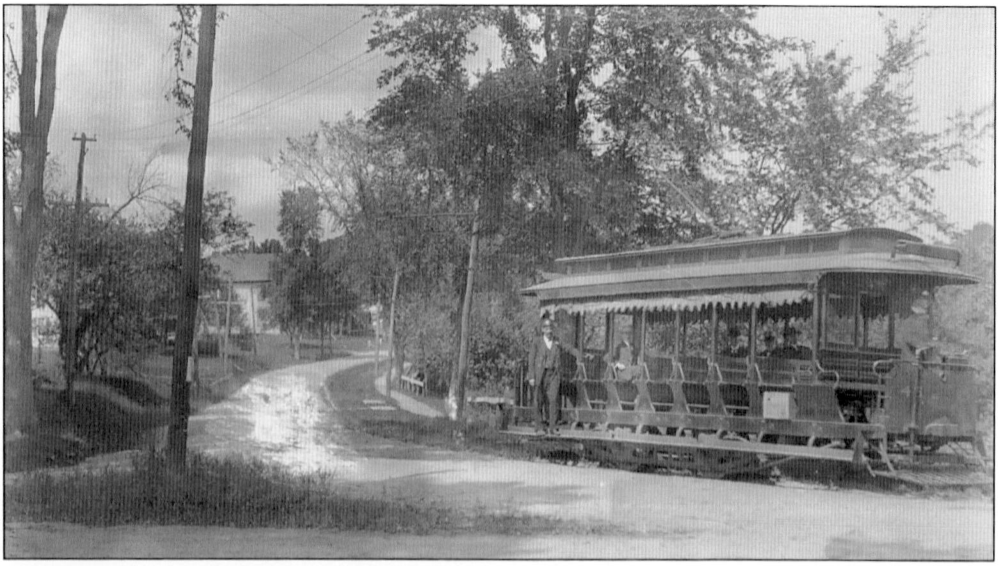

This trolley was photographed on Bridge Street in Montague Center. (Courtesy Peter S. Miller.)

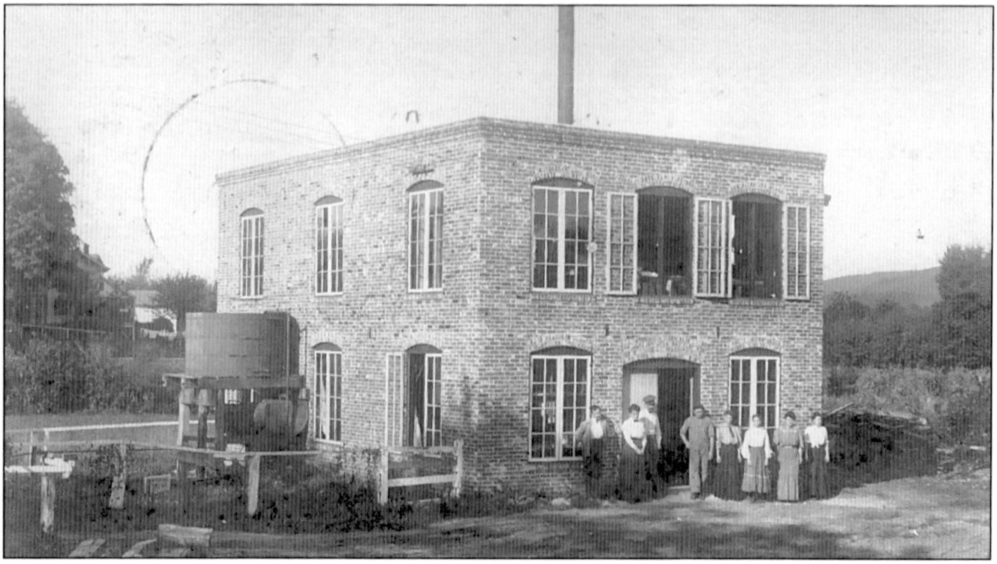

The Alden Brothers Laundry was built in 1905 by Edward Whitney and opened in October 1905. (Courtesy Peter S. Miller.)

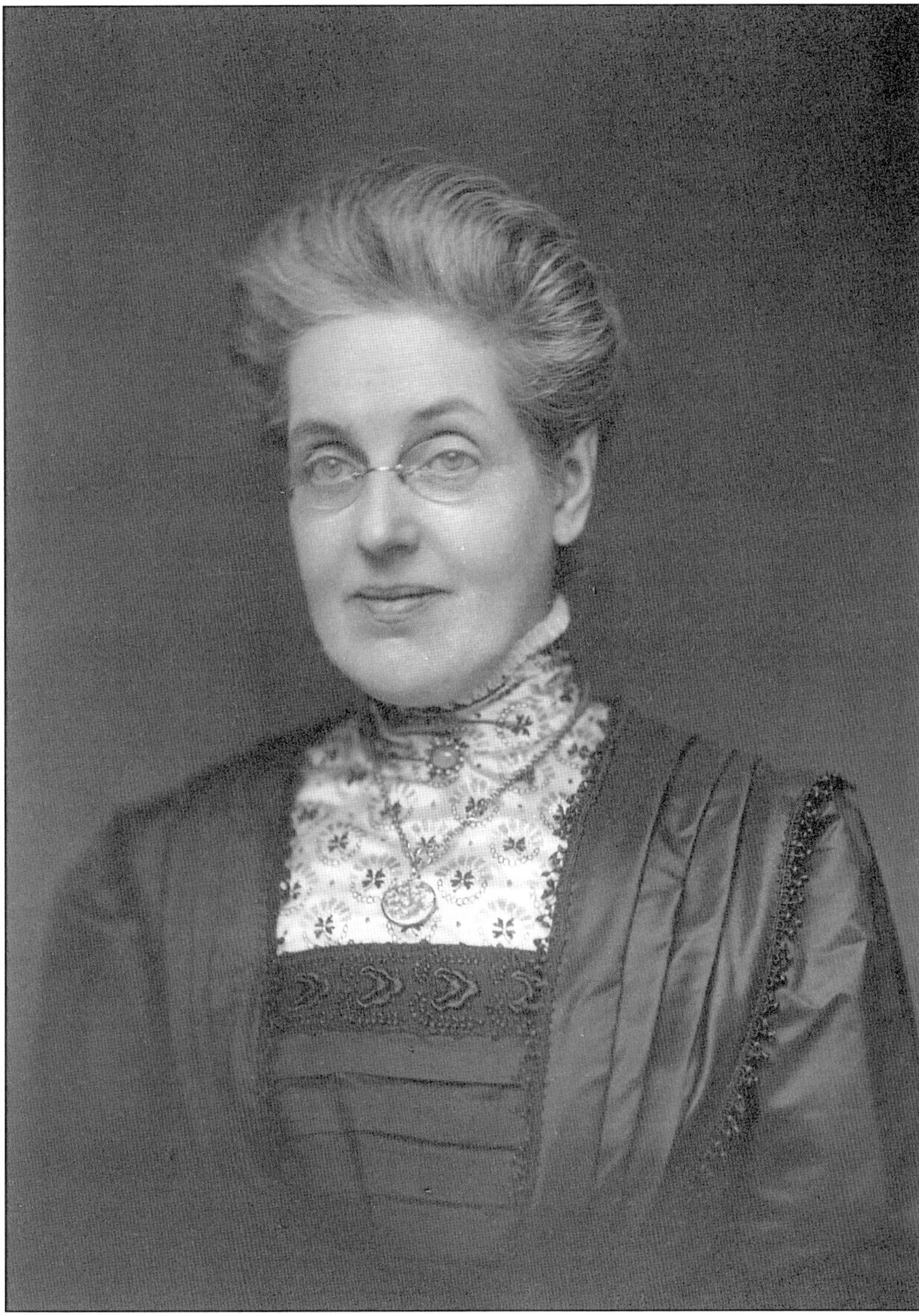

Mary Dean was the daughter of local doctor Ebenezer Dean. She was photographed in 1900. (Courtesy Montague Historical Society.)

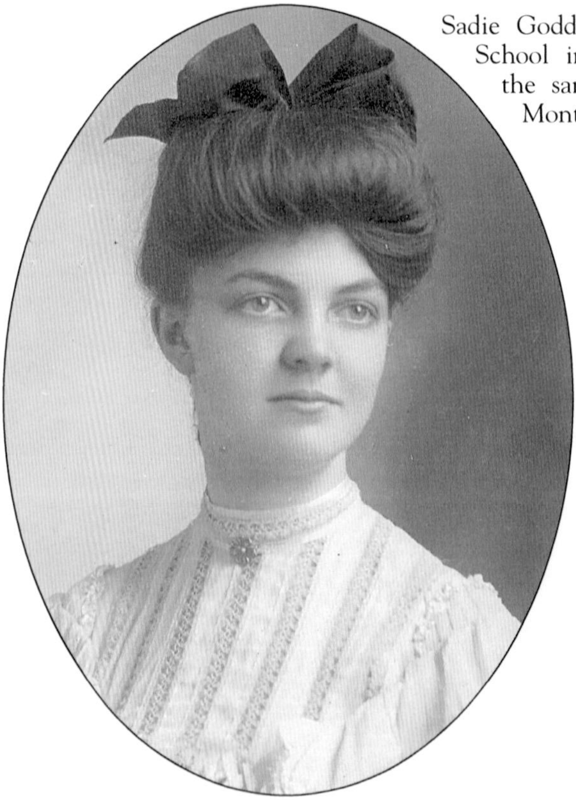

Sadie Goddard graduated from Montague High School in 1904. This photograph was taken the same year by Scott Studios. (Courtesy Montague Historical Society.)

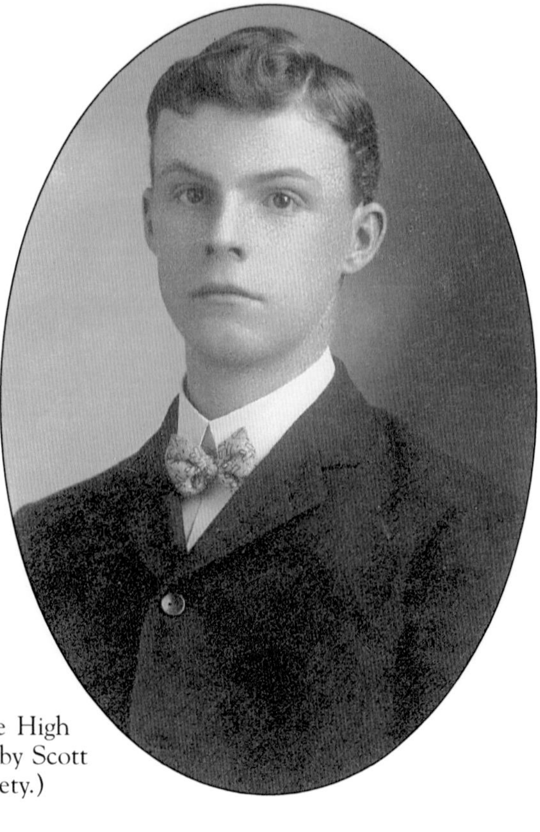

Albert A. Nims graduated from Montague High School in the Class of 1904. (Photograph by Scott Studios; courtesy Montague Historical Society.)

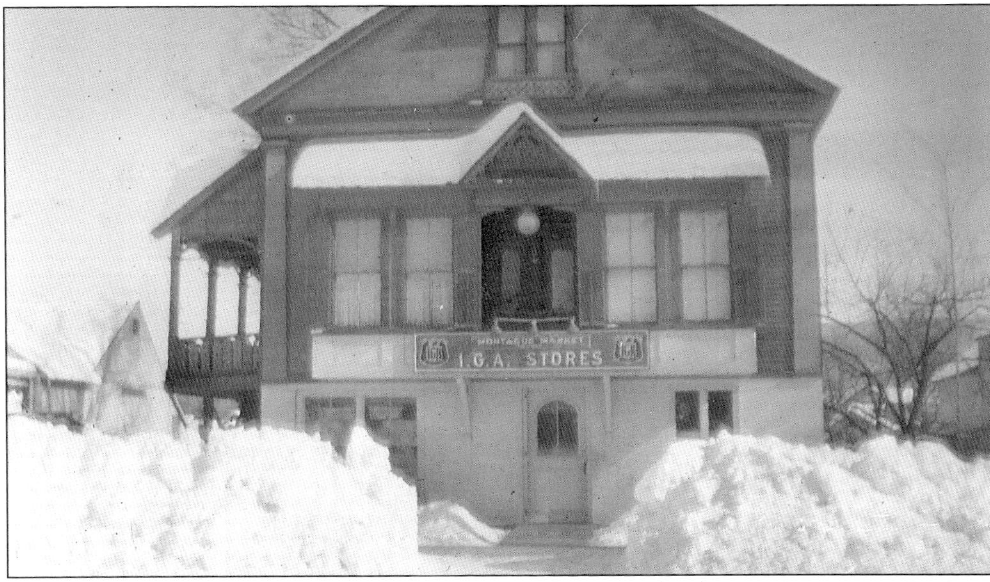

The original town hall of Montague was built on the east side of Main Street in 1837. Later used as an IGA market and later Jim Manning's Auction House, the building was destroyed by fire. (Courtesy Montague Historical Society.)

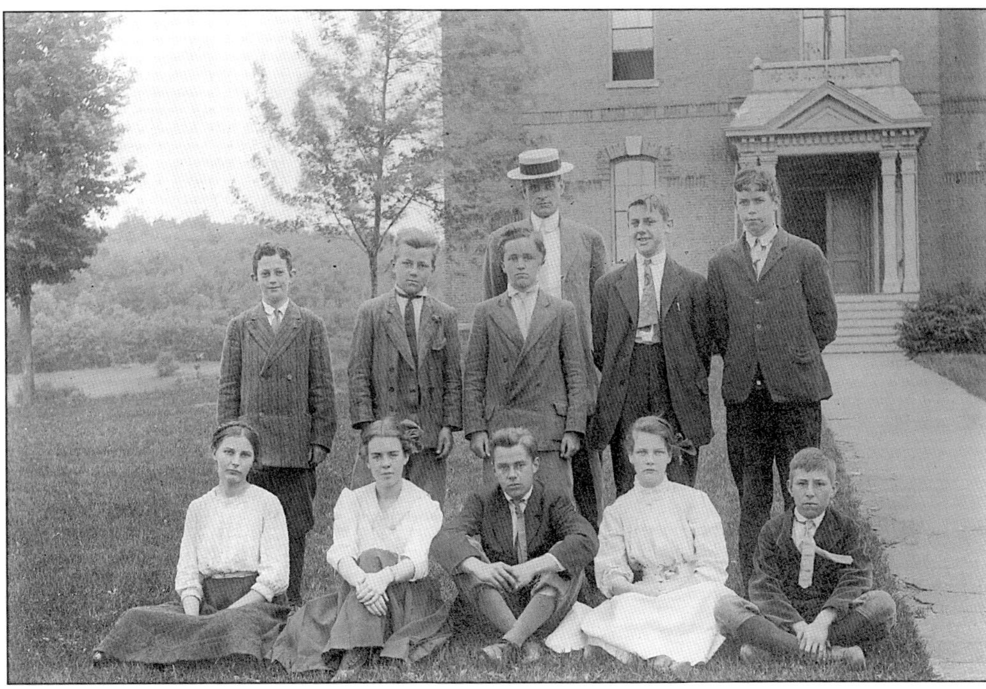

This June 1911 photograph of the Montague Agricultural High School shows, from left to right, the following: (front row) Addie Kimball, Mariam Field, Lawrence Stoughton, Jean Farrell, and William Wonsey; (back row) Harold Martin, Carroll Stoughton, Roger Nims, Everett Lowe, and Frank Bourne. In the rear is Mr. Callister, the agricultural teacher. (Courtesy Montague Historical Society.)

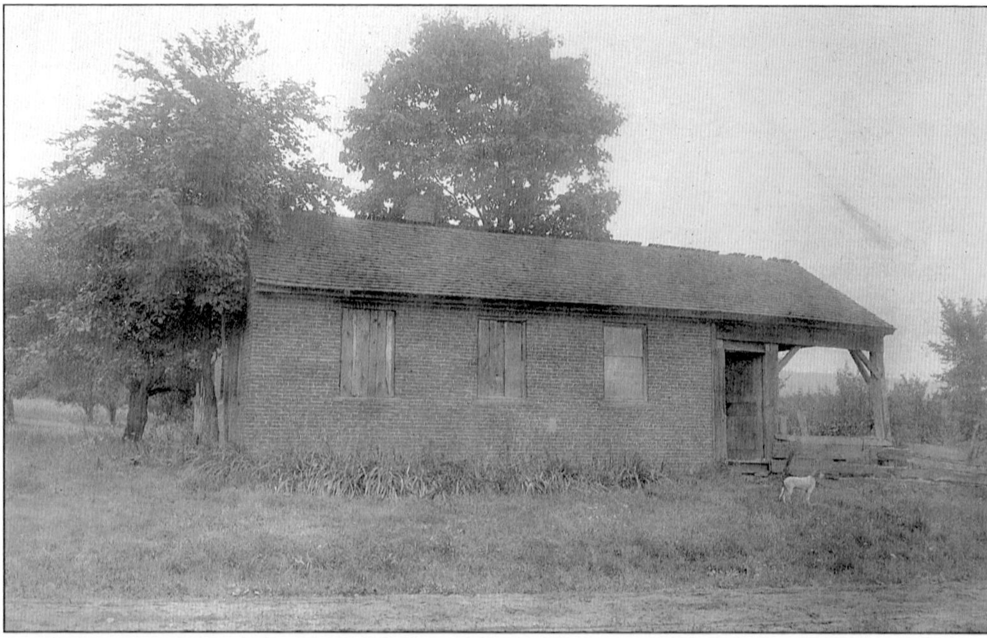

South District School on South Taylor Hill Road was photographed in 1823. (Courtesy Montague Historical Society.)

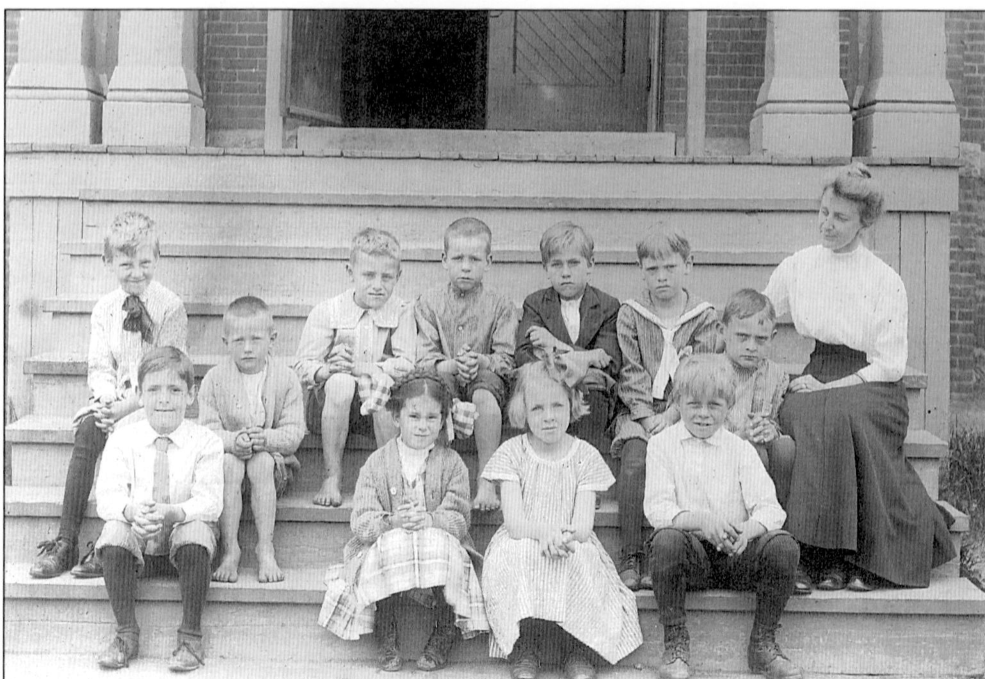

Shown are the first and second grades of the Montague Center School in 1909. (Courtesy Montague Historical Society.)

This photograph shows local residents Richard Clapp and the Allen boys with their catch.

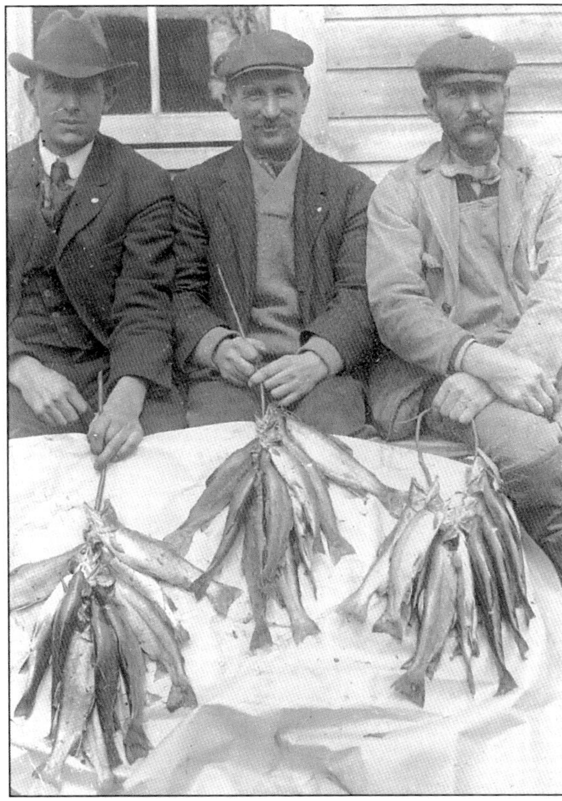

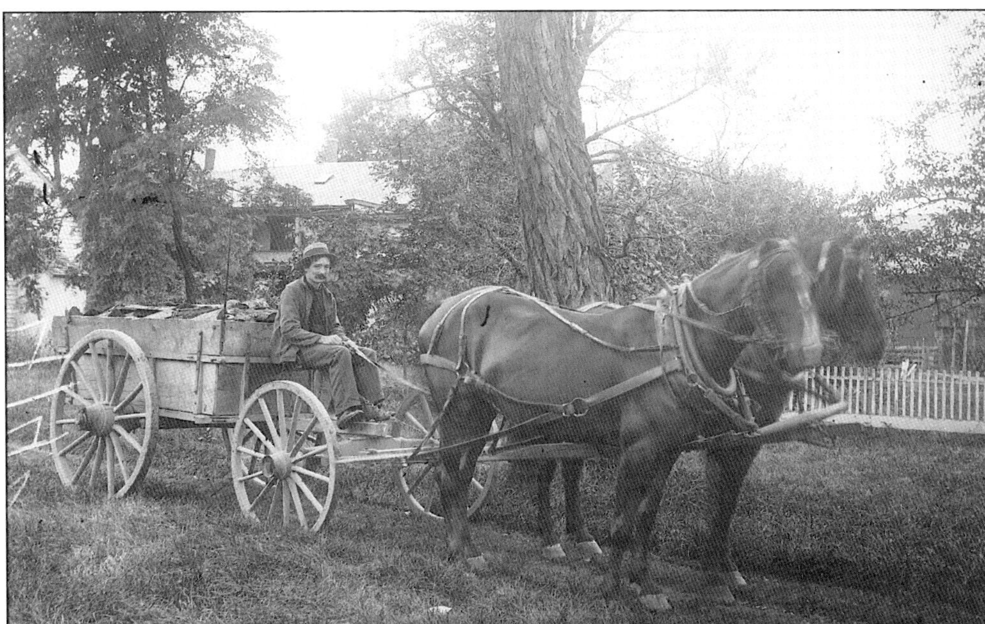

This photograph of a man and a wagon, with a load of wood, was taken on Central Street in Montague Center by the Howes Brothers. The photograph was made from a glass-plate negative. (Courtesy Montague Historical Society.)

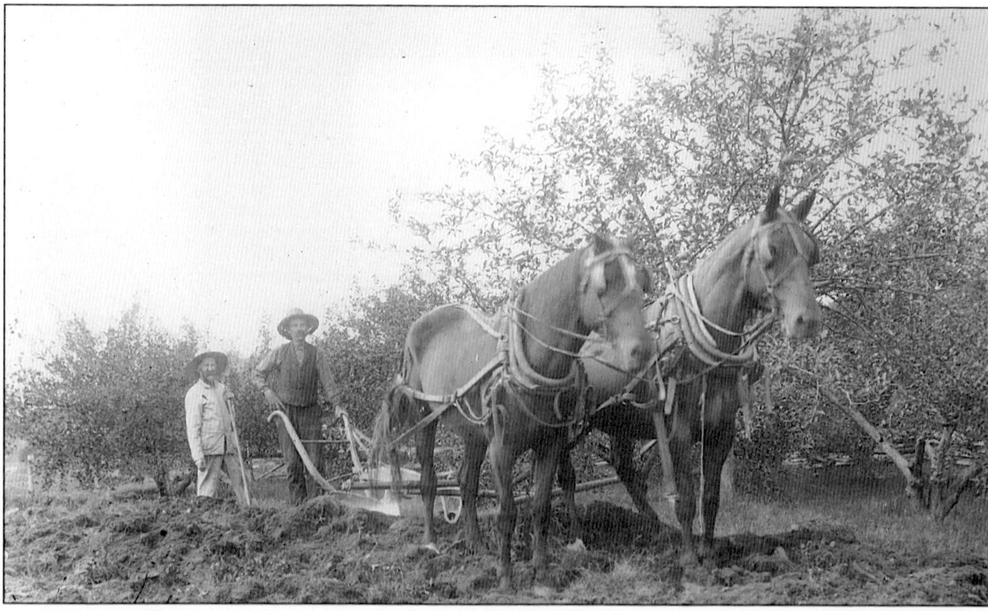

Two local farmers are plowing with horses just south of the village center. This 1908 photograph was also made from a glass-plate negative by the Howes Brothers. (Courtesy Montague Historical Society.)

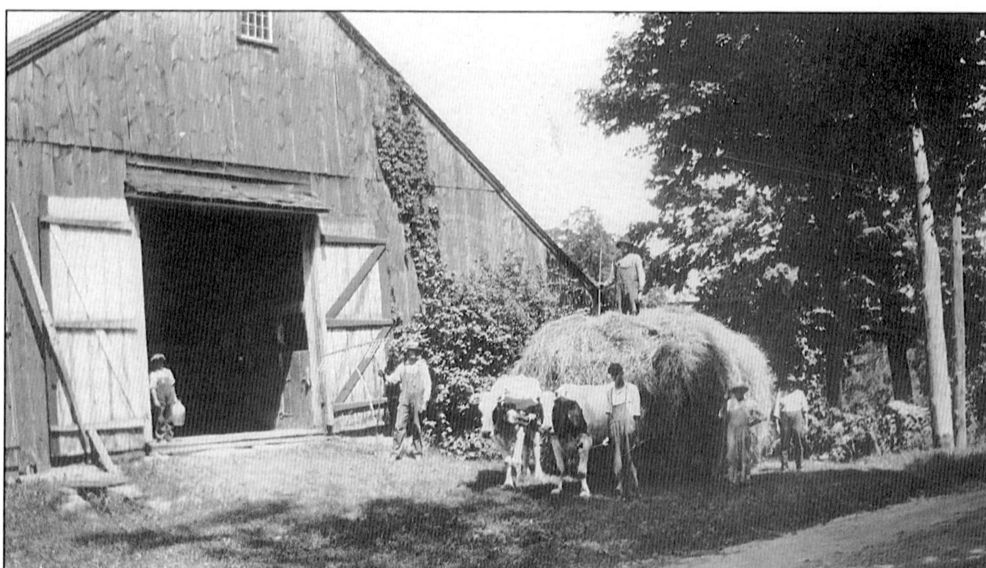

This view of the H. Root barn on Federal Street in Montague Center shows workers with cattle and hay. (Courtesy Montague Historical Society.)

Ruby M. Hemmingway's graduation photograph from Montague High School dates to 1903. She was the author of *I Remember When*, a well-known series of articles in the *Greenfield Recorder*. (Courtesy Montague Historical Society.)

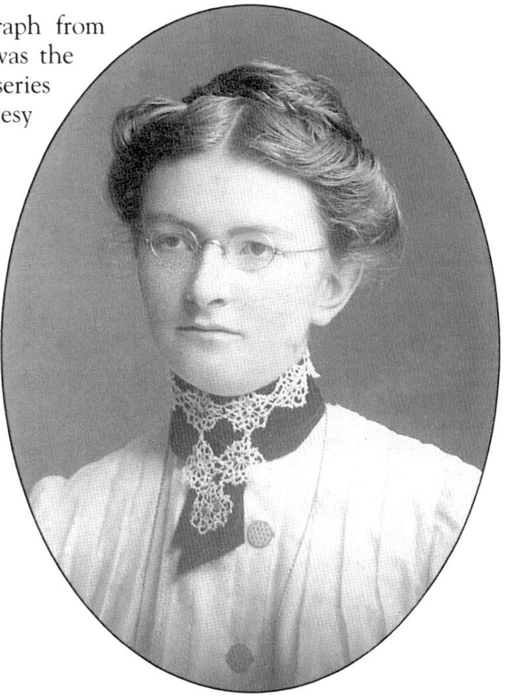

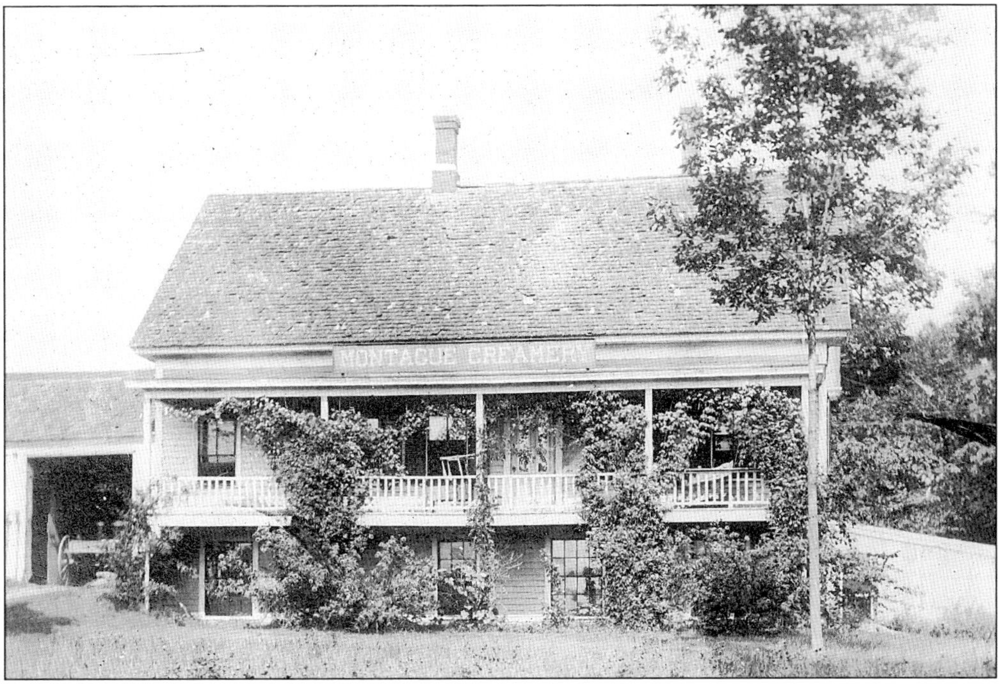

George Andrews was contracted to build the new Montague Creamery, and work was started in June 1891. The creamery opened for business on October 1, 1891, and was located a mile north of town on Greenfield Road. The creamery was well respected and well run, taking two medals at the Paris Exposition in the 1890s. On March 11, 1908, the creamery closed. (Courtesy Montague Historical Society.)

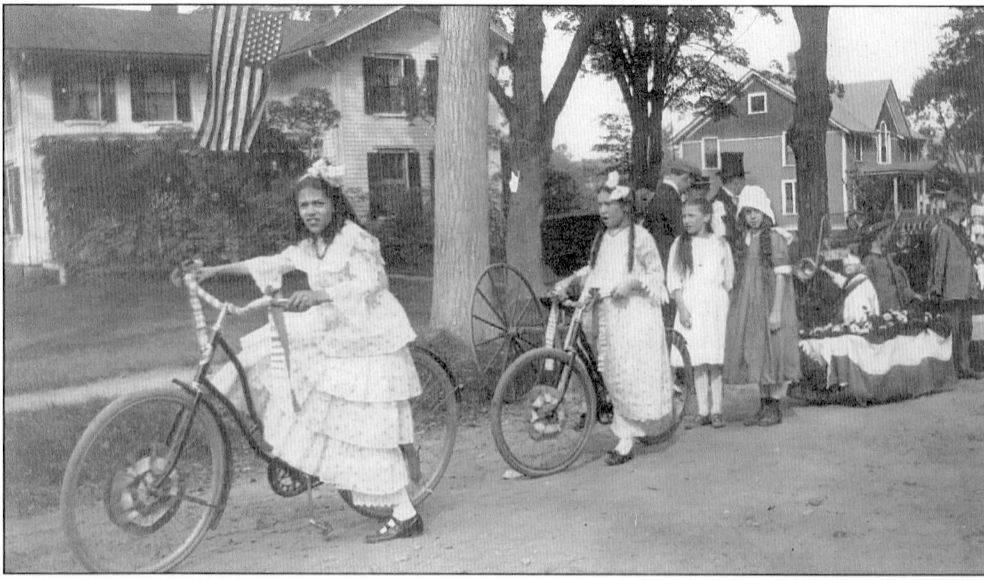

These girls are on bikes for a parade in Montague Center, c. 1920. (Courtesy Montague Historical Society.)

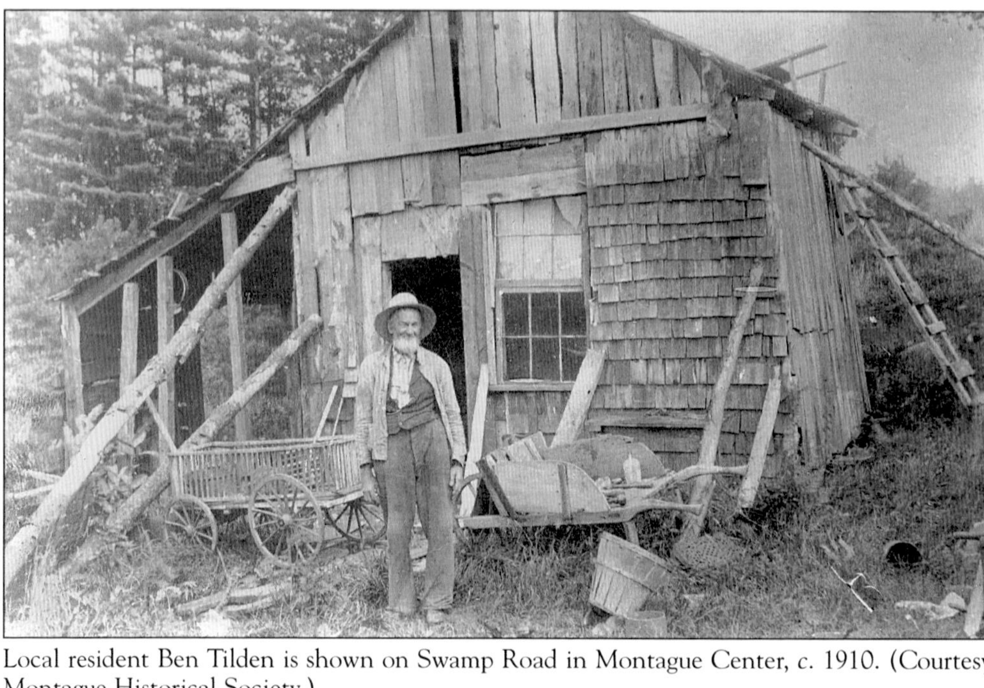

Local resident Ben Tilden is shown on Swamp Road in Montague Center, c. 1910. (Courtesy Montague Historical Society.)

Four

LAKE PLEASANT

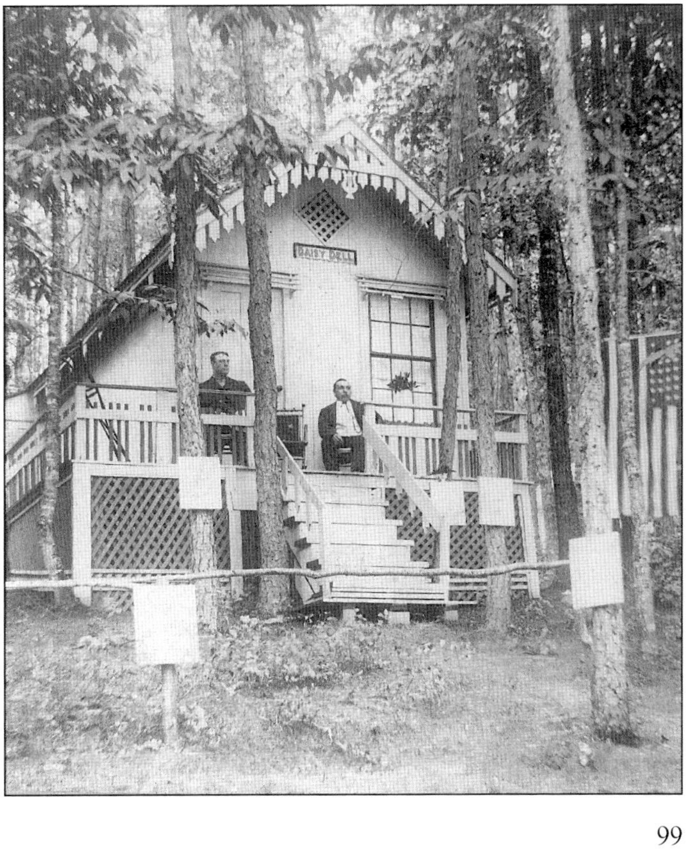

Each cabin in Lake Pleasant normally had a name given to it, such as this one, the Daisy Bell. These cabins replaced tents that had been secured on platforms. Note the gingerbread work of the upper roofline and the flag with only 35 stars. (Photograph by Frank Crosier; courtesy Peter S. Miller.)

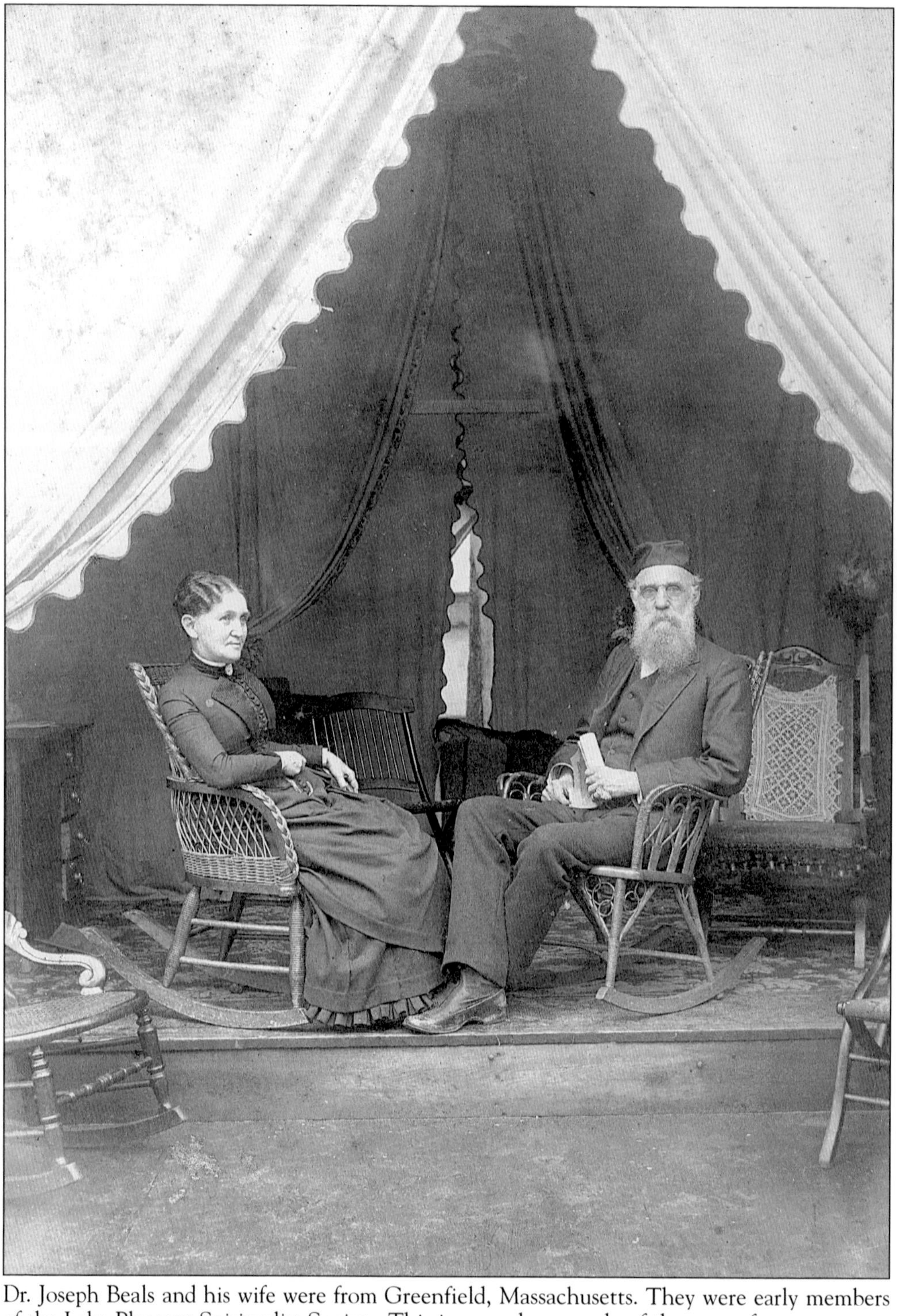

Dr. Joseph Beals and his wife were from Greenfield, Massachusetts. They were early members of the Lake Pleasant Spiritualist Society. This is an early example of the type of tent structure found in Lake Pleasant. The tent would often sit on a platform area with special ornamentation. (Courtesy Louise Shattuck.)

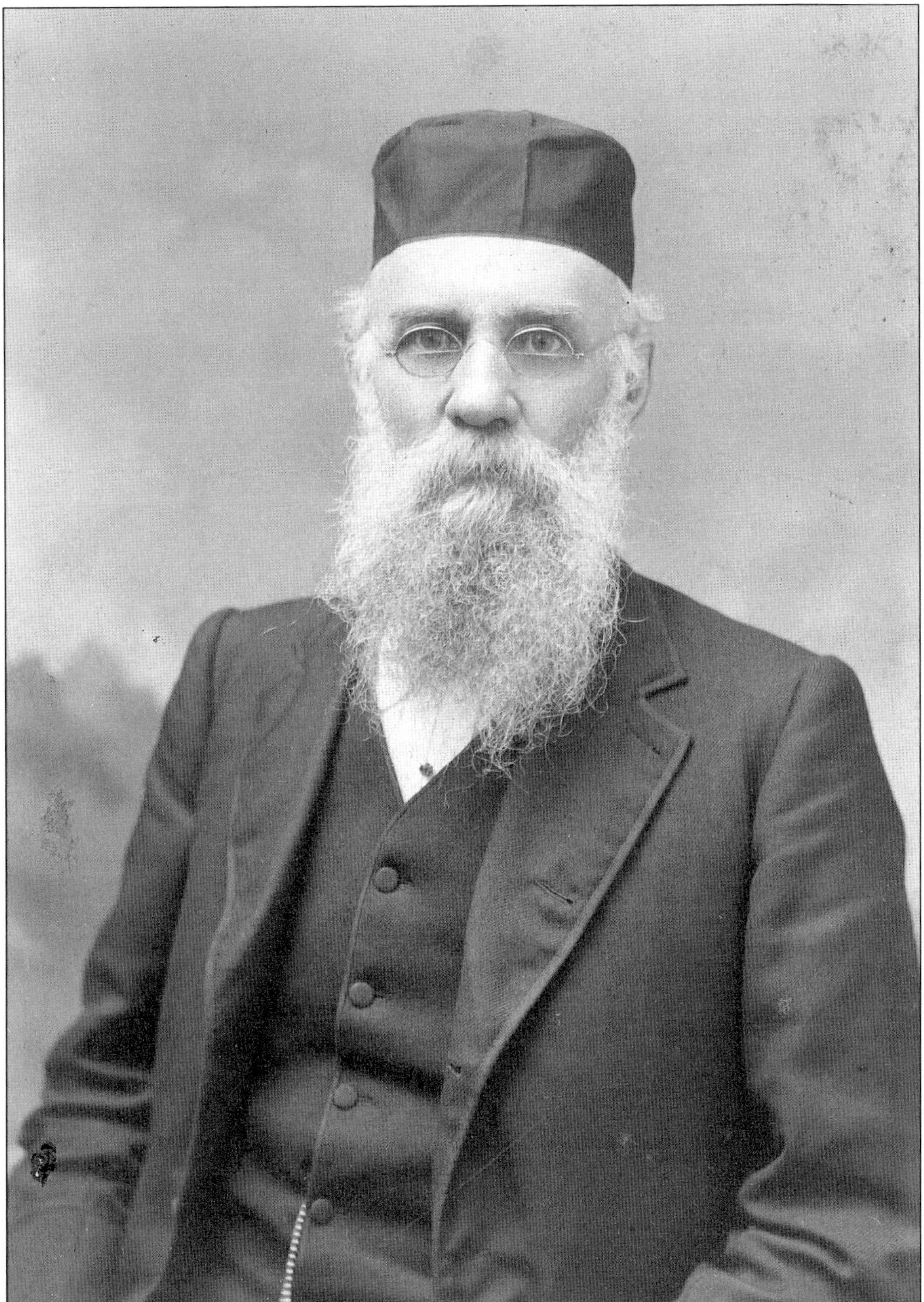

Dr. Joseph Beals, 1821–1896, was the first president of the Spiritualist Camp of Lake Pleasant. A dentist and prominent member of the Unitarian Church of Greenfield, he first became interested in spiritualism through Anna M. Bickford, another early member. (Courtesy Louise Shattuck.)

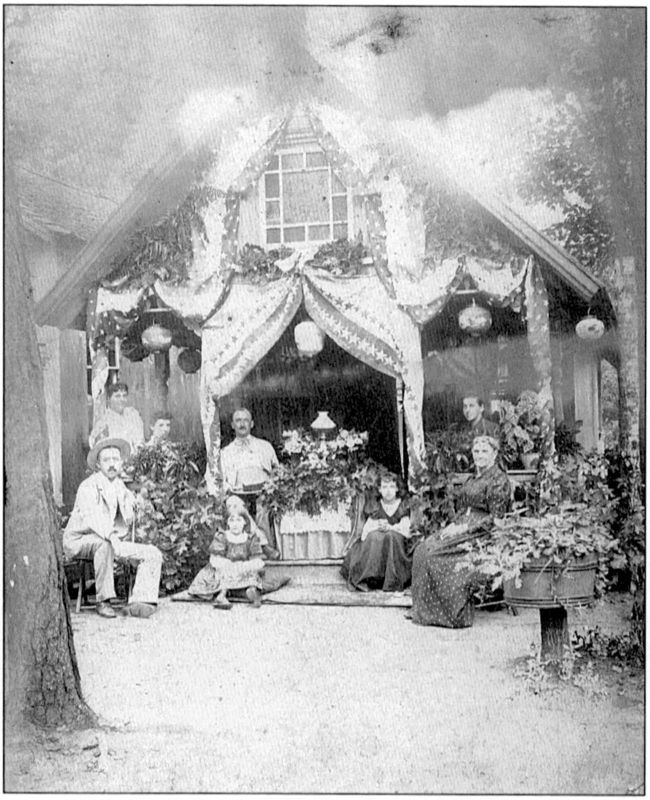

This c. 1890 photograph shows an example of an early house replacing tents. It was taken on what was known as "illumination night," where all of the sites were decorated with Japanese lanterns or various other lights as well as flowers. This was considered to be one of the highlights of the season. (Courtesy Louise Shattuck.)

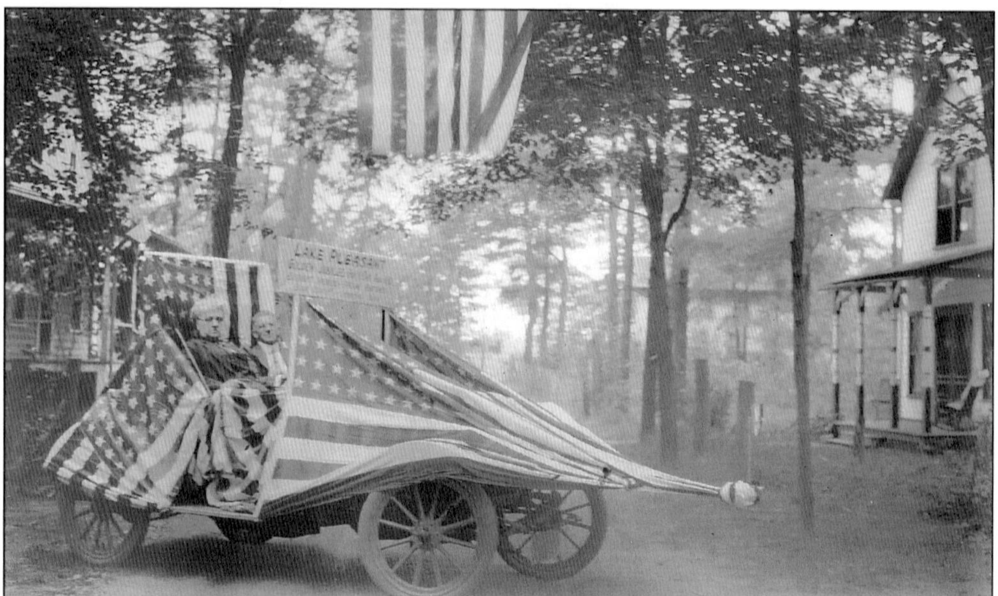

This vehicle is decorated with an American flag for an upcoming parade, c. 1906. (Courtesy Peter S. Miller.)

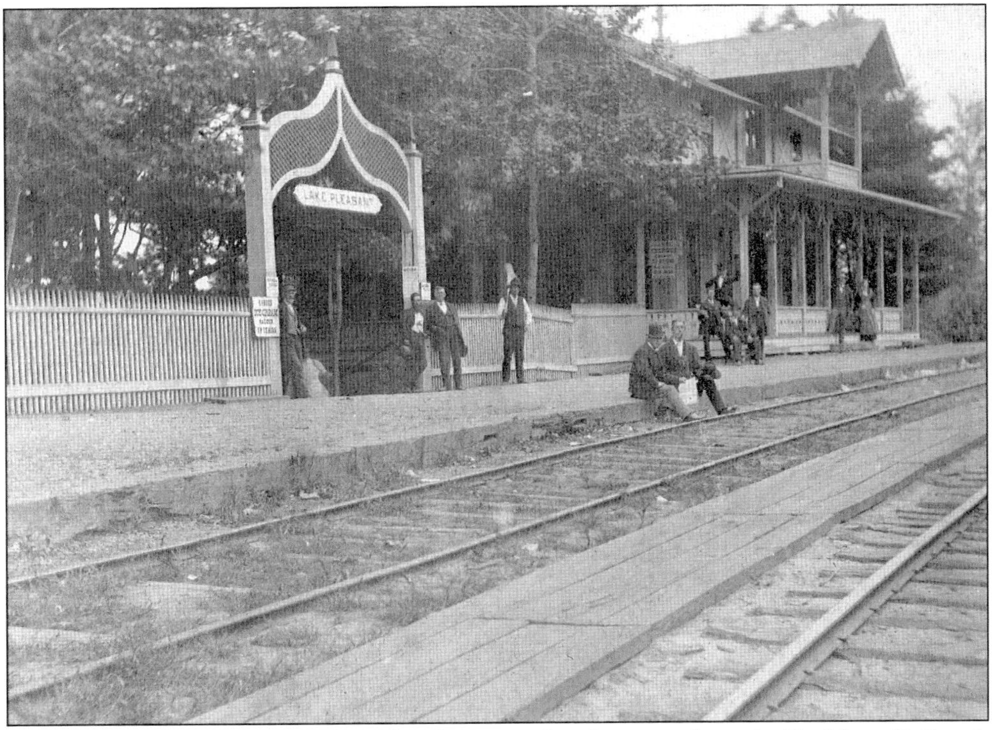

This photograph was taken at the Lake Pleasant railroad station along the Fitchburg Railroad. After the fire of 1907, the building was moved and became the Inn at Lake Pleasant. (Photograph taken by J.A. French in September 1877; courtesy Peter S. Miller.)

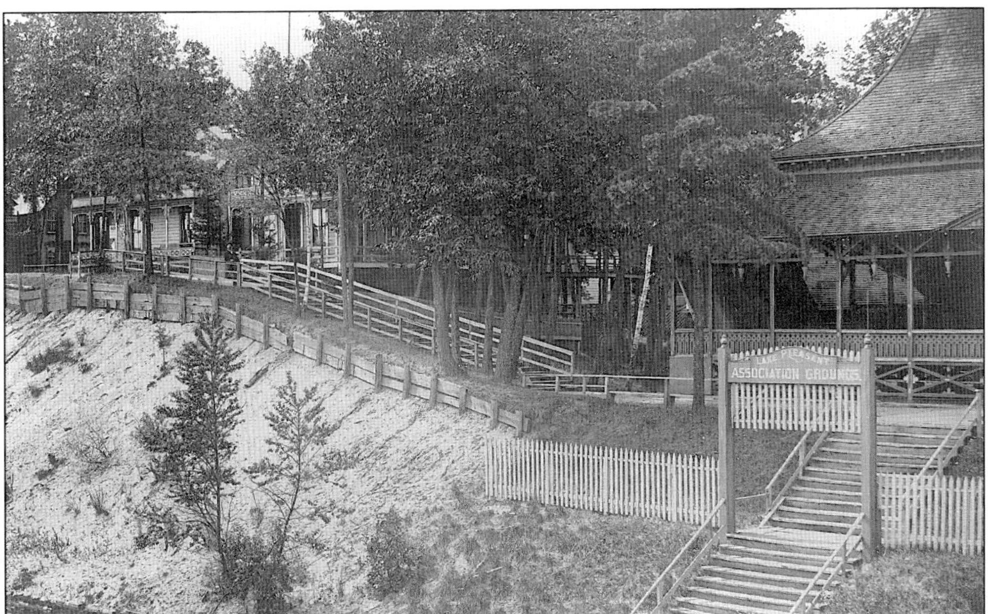

The entrance to the Lake Pleasant Association grounds was photographed from the railroad station, *c.* 1905. The dance pavilion, shown to the right, burned in the 1907 fire. The area is known as "the Bluff." (Courtesy Louise Shattuck.)

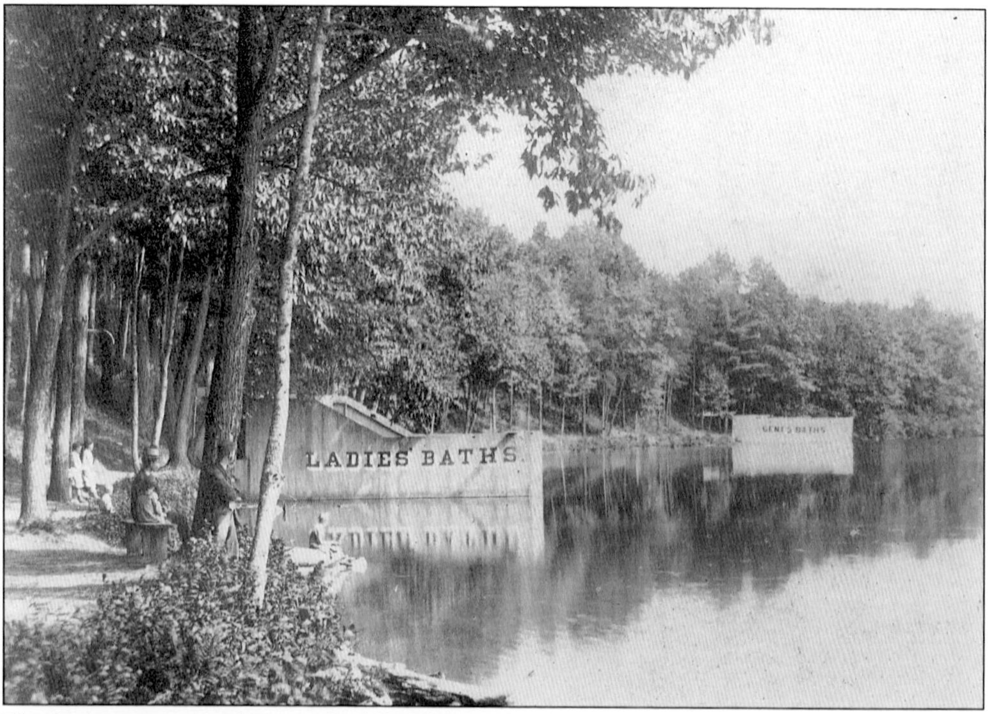

The bath areas were photographed from along the shores of Lake Pleasant. This image shows the ladies bath area in the foreground. Behind it at the far right is the men's bath area. The walkway at the left is Lover's Lane, which surrounds the lake. (Photograph by F. Crosier; courtesy Peter S. Miller.)

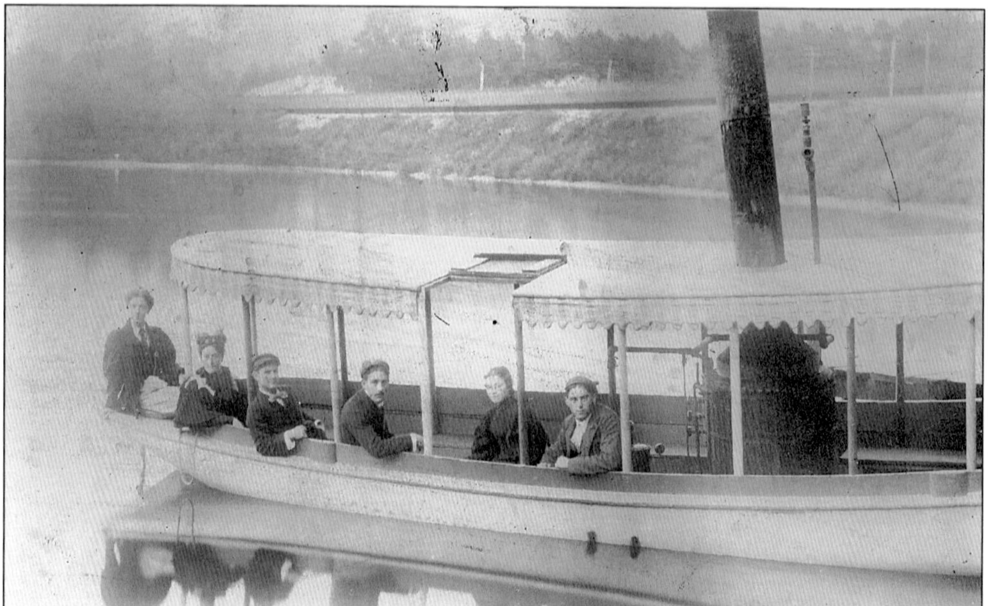

The steamboat *Uncle Sam* sunk in Lake Pleasant. Legend says that it remains in the lake to this day. The photograph shows the *Uncle Sam* just returning from a trip around the lake. (Courtesy Louise Shattuck.)

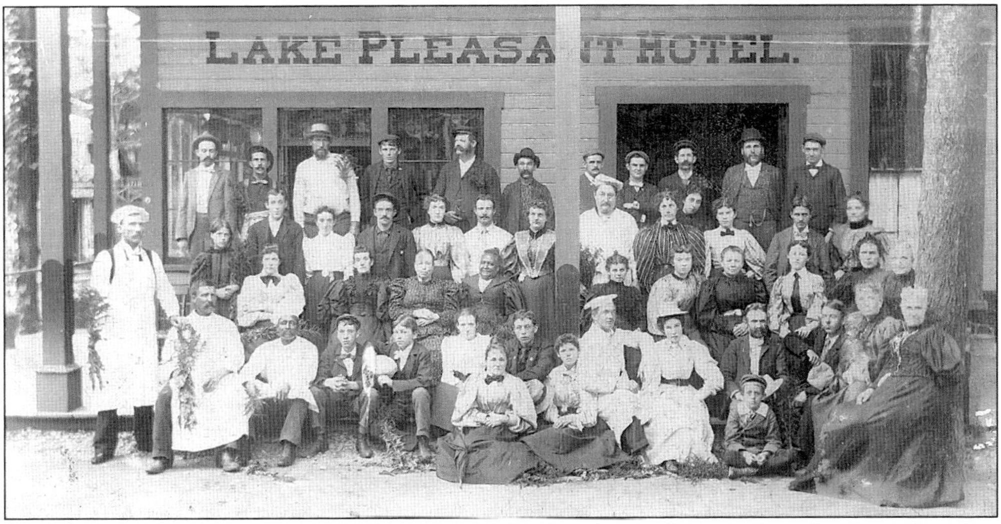

The Lake Pleasant Hotel is shown *c.* 1900. The hotel was destroyed in the great fire that swept through the area in 1907. Shown in the front row with the flat white hat is Charles M. Bickford, bandmaster of the military bands of Greenfield and later Turners Falls. Directly to his right is his sister, Sarah Bickford. (Photograph by Frank Crosier; courtesy Louise Shattuck.)

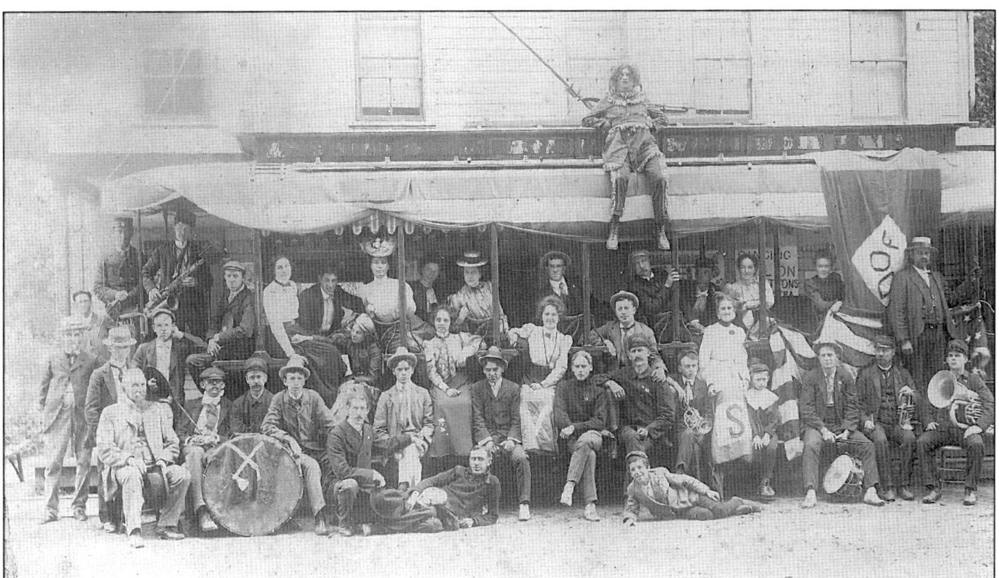

A group waits for a trolley excursion to leave for the town of South Deerfield, Massachusetts. The group is made up from Odd Fellows and members of the Independent Order of Scalpers. (Courtesy Louise Shattuck.)

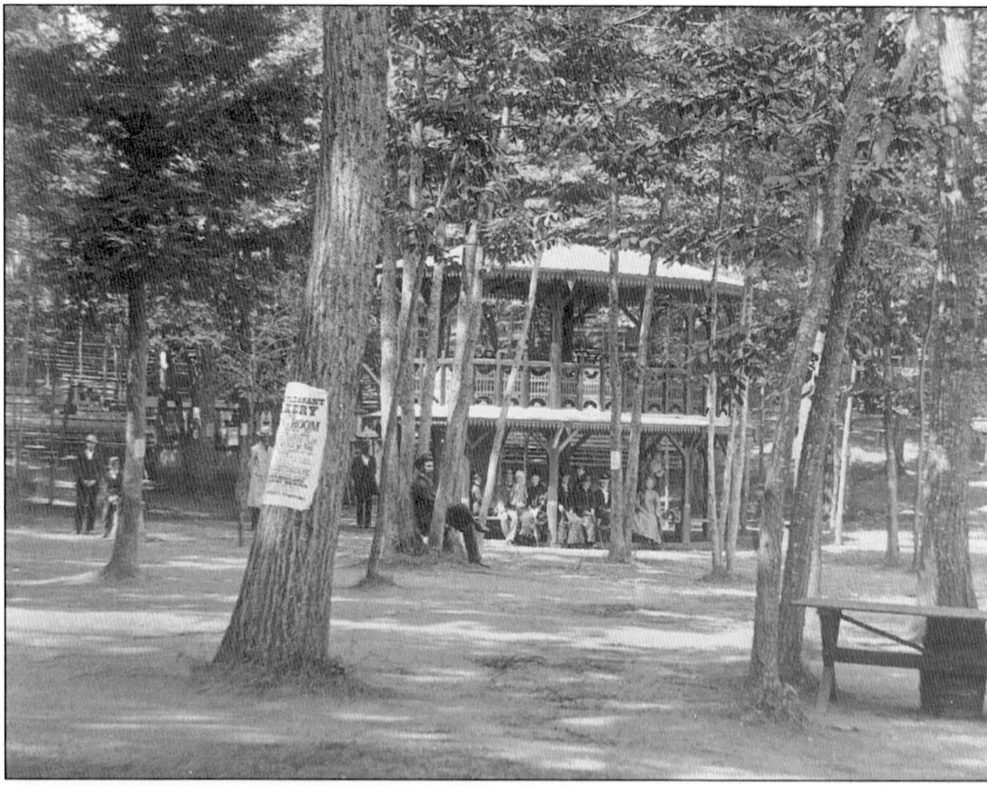

The Lake Pleasant area bandstand was often used for speeches, musical bands, and many other activities, not just those of a spiritual nature. This photograph dates to 1880. (Courtesy Louise Shattuck.)

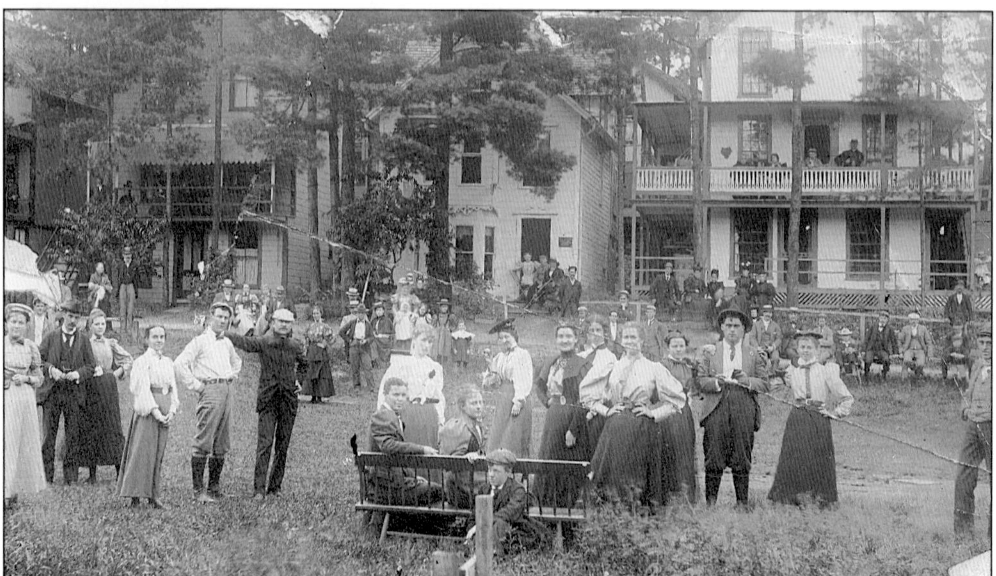

This photograph of visitors to Lake Pleasant was taken just before the great fire of 1907. According to the picture, "All had a wonderful, good time." (Courtesy Louise Shattuck.)

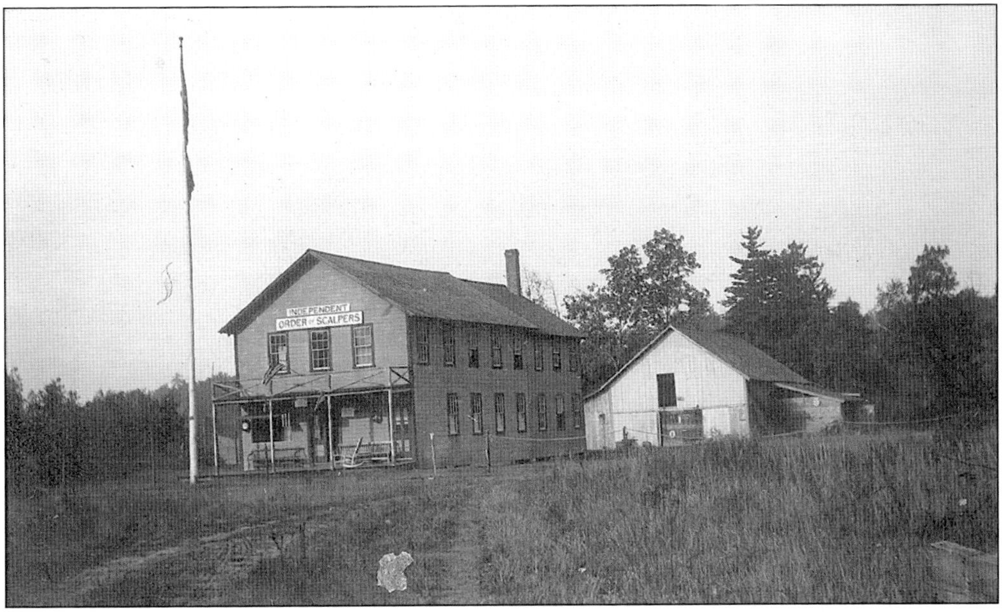

This early view shows the clubhouse of the unique Scalpers Club. Started in 1897 by the Bickford family, the group was set up to be a local club that met at midnight. The members often dressed in Native American attire and took Native American names. (Courtesy Louise Shattuck.)

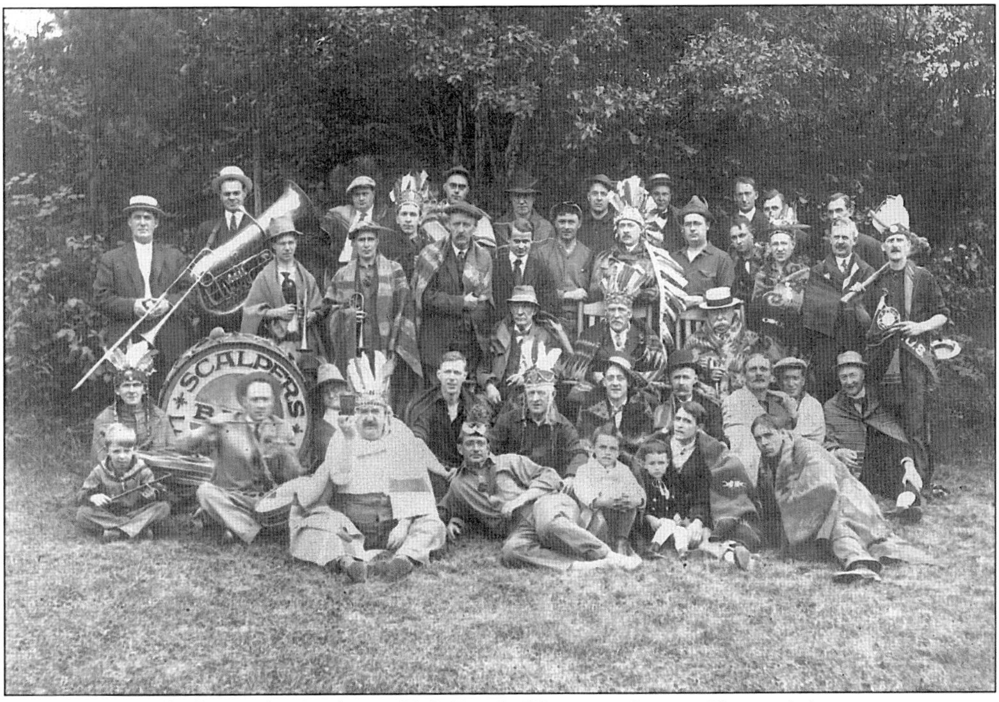

This photograph shows the Scalpers Club Band. (Courtesy Louise Shattuck.)

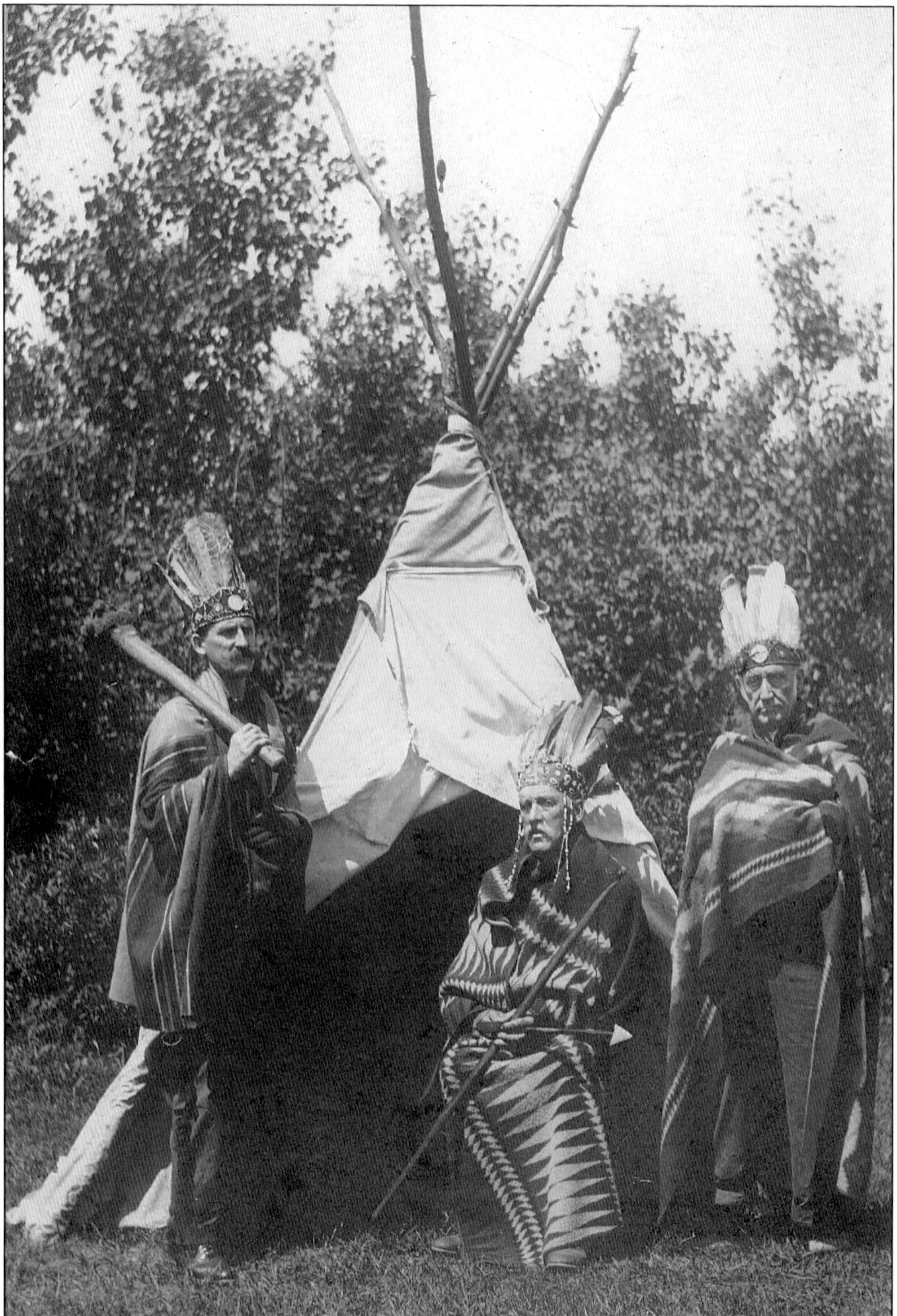

Three members of the Scalpers Club are, from left to right, Jessey Stratton (Sitting Bull), Frank A. Bickford (Grey Eagle), and R. Edwards (Big Owl). (Courtesy Louise Shattuck.)

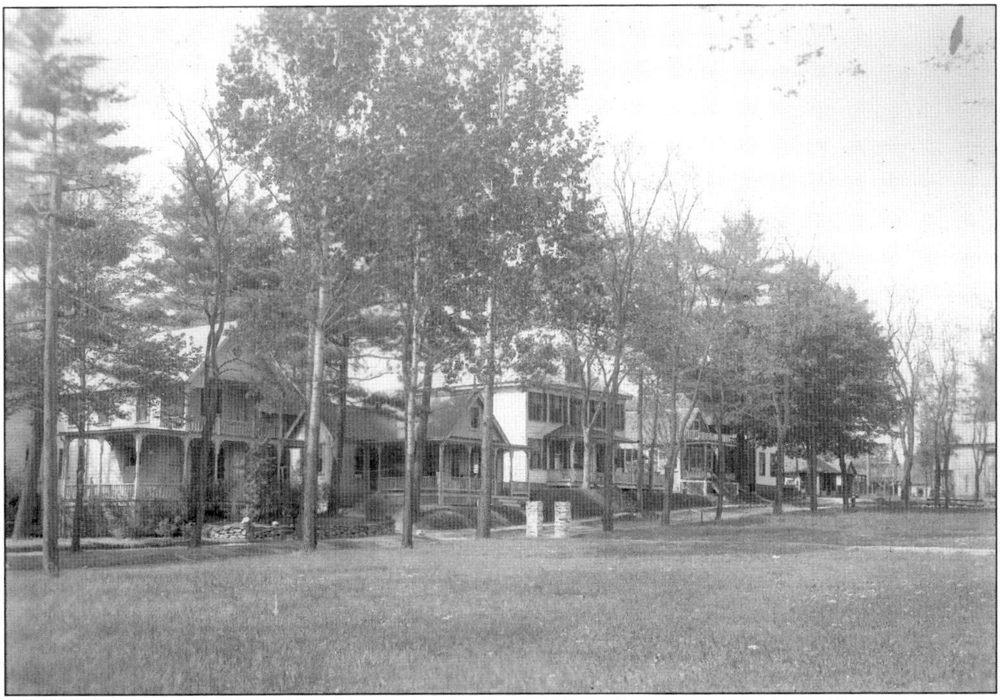

Only two of these homes on Montague Street in Lake Pleasant still stand—the center large white house and the house on the far left. (Courtesy Louise Shattuck.)

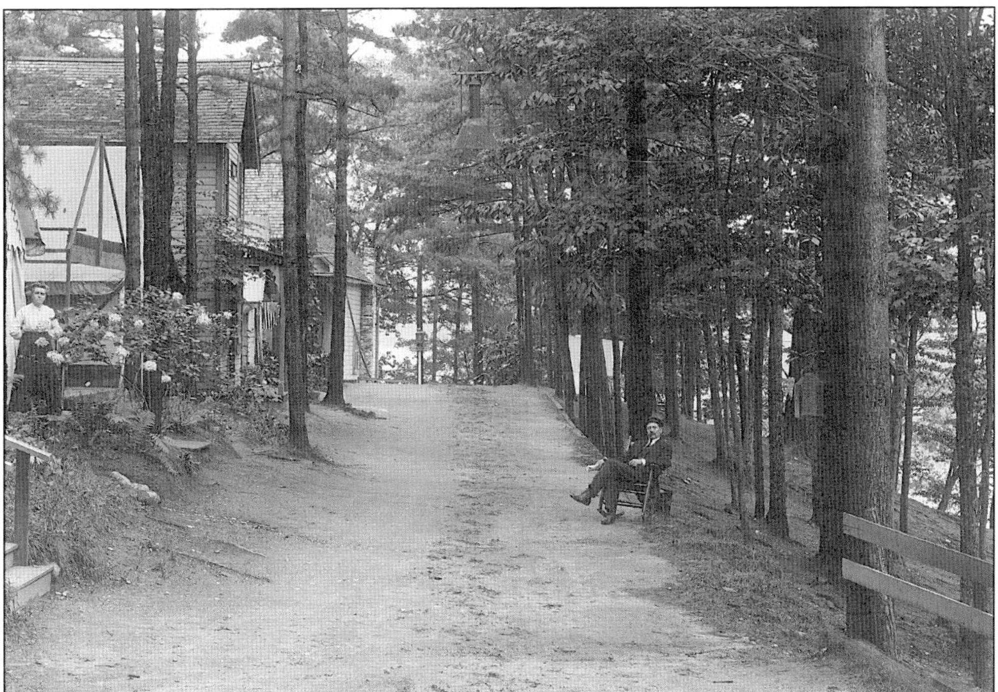

This early-20th-century photograph of an unidentified Lake Pleasant street shows a mixture of tents and cabins. (Courtesy Louise Shattuck.)

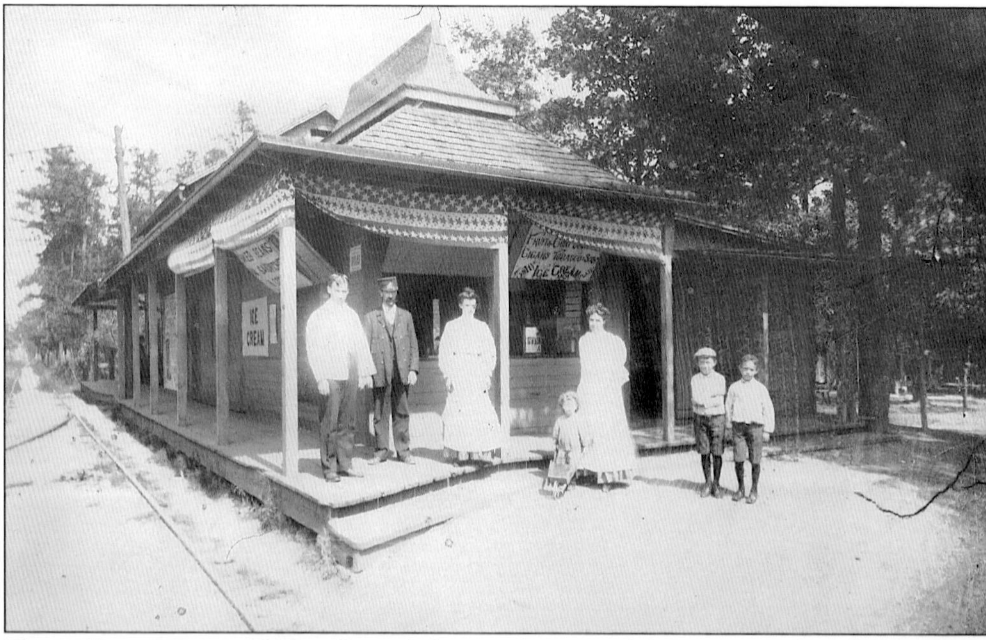

This trolley station, c. 1900, still stands but much is remodeled. It is now located on County Road in Lake Pleasant. The photograph is thought to have been taken by O.C. Leonard. (Courtesy Louise Shattuck.)

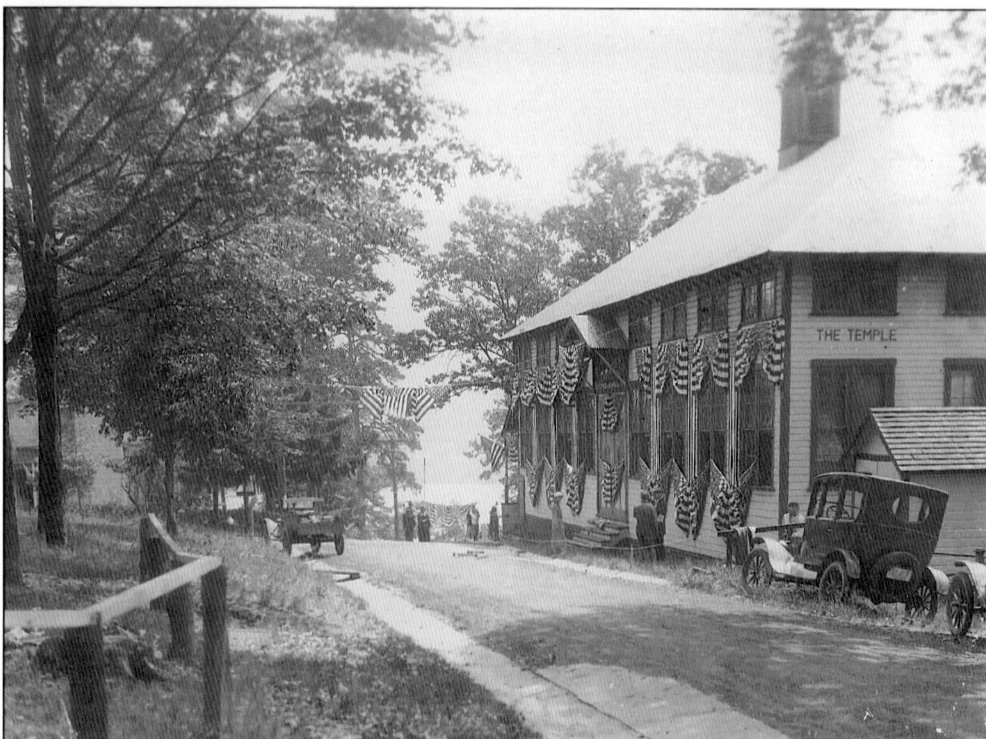

This photograph of the Spiritualist Temple was taken a short time after the fire of 1907. (Courtesy Louise Shattuck.)

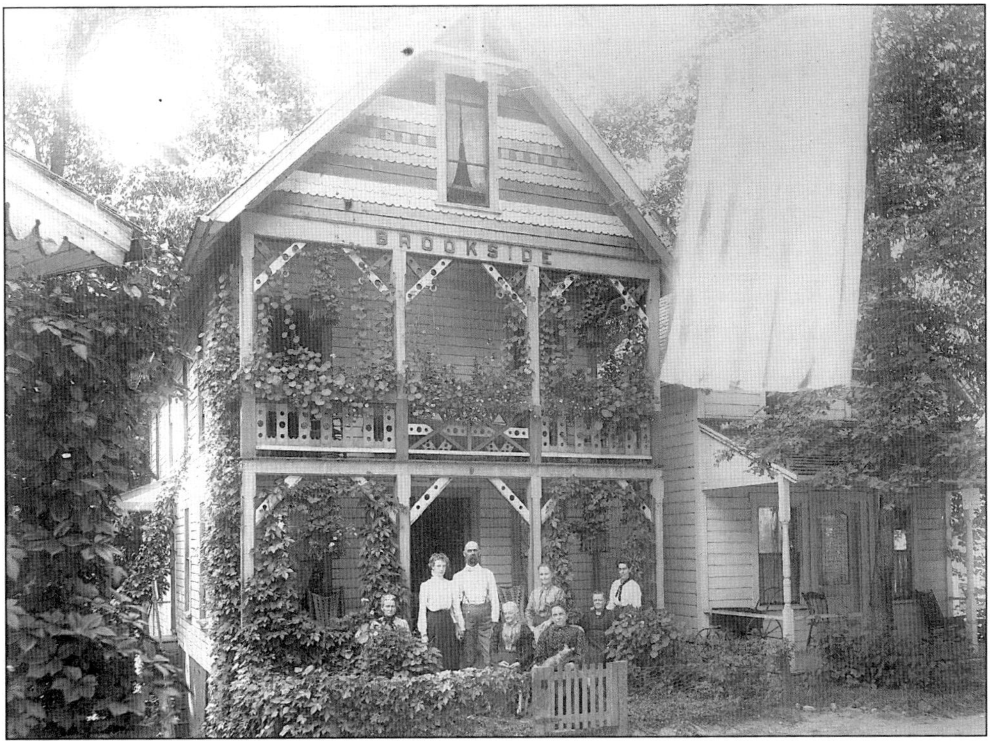

This photograph shows Brookside. Naming homes was common in Lake Pleasant. Note the vines and the ornate gingerbread woodwork around the structure. (Courtesy Louise Shattuck.)

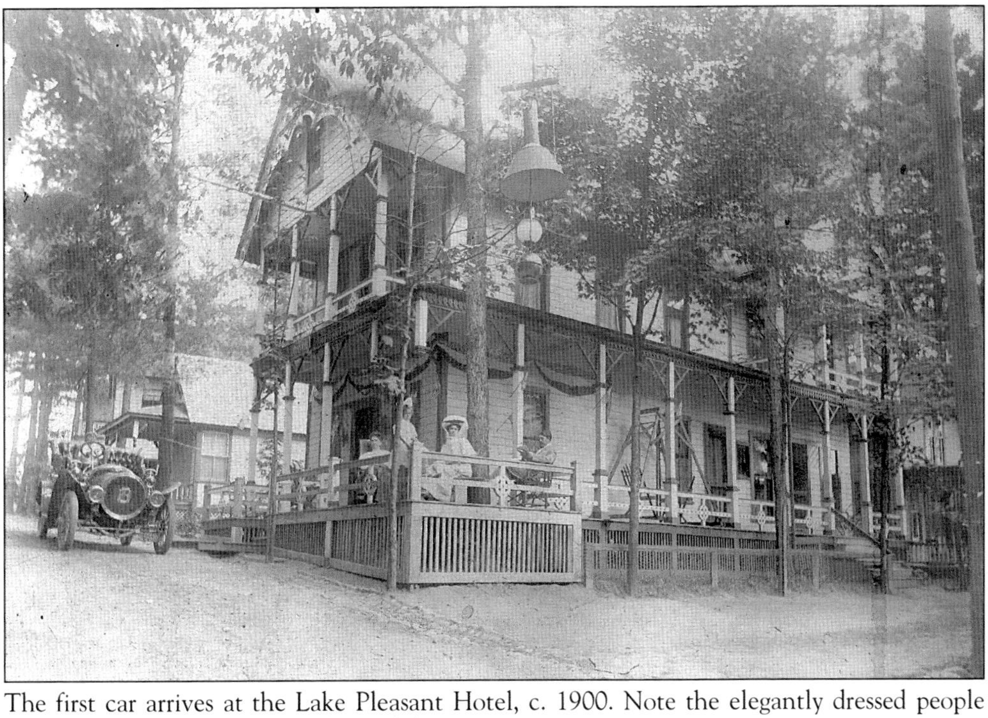

The first car arrives at the Lake Pleasant Hotel, c. 1900. Note the elegantly dressed people looking on. (Courtesy Louise Shattuck.)

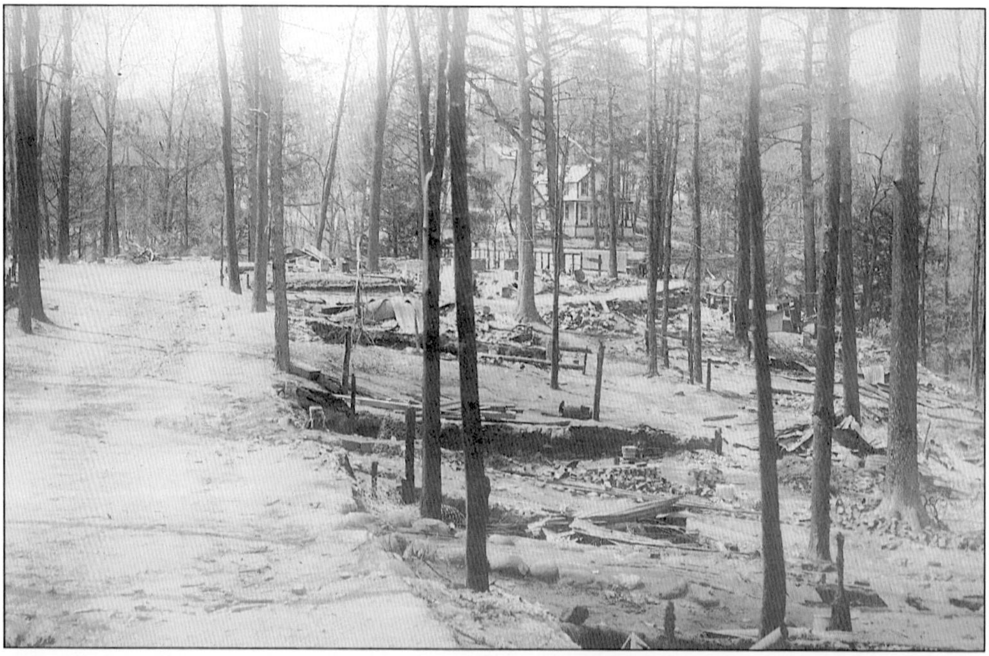

This photograph shows the destruction caused by the 1907 fire that engulfed the area and caused heavy damage. (Courtesy Montague Historical Society.)

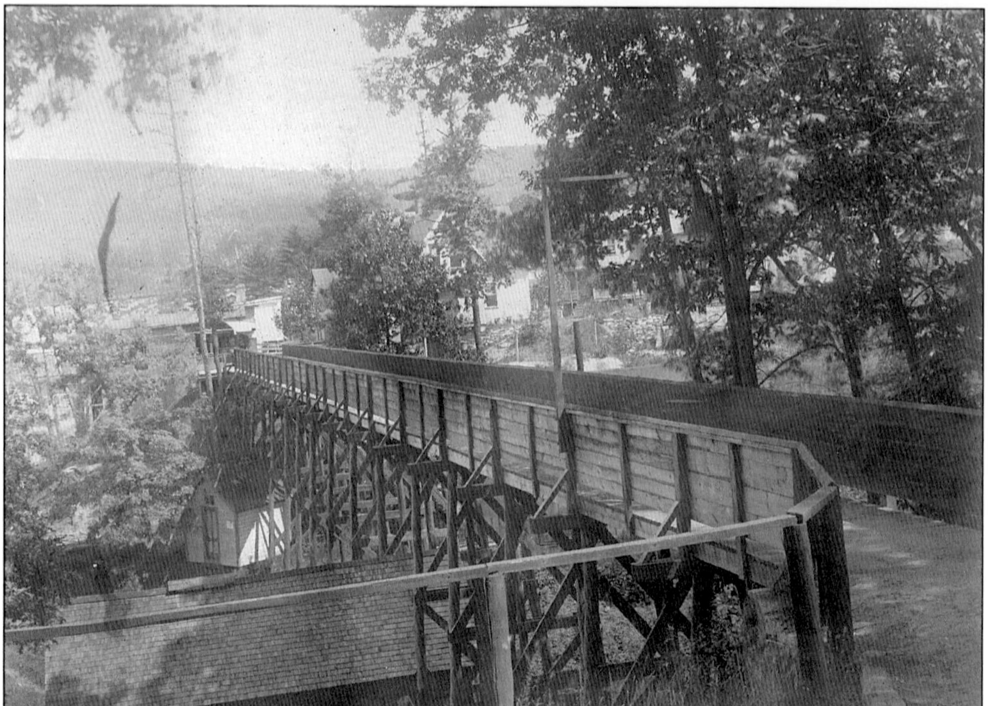

Shown is the footbridge as it appeared before the 1907 fire. The bridge linked both Lake Pleasant villages and was built by Frank Bickford c. 1900. (Courtesy Montague Historical Society.)

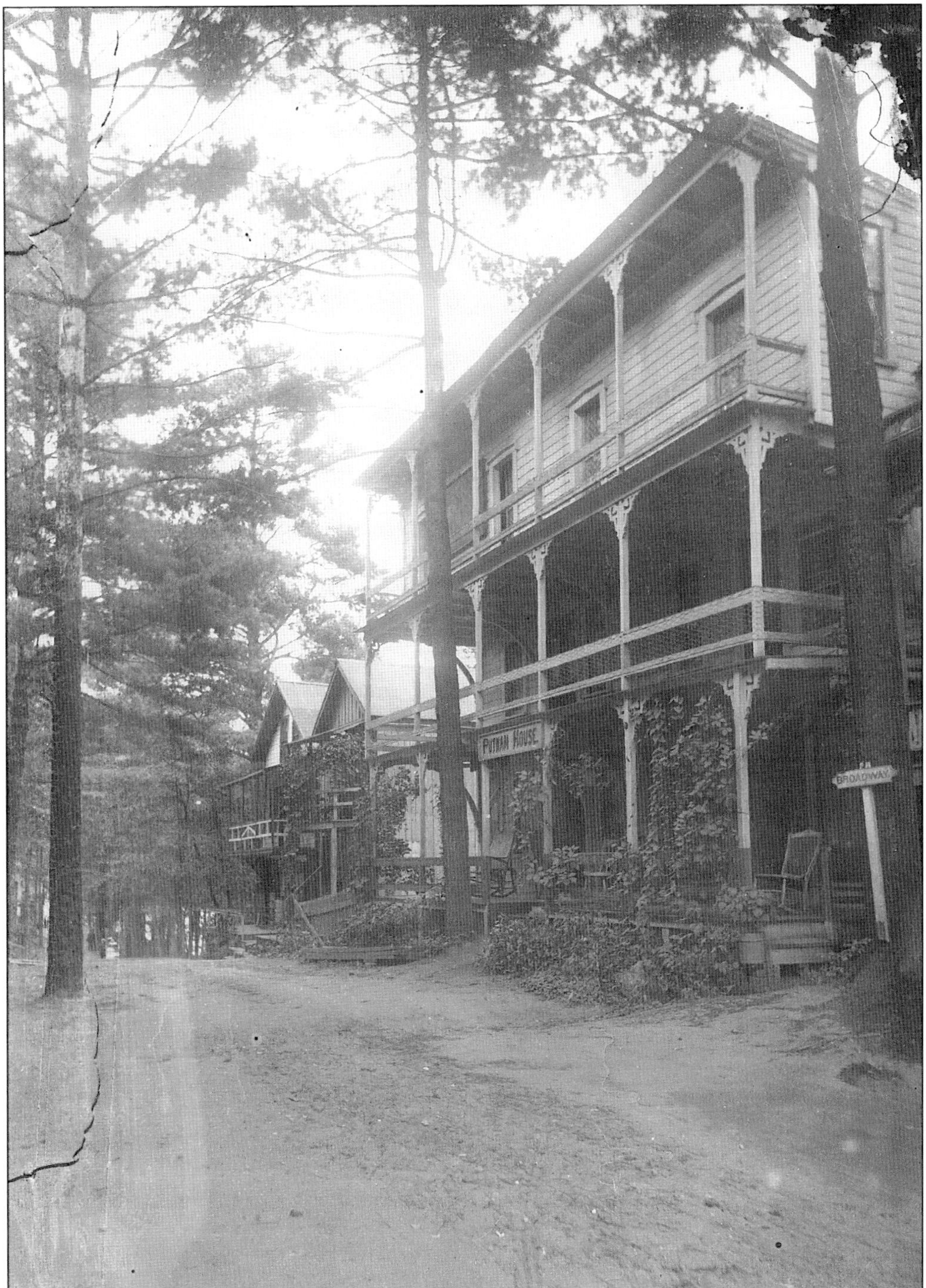

The Putnam House was located in Lake Pleasant. (Courtesy Louise Shattuck.)

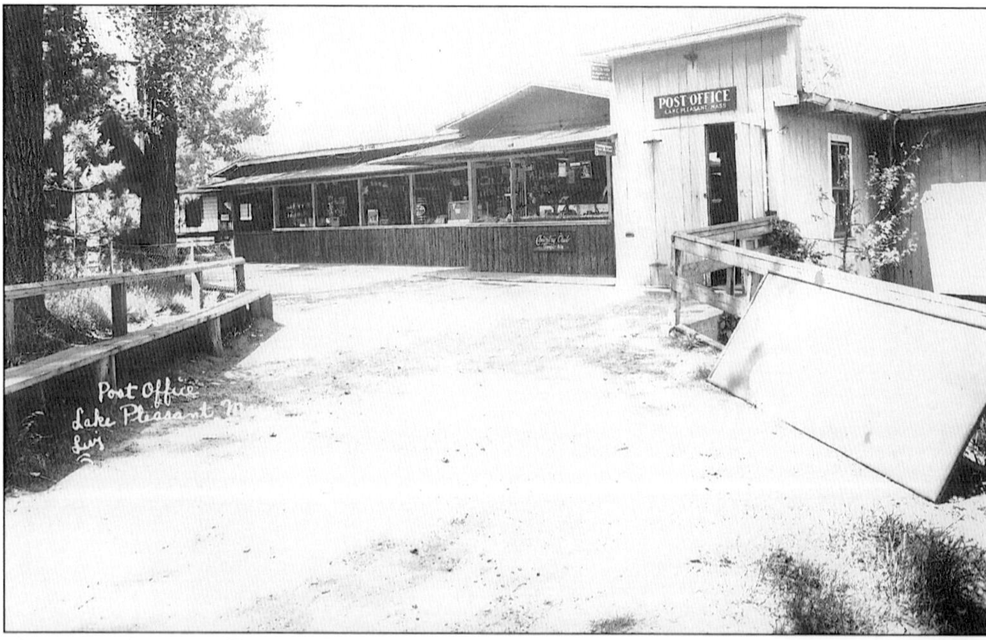

Shown are the post office at Lake Pleasant and a refreshment stand, where ice cream and other items were served. Built after the fire of 1907 at the south entrance to the bridge, the structure was later taken down by the areas water department. (Courtesy Louise Shattuck.)

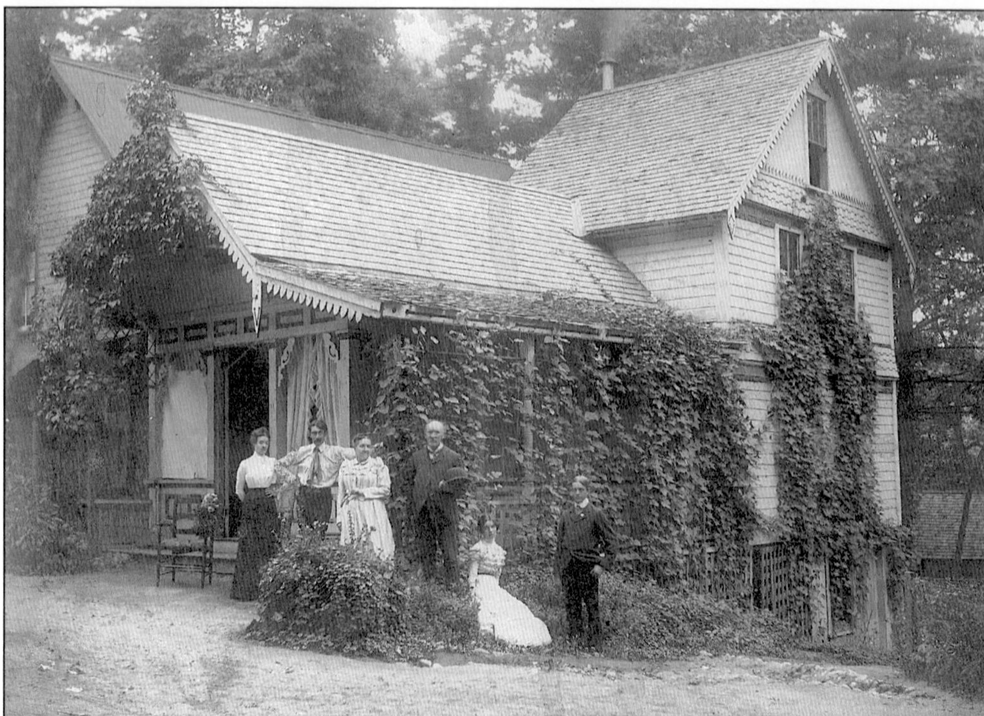

The Bickford family, early members of Lake Pleasant, vacationed at the lake in the summertime. This site is now the home of Louise Shattuck. (Courtesy Louise Shattuck.)

Five

MONTAGUE CITY

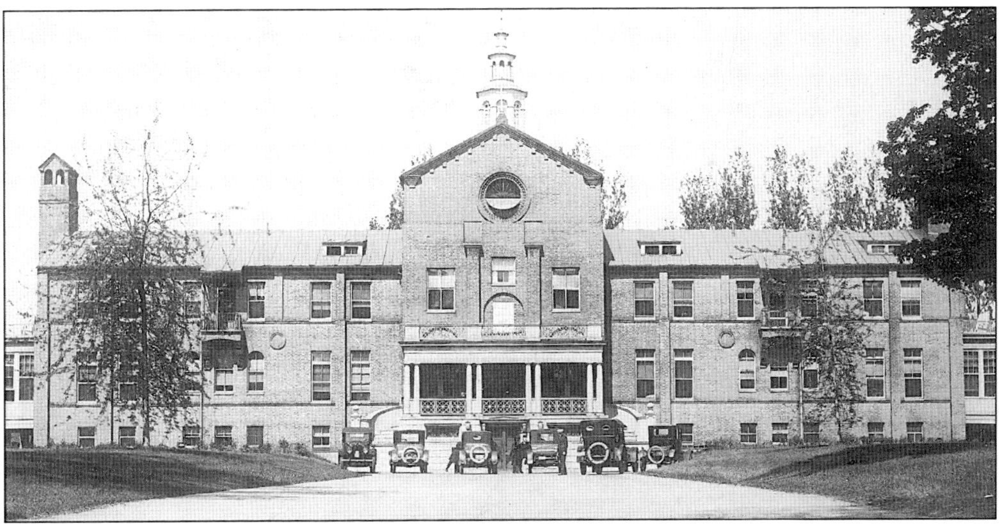

This photograph shows the Farren Memorial Hospital, located in the village of Montague City. The hospital was built by Bernard N. Farren, a pioneer in railroad construction and one of the leading developers in Turners Falls. He was a native of Philadelphia. The hospital was constructed in memory of his only son, B. Frank Farren, who died early in life. The hospitals formal dedication took place on October 23, 1900. Bernard Farren was a generous donor to the Catholic Church. By his choice, management of the facility was handed over to the Sisters of Providence. Nurses were also trained at the hospital until 1941, when the program was suspended. While it can not be proven, it has always been a legend that Joyce Kilmer penned the famous poem "Trees" while on one of his regular visits to the Farren. Part of that tree is visible on the right. (Courtesy Montague Historical Society.)

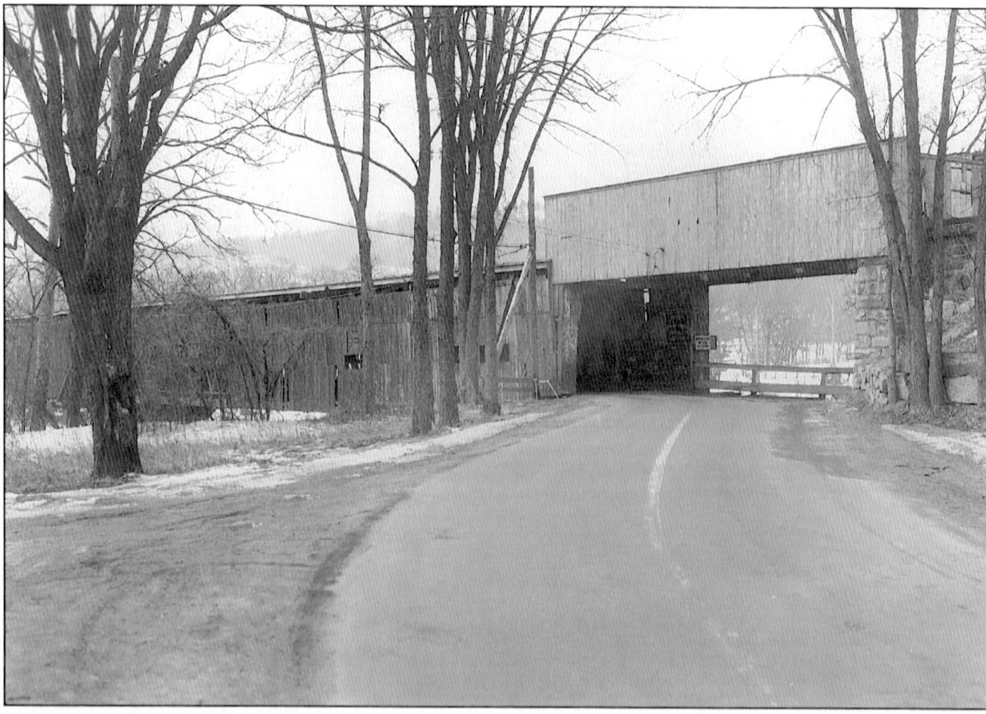

The East Greenfield entrance to the Montague City covered bridge on the eastern approach to the bridge is seen from Montague City Road, *c.* 1935. (Photograph by Alex M. Gamelin; courtesy WMECO.)

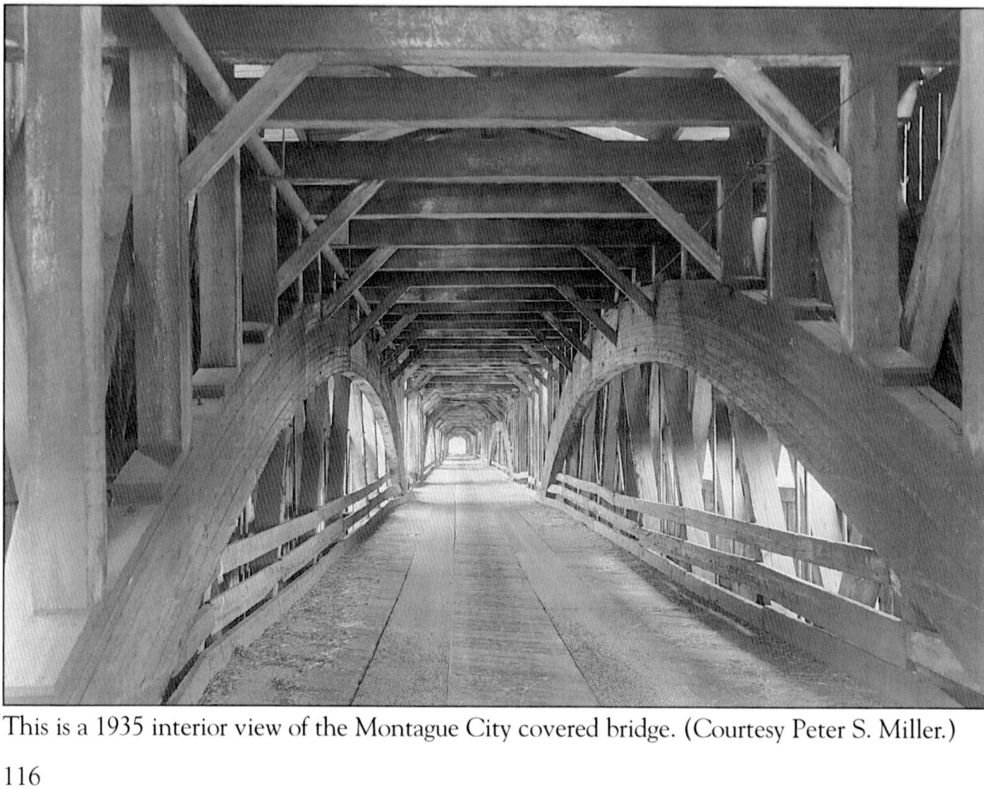

This is a 1935 interior view of the Montague City covered bridge. (Courtesy Peter S. Miller.)

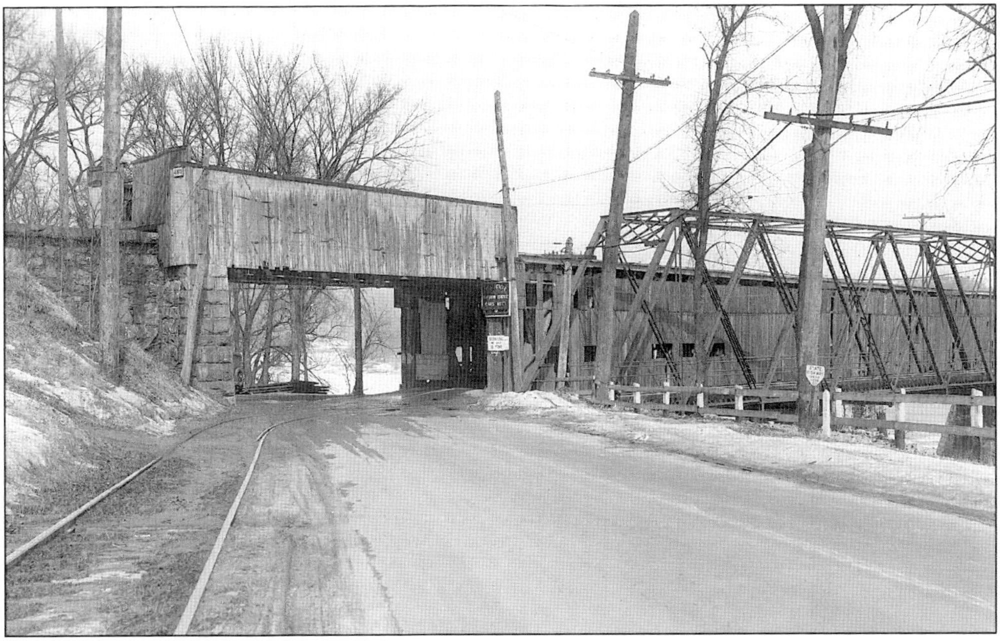

The East Greenfield entrance to the Montague City bridge is seen from the northern approach from Montague City Road. The trolley trestle bridge can also be seen in this *c.* 1935 photograph. (Photograph by Alex Gamelin; courtesy WMECO.)

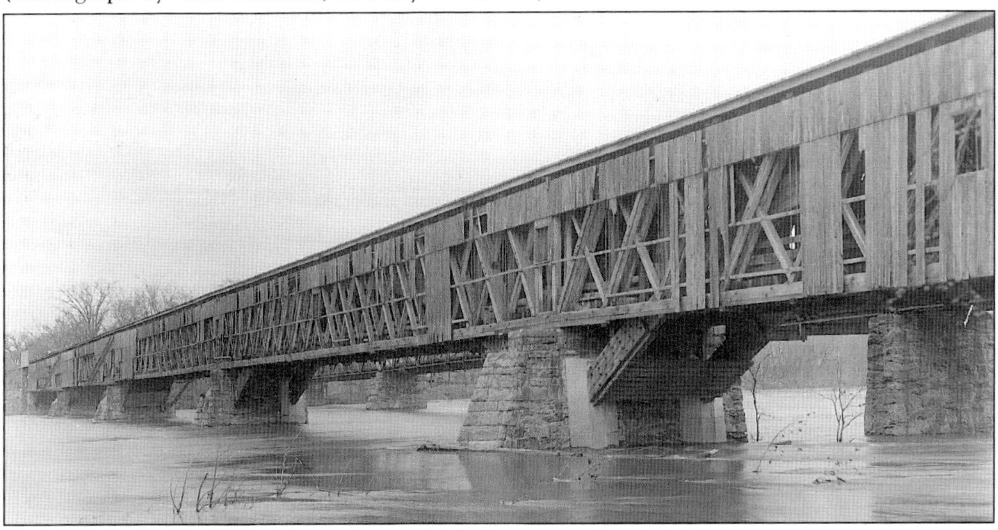

The covered bridge from East Greenfield to Montague City was photographed from the Greenfield side of the Connecticut River. This bridge was built by Col. Alvan Crocker and his associates after they purchased the remains of the previous bridge on this site, which had been washed away by a freshet. Additional arches to the supports were added in 1901 so that the Boston and Maine Railroad could go over the top of the bridge. Twenty years later, the bridge was declared unsafe for railroad passage, and thus the railroad had to find another river crossing point. This bridge was washed away during the 1936 flood, taking the trolley bridge and two of the three spans of the New York, New Haven, and Hartford Railroad with it. The General Pierce Bridge, built by 1948, replaced the covered bridge. This photograph dates from *c.* 1935. (Photograph by Alex Gamelin; courtesy Peter S. Miller.)

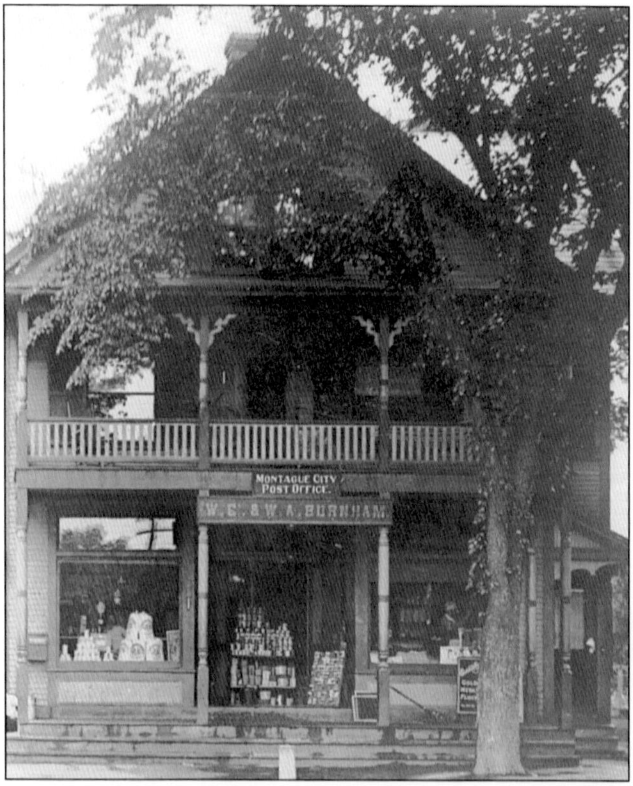

The Burnham brothers' store, built in 1895 at Depot Street and Montague City Road, served as a post office for Montague City. The building still stands, but the store is long gone. Note the stacked grocery displays in the windows. (Courtesy Millers Falls Library.)

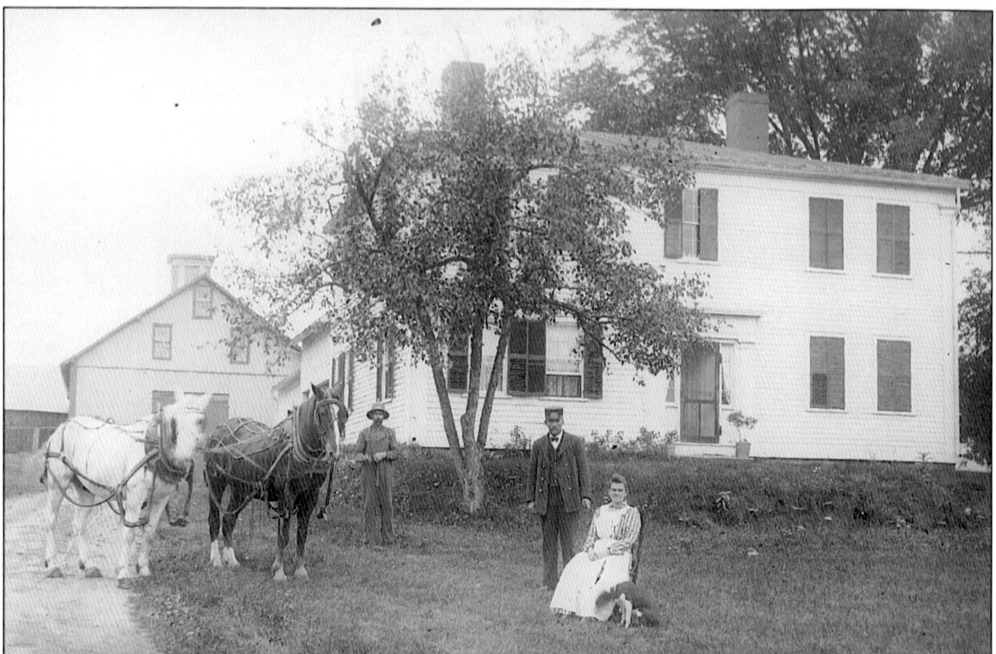

This photograph shows the Allen C. Burnham farm. Before the Burnhams' ownership, it was owned by V.D. Warner. The Montague Internal Medicine offices are now located on this land at Main Street in Montague City. (Courtesy Montague Historical Society.)

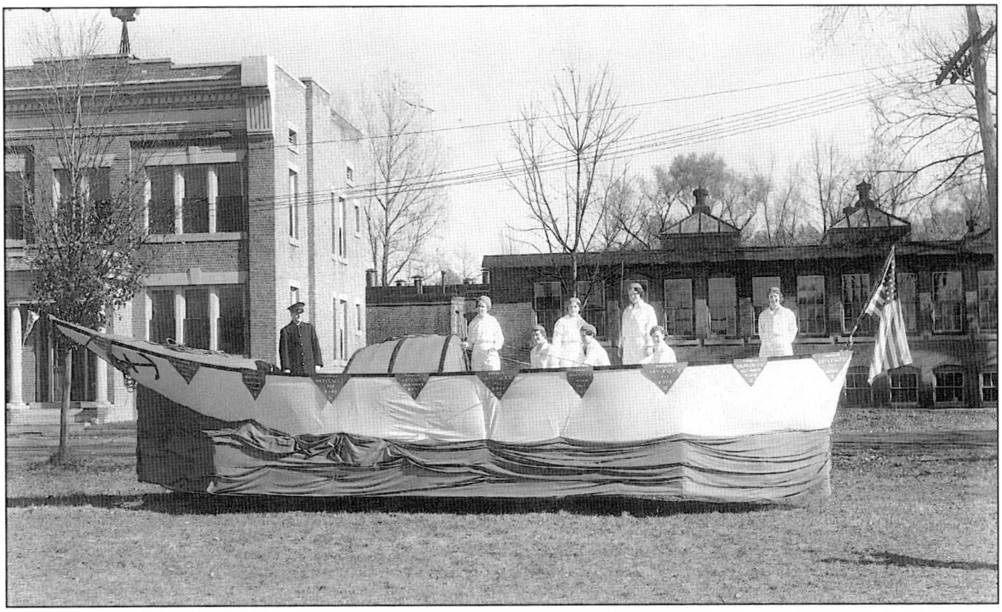

This view of the Montague Rod Shop's parade float shows the company's factory in the background. The ladies present in the photograph are, from left to right, Betty Day, Anita Paul, Lucy H. St.Germain, E. Annear, Evelyn Braun, Dot Ulrich, and Florence Passanait. The Rod Shop was originally started by Bernard Farren, L. Bartlett, and Charles W. Hazleton in 1885. It became the pattern by which other rod makers operated, using the latest techniques in rod manufacturing. As the company grew, the newer Montague City plant was taken over by L. Bartlett and his brother, Eugene. The company was acquired in 1934 in part by Ocean City Reels and continued operations for many years. They finally closed the Montague City factory in 1953, shifting operations to its other locations. (Photograph by Alex Gamelin; courtesy Turners Falls Library.)

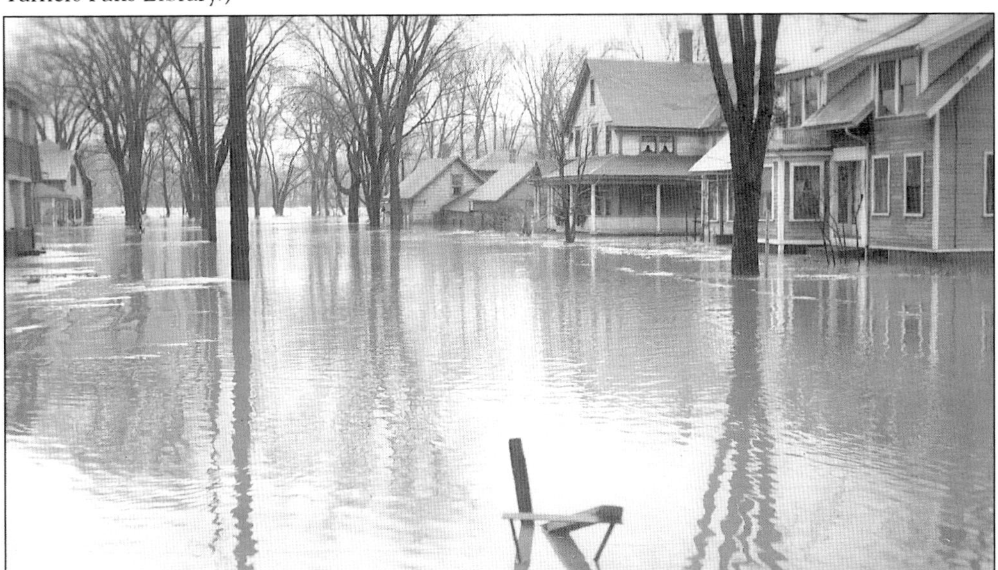

This photograph shows the Montague City area, which was hit hard by the flood of 1936. (Courtesy Peter S. Miller.)

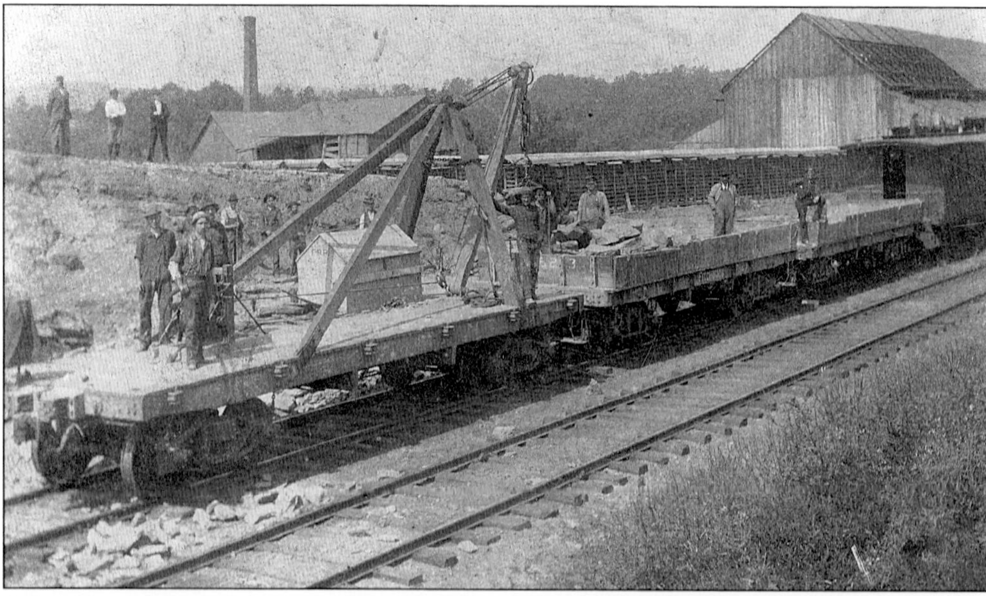

This photograph may show the Thomas Brickyard, and the double tracks could be the New York, New Haven, and Hartford Railroad line. Many millions of bricks were made in the town of Montague. The mills, block, and housing buildings in Montague were built of this brick. The brick was sent all over New England and was used in the construction of the Hoosac Tunnel. (Courtesy Turners Falls Library.)

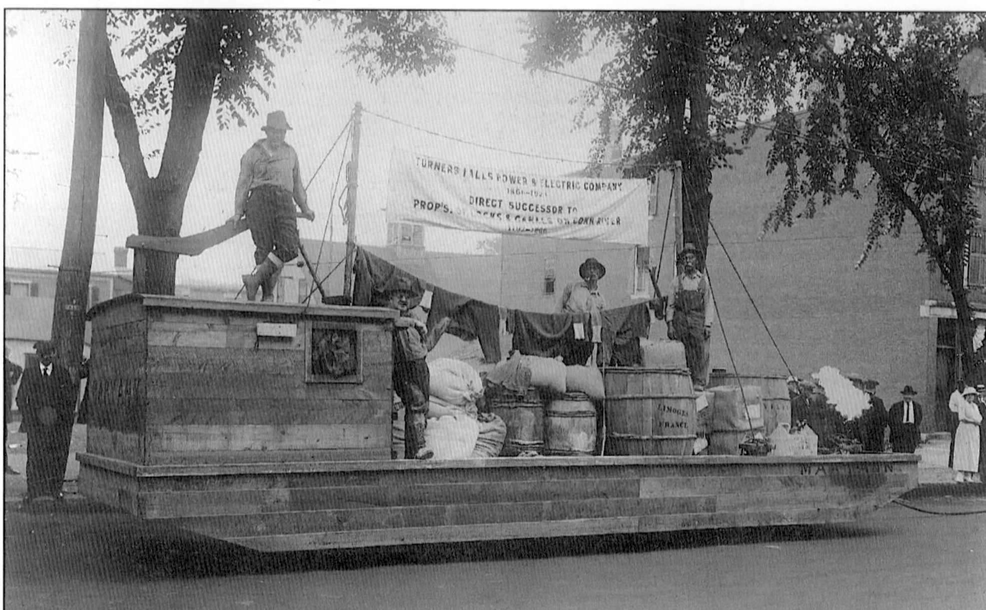

A Fourth of July parade in 1923 included this float. On the float is Louis Abbott, Frank Dubie, Charles Mosher, and George Farmer. The sign reads, "Turners Falls Power and Electric Company, 1866–1923, Direct successor to Props. of Locks & Canals on the Connecticut River, 1792–1923." This type of raft went up and down the river, through the canal in Turners Falls and Montague City until the trains came in 1846. Cheapside was a busy river port. This photograph was taken in Turners Falls. (Courtesy Turners Falls Library.)

Six

Turners Falls Revisited

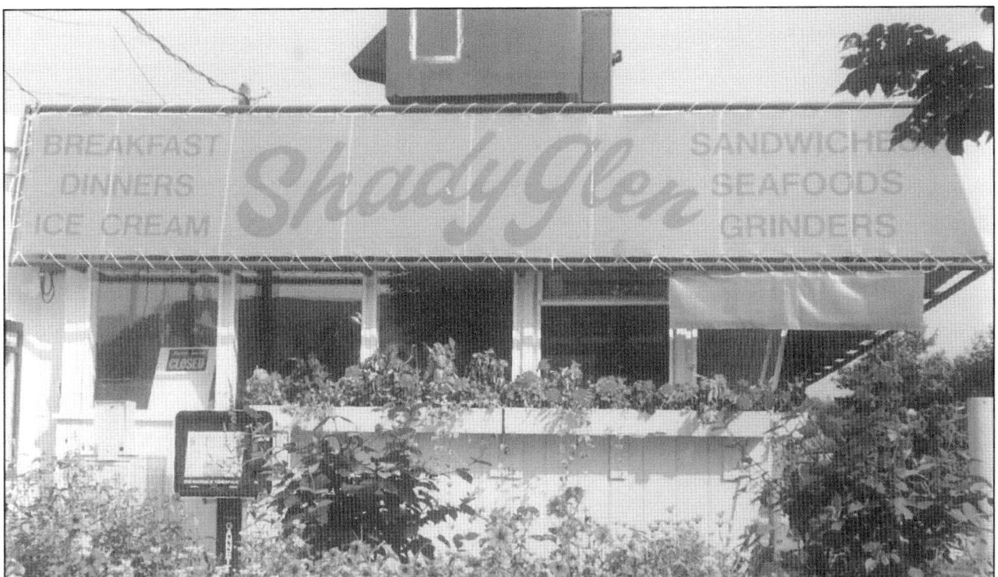

The Shady Glen, on Avenue A near the bridge, has been a local favorite eating spot for many years. It has a large counter space, tables, a juke box, a faithful, longtime staff, and of course great food. John and Linda Carey, proprietors, care for their clientele. It was originally built in the late 1950s as a drive-up Dairy Queen with car hops. For a short time, under the ownership of Richard and Shirley Brodrick, it was changed into what it is today—a restaurant. In 1962, Frances Carey Humphrey owned it. In 1963, John Carey purchased the business. Today, John and Linda Carey both own and work the business. (Courtesy John Carey.)

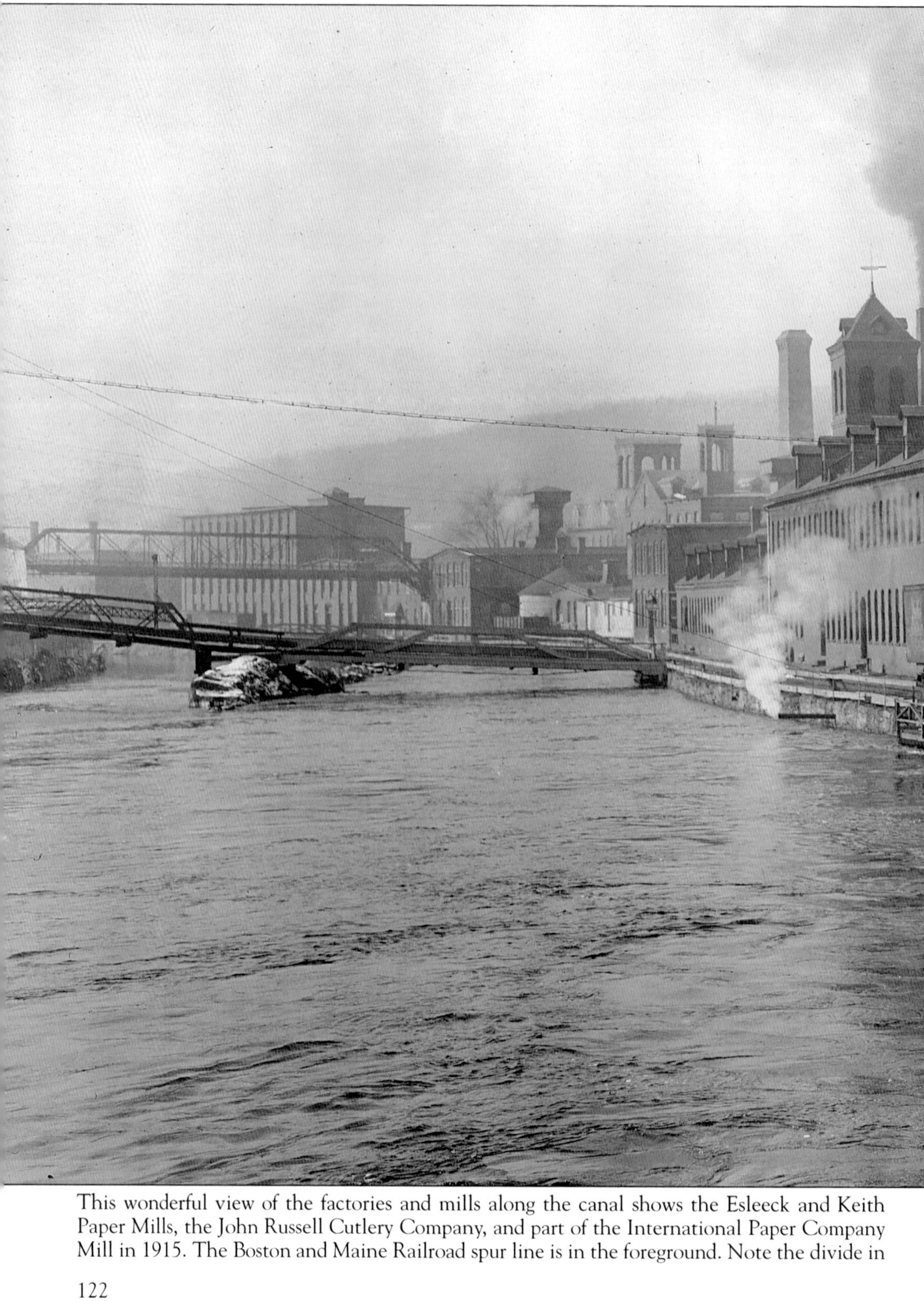

This wonderful view of the factories and mills along the canal shows the Esleeck and Keith Paper Mills, the John Russell Cutlery Company, and part of the International Paper Company Mill in 1915. The Boston and Maine Railroad spur line is in the foreground. Note the divide in

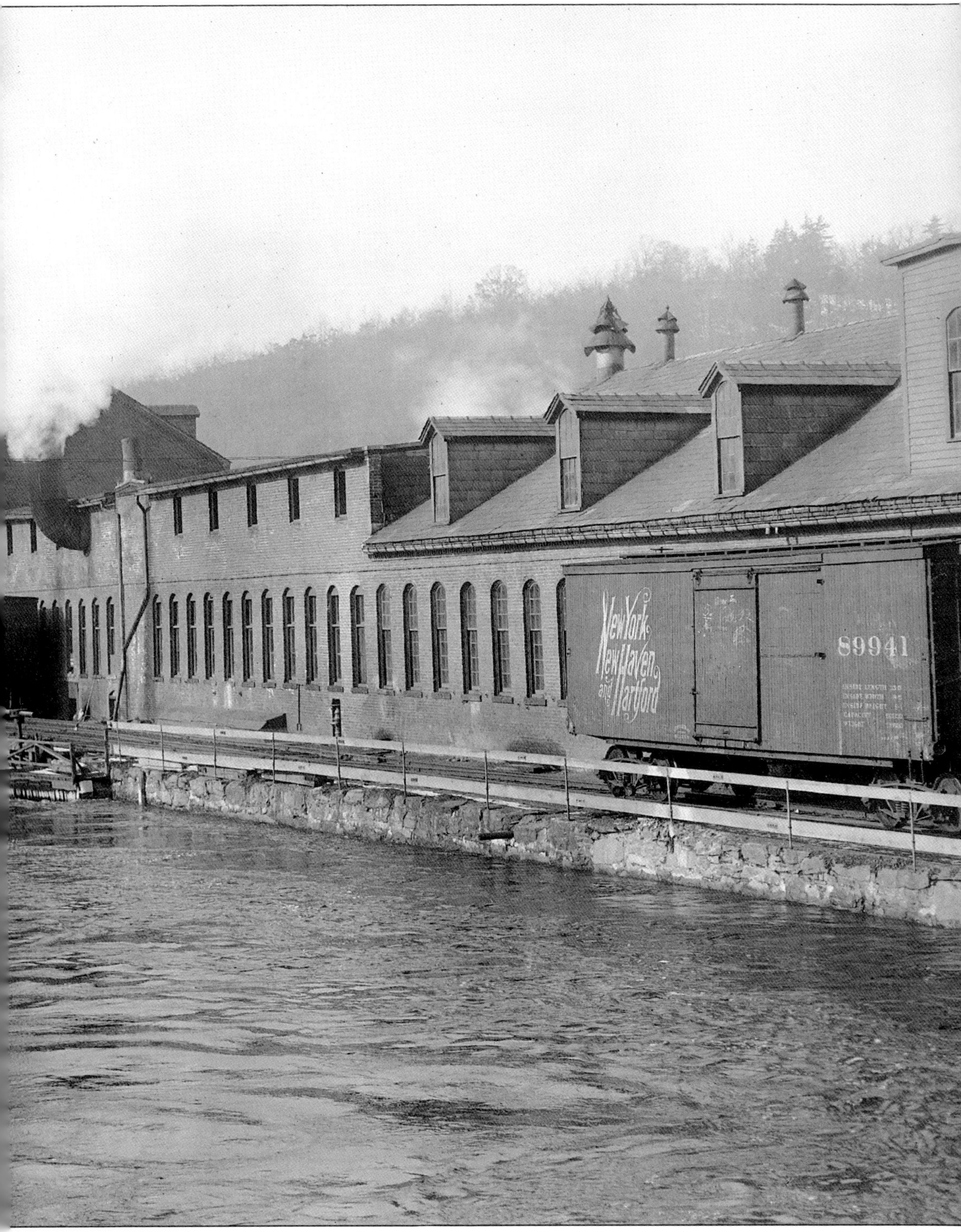

the middle of the canal. Perhaps this was a temporary divide between the old and new addition to the canal. (Courtesy Kyle J. Scott.)

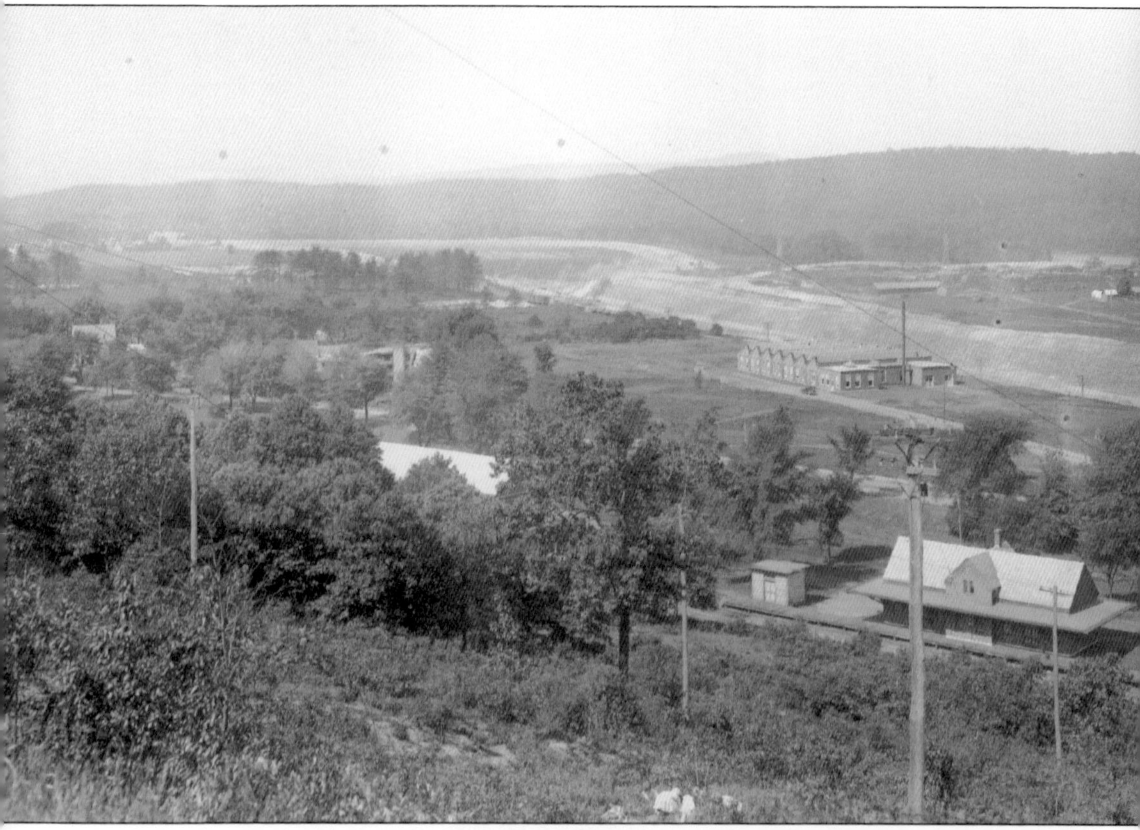

In the background of this view is Avenue A, the McLean Silk Mill, the new power canal, and the Patch section of Turners Falls. The station for the New York, New Haven, and Hartford

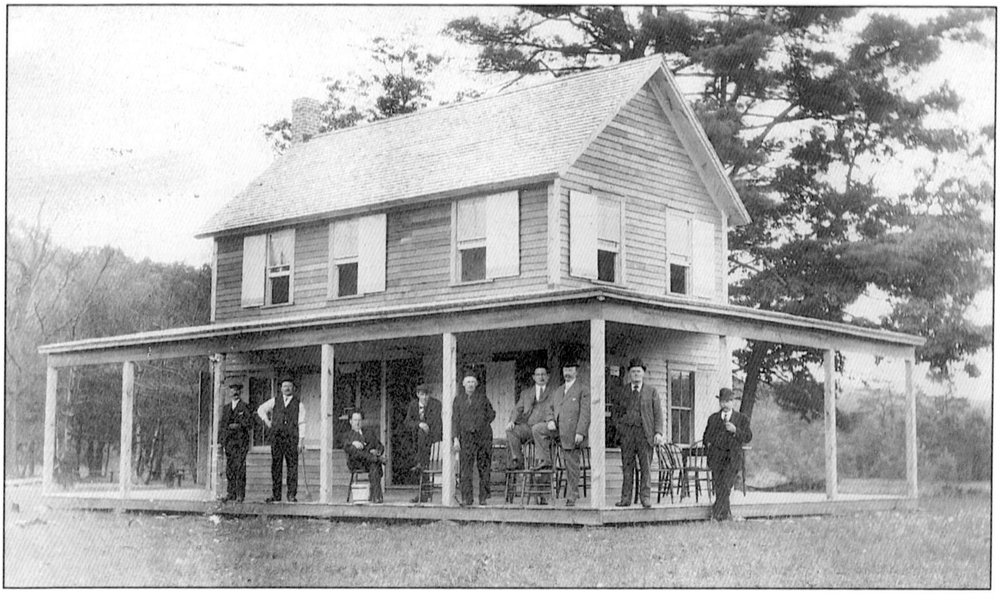

The Schutzen Verien Club, a German social club, met in Riverside Gill, *c.* 1908. (Courtesy Peter S. Miller.)

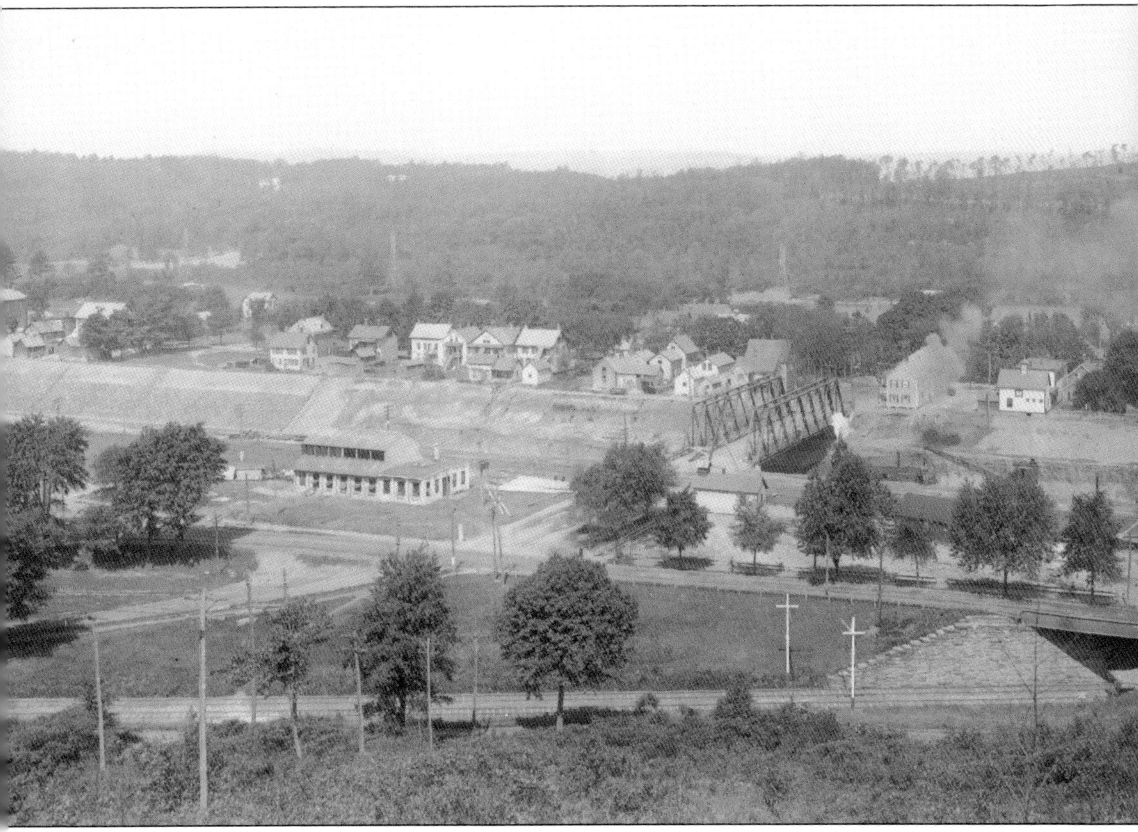

Railroad is visible in the foreground. (Courtesy WMECO.)

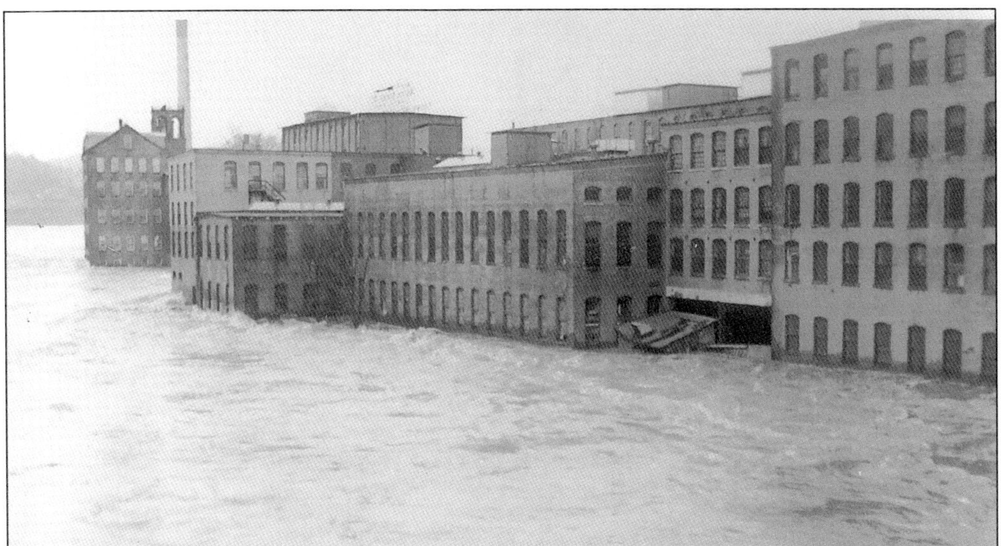

The 1936 floodwaters along the Connecticut River are shown behind the Keith and Esleeck Paper Mills. Of the three bad floods—1927, 1936, and 1938—the 1936 flood, which had the highest water level, was the worst. (Courtesy Peter S. Miller.)

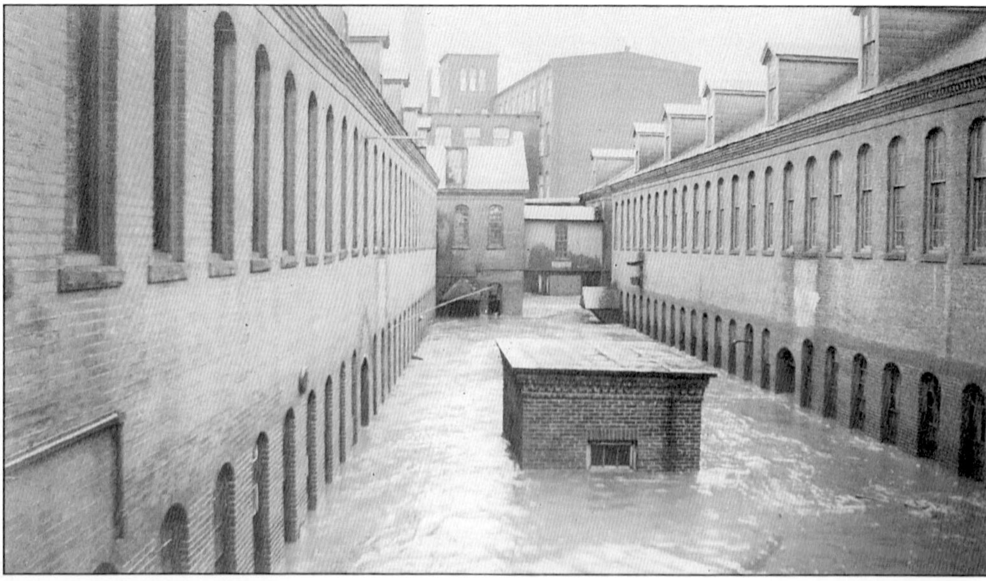

This photograph possibly shows the 1936 floodwater level between the different buildings of the John Russell Cutlery Company. (Courtesy Turners Falls Library.)

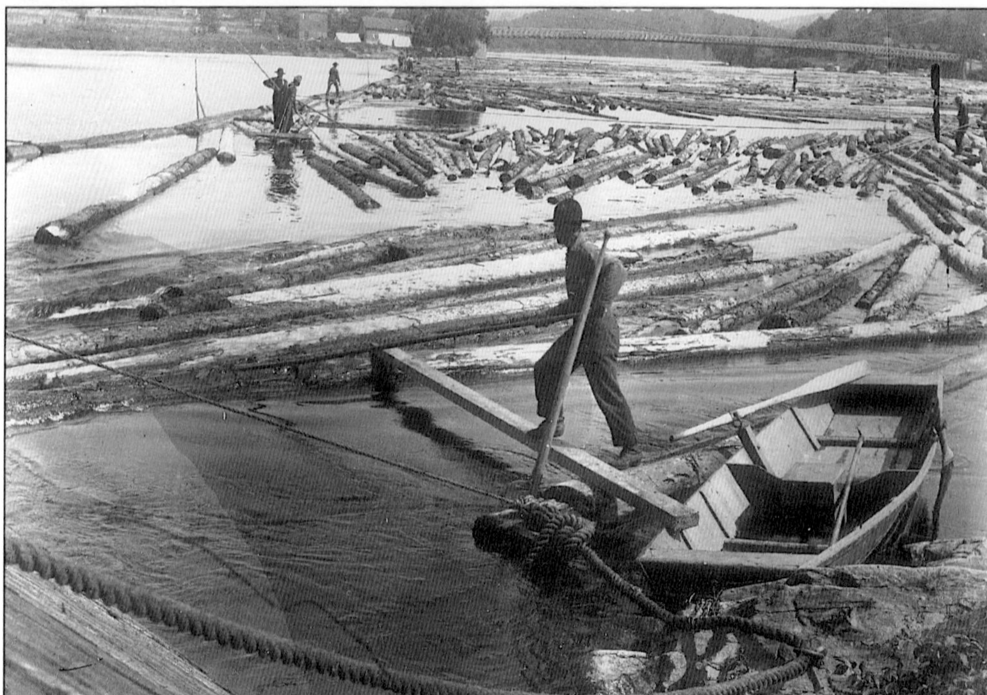

Log drivers on the Connecticut River are getting ready to send some logs down the river. The boat is tied to the island in the middle of the river. The log chute is nearby, and the Red Bridge is in the background. The building in the back was used by the loggers. From one of these buildings, the cook (only on Sundays) would sell baked beans freshly made the day before. Carl J. Schuhle, formerly of Turners Falls, can remember his mother sending him across the Red Bridge to purchase these beans. (Courtesy WMECO.)

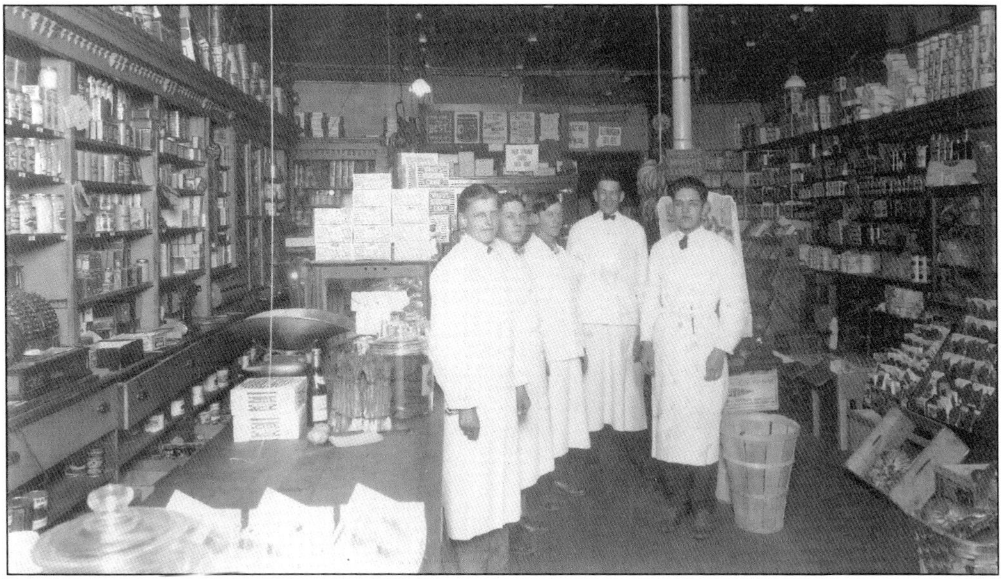

This *c.* 1925 photograph shows the interior of Koch's Grocery Store on Avenue A in Turners Falls. Shown are Joe Kuklewicz, Eugene Koch, Roland Bowman, Fred Shulda, and Felix Verrier. The former site of the store currently houses Turners Falls Oral Health and Booskas Flooring. Before these businesses, but after Koch's Grocery, it housed Eugene Singley's furniture business. (Courtesy Pamela Hubert.)

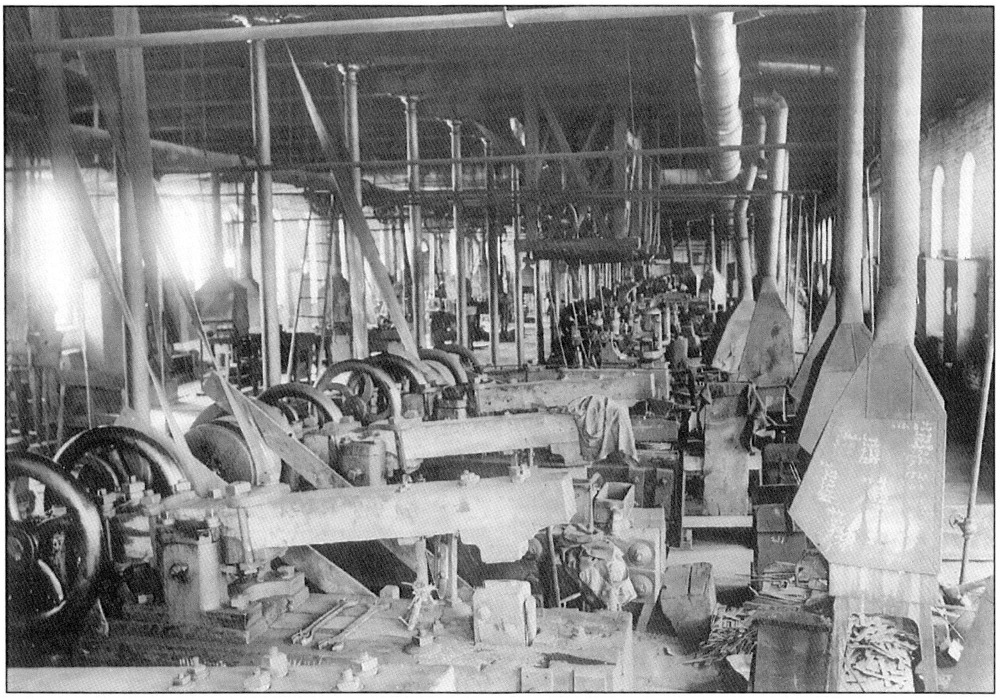

This picture shows the trip hammer and forge room at Russell Cutlery. In this room, the forgers would remove heated steel from the furnaces on the right. The metal, white-hot and glowing, would be worked with the water-powered trip hammers on the left. The machines were driven by a central belt system. (Courtesy Russell-Harrington Cutlery Company.)

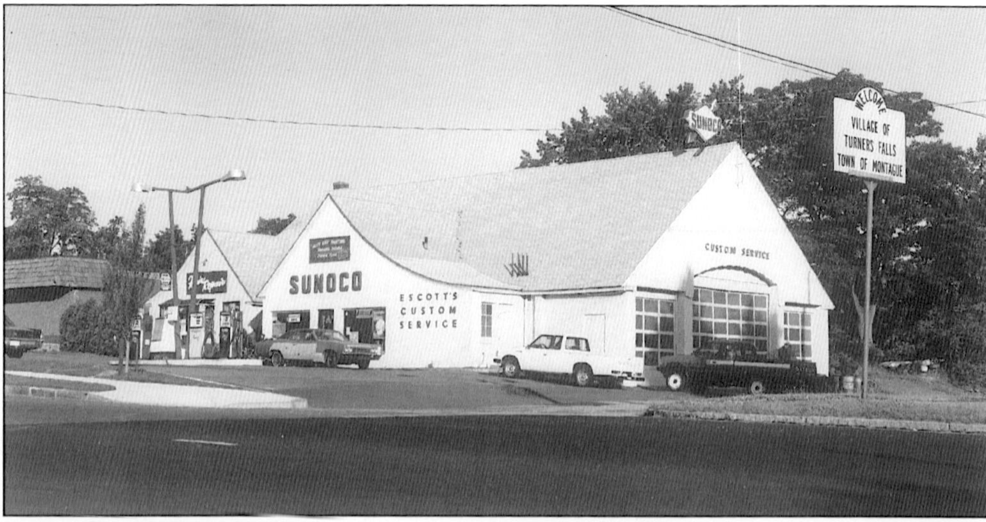

Escott's Sunoco station, a fixture on Avenue A in Turners Falls for many years, was located near the end of the Gill-Montague Bridge. Owned and operated by Robert "Skip" Escott, the service station was demolished for a planned Heritage Park. In the same building as the service station was a beauty salon operated by Mrs. Barbara Escott. The former Cumberland Farms store can be seen far left in the photograph. (Photograph by Peter S. Miller.)

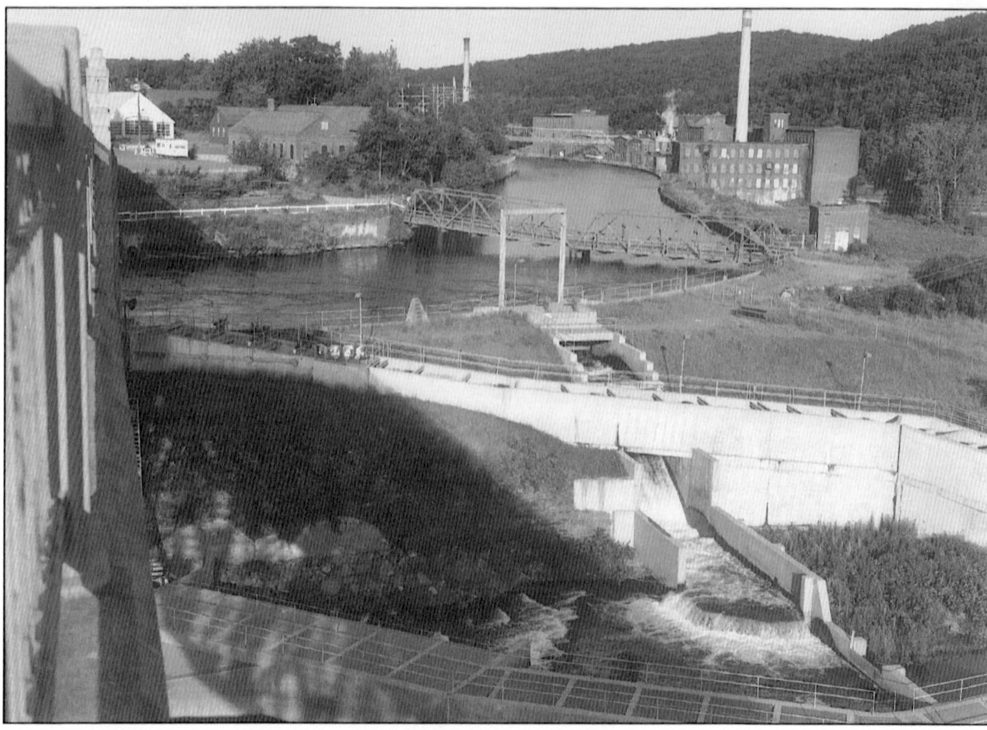

This c. 1986 photograph shows the edge of the Gill-Montague Bridge to the far left. In the center is the fish ladder that salmon and other species of fish use to overcome the obstacle of the Turners Falls Dam on the Connecticut River. Note that the Indeck Electrical Plant had not yet been built on the former John Russell Cutlery Company site. (Photograph by Peter S. Miller.)